Thoughts in th

Thoughts in the Mind of God

An American Woman's Spiritual Quest
Among the Himalayan Shamans

Ellen Winner

ISBN 1-59457-231-3

Cover photo: NASA and Hubbell Heritage Group

To order additional copies, please contact us.
BookSurge, LLC
www.booksurge.com
1-866-308-6235
orders@booksurge.com

Thoughts in the Mind of God

CONTENTS

ACKNOWLEDGMENTS

This book would not have been possible without the loving support of my husband, Joe O'Laughlin, the encouragement of my children, Thomas David Denberg, William Aaron Denberg, Evans Hawthorne Winner III, and Keridwen Morgan O'Kennedy Winner, and my mother, Evaline West Plucknett.

Special thanks are due to Patricia Sandler Denberg, Sarah Irvine, Albert Plucknett and Mary Harvey Byers for their thoughtful reading and editing of the manuscript and their many helpful suggestions, and to Hal Zina Bennett for his professional guidance and encouragement.

To my teachers, Michael Harner, Mohan Rai, Maile Lama, and Jebi Bhandari, great love and gratitude.

INTRODUCTION

Most of us—believing in a God or not—have experienced the death of a loved one and found it impossible to conceive that someone so "real" could just disappear. Our sense of reality is shaken. And on occasion, most of us have lain awake in the wee hours wondering, what happens after *I* die? We can't really imagine ceasing to exist.

When a Tibetan Buddhist dies, if he's lucky, his friends and relatives will read over his body from an ancient text to remind his soul that it need not return for another birth, but now has a precious opportunity to be free from the wheel of suffering.

These Buddhists believe that the soul, newly released from its physical body, will see visions of extreme intensity, much like the strong visions experienced by young children who are new to their physical bodies and haven't yet learned to put up defenses against their own powerful imaginations. Most of us can remember going through a stage of being afraid of monsters in the closet or under the bed, or our parents may have told us that when we were little we had an imaginary friend. Similarly, the dead person's soul may see both wrathful and peaceful deities while it is in the in-between state between life and death called the "bardo."

But no matter what visions the dying soul sees, no matter how frightened or overcome with awe the soul may be, the Tibetan Book of the Dead urges it again and again to think: "I will recognize whatever appears as my projection and know it to be a vision of the bardo; now that I have reached this crucial point I will not fear the peaceful and wrathful ones, my own projections."

My own projections?

The idea is that once the soul understands what it sees as a creation of its own mind, the soul gains freedom—becomes enlightened, and escapes from suffering forever.

This teaching is not only for the dying. It also applies to ordinary life. Buddhist wisdom holds that there is a bardo (a gap) in which enlightenment can be gained, not only between life and death, but also between one thought and the next in any living person's mind. We need only realize that whatever we are seeing, sensing and feeling is but a projection of our own minds—that whatever we think is happening "ain't necessarily so"—and then we will be free.

I am not a Buddhist. I don't have the patience for the hundred thousand prostrations, the hundred thousand mantras, the hundred thousand offerings required before one is considered fit to receive the higher teachings. But I'm convinced the Buddhists are right about this material world being a projection of our own minds.

When I was little, my father assured me the scary faces floating over my bed at night weren't real, but that cars and refrigerators and trees and rocks were. Ever since then, I've been wild to figure out why. Seeing those scary faces definitely had a stronger impact on my mind than opening the refrigerator door. Then in my teens, I had another strong, nonmaterial experience—one of those quick glimpses of higher truth you can't hold on to but can never forget. At the time, that experience seemed more real than even my own perishable body.

If you think you don't share "reality" with the people around you, you start to worry that you might be crazy. Maybe I was crazy. I'd been granted that brief "knowing" that Consciousness is One when I was fourteen, but right away, my brain took over and reasoned that since I was the one who possessed the only consciousness I knew, that One Consciousness must be mine. And this made me responsible for all the pain and suffering in the world. Anyone who's ever been there, stuck on the "reef of solipsism," knows the bottomless hell of that black and dreadful guilt. It is accompanied by a strong sense of taboo—this must never be spoken. I am now determined to break that taboo.

My education in science and law offered a safe and predictable worldview where only repeatable phenomena are considered real. My husband, Evans, agreed. He scoffed at the very idea of spirits. I wanted to be of the same mind because I didn't want to be crazy. But I couldn't, though I tried very hard.

After being initiated into shamanism by Michael Harner (founder of the Foundation for Shamanic Studies and author of *The Way of the Shaman*), I took a lucky chance to go to Nepal, hoping the mountain shamans could help me figure it all out. I studied there with Mohan Rai (whose life story is told in *World Shaman: Encountering Himalayan Spirits in our Time* by Ellen Winner with Mohan Rai).

Shamans take a broader view than most people—that not only

are material objects real, but our non-material visions and feelings, which are spirits, are also real. This makes sense because when you come right down to it, the only way we know about anything is through impressions on our minds—which come in through our senses or by other means—the way thoughts enter our minds.

Spirits, which like everything else, are impressions in the mind—or I should say in the One Mind we all share—are real in the sense that we experience them. Material objects are real in exactly the same way. And both can be changed in ways that seem miraculous by nonmaterial methods, such as mantras, rituals, and prayers.

Buddhists teach that the world is illusion. They show us the world we see is not necessarily the vale of pain and suffering (mingled with just enough physical satisfaction to keep us hooked) that we think it is. There are other, less painful ways we can experience our beingness. It's natural to think that if we witness a miracle—a dead body that fails to decay, a man who turns into an animal, or a terminal cancer miraculously healed—this proves the Buddhists right. If the hard-edged physical world can be changed by the power of a shaman's will, it must not be real.

The trouble is, as I discovered when I returned home from Nepal to confront my husband's illness and death, we can't always change things when and how we want using mantras, rituals, and prayers. There must be a greater Will than ours at work within the One Consciousness. And if so, we must find a way to join it.

When I was quite young, my mother explained to me how water striders stay up, skating along on top of the river, by distributing their weight on all their legs. If they pulled in their legs, they would break through the surface tension and get wet. Later, that became a metaphor to me for how we keep ourselves in place in ordinary reality. Ordinary daily reality is like the flat, two-dimensional surface of the water. We project our desires and fears out upon it like the water strider's legs. To free ourselves from this flat existence, we need only pull in our projections and allow ourselves to sink into the flowing river of love and compassion that underlies our existence and will carry us home. As you read what follows, you will see what I mean.

I've written this book like a novel to give you a sense of living my difficult lessons without spending years of your own precious life in the same cul-de-sacs where I got stuck. I hope you will let me know your own thoughts, so that we can all help each other arrive sooner at that sea of love and total acceptance we know is our true and real home.

This is a true story.

All the spiritual experiences described as my own really happened. I've added bits of dialog and changed the order of some events for dramatic effect, but never to give the impression of synchronicities or magical happenings where none, in fact, occurred.

Some names and many incidental characters have been changed. Every good story needs villains, so I made up or exaggerated irritating qualities of some of the people appearing in these pages, but these descriptions may not be true.

Ellen Winner
Boulder, Colorado
ewinner@worldshaman.org

BOOK ONE

GO LIKE A PIRATE

I was thinking up arguments for an appeal brief when my friend Peter called. It took a moment to shift gears. This was an important case. Our client, Agrigenetics, had finally hit on a way to make an entire corn plant grow from a single leaf cell, a sort of Holy Grail for plant scientists since the early eighties, but the Patent Office didn't believe it would work. It had not been thought possible before. How could I convince them it was real?

I picked up the phone. Outside my office window, through knobby pine branches and clumps of dark green needles, the grey granite Flatirons on the front of Boulder's foothills tilted toward the summer sky. "I know you're interested in shamanism," Peter said. "I'm finally getting my shaman school started, and want you to come to Kathmandu and be part of the first group. You'd like it."

"I wish I could." I was still thinking burden of proof, wondering if the sketch in the inventor's notebook of a multi-celled embryo, complete with head and root poles, would be proof enough for the Board of Appeals.

"But you can." Peter's tone was insistent. "It's only three weeks, and won't cost you a thing but airfare. I wouldn't charge you. Think of it as a thank you for the legal work." Earlier that year, I'd helped set up a nonprofit corporation for his Institute for Shamanistic Studies.

"I don't know what Evans would say..."

"What can he say? It's your money. You're the one working, supporting him all this time. Don't ask him. Tell him."

We'd known Peter Skafte, a tall Dane, as a rafting and climbing companion since his undergraduate days in Boulder, but we rarely saw him now that he'd earned his PhD in anthropology and lived in California.

"I've got my Rai guy, Mohan Rai, arranging everything. He really knows how to make Westerners comfortable."

"Mohan Rai—your trekking agent?"

"Right. It turns out his father was a famous shaman in Bhutan.

He's found some really good shamans to teach in our school. One of them can make you shake just by touching you. It's incredible."

"Why would you want to shake?"

"It's a sign of possession by the tutelary deity. The shamans shake when the god comes on their bodies. Then the god speaks through them." His voice held awe.

"They can teach that?"

"If we're suited for it, yes. They'll test us. But Ellen, this is like nothing you've ever seen before. These are *real* shamans in a shamanic culture—not a weekend seminar for new-age wannabes."

I felt put down. Peter knew my interest in shamanism had started with Michael Harner's basic workshop in core shamanism a few years earlier. Its echoes still resounded through my life. "Evans makes fun of me too. But even—."

"This is real. Think about it. But let me know soon."

Peter lived a glamorous life—international travel, National Geographic expeditions, study with shamans in remote mountain villages—out of my league entirely. I said goodbye and returned to the outline on my yellow tablet.

❧

At dinner, I brought up the subject of Peter's invitation. Evans had scarfed down his food with mechanical efficiency, and taking his ashtray in his lap, leaned back and began to hold forth to our seventeen-year-old son, Thorne, and his high school friend, Paul. Six-year-old Keri and I listened from the other side of the table. I had two sons from a previous marriage, but Tom was off at college, and Aaron, home for the summer, worked nights.

"Einstein? One of the three great villains of all time, along with Freud and Korzybski," Evans lectured. "It's all relative. Everything's unconscious. Thoughts don't correspond to reality." The once-dark beard on his narrow face was salted with white, and long white strands of eyebrow sprouted out above his deep-set eyes. "Major destroyers of rational thought. As far as I'm concerned, they're bee-oh-dees."

"Bods," said Keri.

"Better Off Dead."

Thorne thought it over in his serious way, and didn't even point out the obvious: they *were* all dead. With his beard coming in dark, and his clear blue eyes, Thorne was even more handsome than his father when we'd met.

Paul's eyes were riveted on Evans' face, gulping in his words, probably to use later to impress his friends.

"Everything's relative. Oh well. Might as well lie. Might as well steal. Nothing means anything. There aren't any standards, so why not?"

I'd heard it all before. And pointed out the flaws. I wouldn't say a word. I blinked back a prickling in my eyes. Once I, too, had sat at Evans' feet, awed by his brilliance, drinking in certitude, loving the consciousness alive in those knowing eyes of his—eyes that glossed with rancor when they fell on me now, their light reserved for others, like Paul, who wouldn't ask for more than Evans could give.

I dug my thumbs in under my cheekbones until it hurt, willing him just to shut up. I didn't want to hear his tired old ideas, or be pinned down among them like another dead butterfly in his collection, have him rap his knuckles on the table top—or the side of my face—to prove what was real. I closed my hand around my water glass, *relatively* cold and hard against the warm, soft flesh of my palm, or so the message to my brain alleged. I took in a shuddering breath, refusing to give in to the old confusions.

"Peter called today," I said when Evans stopped to light a cigarette. "He invited me to Nepal—as part of his shaman class."

"His what?" Evans' voice slid to a high note of mock affront, which I ignored.

"He's made up a three-week program for Americans. With shaman teachers. You know he works with shamans over there."

Evans tapped off an ash with his long, stained finger. "If you want to be a witch doctor, you should ask *me*. I can teach you more than any shaman from Nepal."

"So can I," said Paul.

"Right, since there's nothing to be taught," Thorne added.

"You don't even believe in spirits," I pointed out.

"Why should I believe in something that isn't real?" Evans sucked the white tube of his cigarette and blew smoke.

"I suppose you know what's real." I kept my voice flat.

"Reality is what can affect me. No spirits have affected me yet."

This was an old argument. I refused to let him hook me in. I'd been in therapy. I knew how it worked. Simple projection. I didn't want to own my load of doubts, and so projected them on him, while he, stubborn and close-minded, projected his intuitions of a spirit world beyond his control on me, accusing me of superstition. We'd been at it for years, twin planets locked in a tight little orbit by equal and opposite forces of attraction and repulsion, love and hate.

"Right," I said. "Then what makes you think you know the first thing about shamanism?"

He ground out his butt. "What's to know? Shamans were the smart ones of the tribe—more alert than the rest. Maybe someone with superior intelligence noticed a scratch on a tree that only a mammoth tusk could make, and realized he could tell everyone he knew how to call the great mammoth to come and be hunted—for a price. A pretty good gig. And when he figured out that it could support him in his old age, he found ways to keep it going."

"He could claim to make rain," Thorne added, "if he made sure he was first to notice when the clouds began to gather."

"Or maybe smell it coming." Evans snapped his lighter with a familiar, practiced motion that reminded me of the beatnik he'd been before we met—cool, living an artist's life in Greenwich Village. "A group could be sitting around the savanna, and the smart one would see a ripple in the grass, coming closer. He'd say, 'I'm hot, I think I'll call a little breeze to cool me.' The next minute the wind would be there, and everyone would be amazed."

"That makes sense," said Paul.

"What about *really* foretelling the future?" I challenged. "Like an oracle. Shamans were known to do that."

"That's easy," Evans said. "People predict the future every day. For example, if I throw a ball in the air, wouldn't you be able to predict it would come down? The smarter you are, the better your understanding of cause and effect. You know what's likely to happen. Then, if you're a good shaman, you make sure to take credit when things turn out the way you said they would."

"But what if you're wrong?" Paul asked.

Evans raised a humorous eyebrow. "If anyone happens to notice, you say, 'You didn't have faith.'" He deepened his voice. "Or, '*Somebody* hasn't been celibate.'"

The boys laughed. Keri slid from her chair to chase the kitty, and rubbed her face in its soft fur.

"They remember the times you were right because they want to, and conveniently forget when you're wrong," Evans said.

I cleared the table. Thorne switched the radio to the classical station and rocked in his chair, listening to Stravinsky's Firebird. Evans and Paul went off to the basement workroom where Evans made his jewelry—brooches, pendants, goblets, sword hilts, and replicas of ancient ornaments. Paul was helping him put together a chain mail shirt, tediously linking tiny o-rings.

Evans' work was good, intricate with fine, hand-worked detail, but none of it brought in a cent. He refused to take commissions, which meant he'd have to follow someone else's orders, and would rather give his pieces away to his friends than sell them.

I loaded the dishwasher and closed the sliding glass door, caught by surprise at my reflection. My newly-permed hair had suddenly become more white than brown. Prematurely though. My face wasn't old. I lifted my chin for a better angle. A little nerdy in the wire frame glasses, but who cared? Certainly not Evans.

I read Keri her bedtime story on my bed in the study, and she fell asleep there, cradling her cheek in her palm, the long, dark lashes she got from her father resting sweetly on the blue-white skin beneath her eyes.

Last spring, I'd finally worked up the courage to give Evans an ultimatum: get a job or get out. I'd allowed him two months. That's when I started sleeping in the study. But luckily, I hadn't told the kids. Right after that, his back went out. One minute he was fine, getting out of bed, the next, collapsed, writhing in pain on the mattress. At the hospital they said he'd ruptured a disc. Of course I couldn't desert him now.

The healing was slow. Sitting or lying, he couldn't be at ease. His suffering wrung my heart. I'd been meeting with a group of healers, learning to channel energy through my hands, but he cringed away when I asked to work on him. "Don't! It'll make it hurt more." He couldn't stand being touched.

Little by little, his back improved, until now he was able to spend time in his workroom and sit up with his friends. He belonged to a group who dressed up in medieval costumes and pretended to be historical figures. As far as I could see, it was just an excuse to bolster their egos with boasts of imagined feats—an escape from real life. Evans had turned the garage into a "great hall" for their parties, laying a flagstone floor and hanging the walls with swords and coats of arms.

Out in the living room, Paul called goodbye, and the front door clicked shut. I tucked the covers around Keri and went looking for Evans to say I'd decided to accept Peter's invitation. I wasn't sure I really wanted to go, but I did want to make Evans feel he couldn't stop me, that he had no right to object. I could do as I pleased.

Thorne was at the piano, working out the Firebird theme. "Where's your Dad?" I asked.

He struck a dissonant chord, and didn't look up. "He went out."

Through the next morning at the office, the appeal brief took shape. Plant regeneration *was* an unpredictable art. A Monsanto patent application had described it as black magic, requiring incantations, mantras, special vibrations. I'd heard that the attorney who wrote that had been fired for his little joke, but it was true. Technicians with good hands could make regeneration work; others couldn't. I'd need hard evidence to prove it to the Board.

Just as I'd need hard evidence to convince Evans that gods and spirits were real. He hadn't the slightest use for mysticism—though I still found that hard to accept. From the moment we met I'd known our love was ancient, fated, that we'd been together through hundreds of past lives. How could he not feel the same? He knew all the words, talked knowledgeably of the Great White Brotherhood, past lives, karma, the Bardo, ideas his mother, Anna Kennedy Winner, a Buddhist Theosophist and author of *Basic Ideas of Occult Wisdom,* had taught him from childhood. But he'd never outgrown his teenage rebellion against everything she believed.

I wished I could phone Anna Kennedy now, the way I used to, and tell her about Evans' downward spiral and my frustrated desire to heal him. She had always been so caring, focusing on our souls instead of our mistakes. "I feel so trapped," I would tell her.

"Don't worry, dear," she would answer. "It'll all work out if you just remember that you love each other."

But Anna Kennedy had died soon after Keri's birth.

And about a month later, I dreamed I came across her in a maze of hallways and chambers. She was standing, as though stationed there, at a doorway leading into a suite of interior rooms. I heard myself begging, surprised and embarrassed at how pitiful it sounded, but without a thought of taking it back, "Oh, Anna Kennedy, please, please, please, please, *please,* tell me how to reach enlightenment."

"I'll call someone higher up," she answered in her normal, pleasing and instructive voice. She had lifted a phone from the wall behind her, listened, and reported what she heard: "Go like a pirate."

A woodpecker clung to the wooden siding by my office window and started up a rapid-fire knocking. Peter answered on the first ring.

"I'm thinking seriously about Nepal," I said. "But I've never been so far all by myself."

"It's easy," he said, sounding pleased. "Just get on a plane in Denver, and when you get off in Kathmandu, I'll be there."

OUTSIDER CHIMP

I hugged Thorne and Keri goodbye, and leaned over Evans' chair to peck him on the forehead. Aaron helped me load the trunk with my two long duffel bags packed with clothing, a water filter, and plenty of canned food, mainly corned beef hash and beef stew, for Peter had stressed we'd need our own, guaranteed disease-free food stocks.

My stomach held a tight, scared feeling as Aaron drove me to the airport in his taxi, dodging onto the freeway directly into the path of a large moving van. "Slow down!" I yelped.

"What's wrong with you, Mom? You've been acting like a witch all morning." He couldn't understand how anyone lucky enough to be off on a trip to the other side of the planet could be upset—nor could I. I must have sensed, even then, that there would be no coming back to the life I'd known.

Peter had booked me on the plane from Seattle with his other two students. I spotted Diane right off, a good-looking woman in her early forties, with long, brown hair in springy curls around her face, and an easy, exuberant laugh. She was recently divorced, and her only son was grown, she said as we waited in the boarding line, and she was looking for adventure. "It's so good to be free," she exclaimed, throwing her arms wide, oblivious of the other travelers.

When I told her about my marriage to Evans, she grabbed my arm and shook it. "Get rid of the bastard. Take your kids and leave." She tossed her glossy curls. "This is just what you need."

Leonard was a different sort, thin but compact, with skimpy light hair tied up in a ponytail, and wire frame glasses, a San Franciscan who told us right off he was gay. He'd recently taken the basic Harner workshop and decided he was a shaman. "I cured a friend of chronic headaches," he bragged. "I massaged his head and channeled energy through my hands. Then, I had this string with big knots spaced along it, and hid it up my sleeve. I said, 'Now, I'm going to extract the bad energies.' I pulled the string along slowly between my thumb and his head so he could feel the knots go by, and asked if he could feel the bad spirits leaving."

"Do you think that's ethical?" I kept my voice light.

"My goal is healing." His pale eyes, magnified by the big, smooth curve of his glasses, went flat. "If it works it's ethical."

"You don't think the spirits can heal by themselves?"

"Maybe. But nothing wrong with helping them along."

❧

A pretty Thai stewardess, graceful in a pink and purple uniform that matched the pink and purple seat covers and pink and purple fabric panels that separated our section from first class, handed me a glass of wine. I stared out the window at the surface of the ocean, metallic blue and wrinkled with tiny precise waves, so far below it looked surreal. A layer of clouds closed off the view, and I leaned back and shut my eyes, feeling stretched and stressed.

A little old oriental lady tottered by on her way to the toilet in the rear. It was obvious, from her slow, careful movements, and the solicitous way her family treated her, that she was ill, but her face was radiant. I thought she must know some Buddhist secret for distilling joy from pain.

I felt worse by the moment, nauseated and achy. Breathing was a chore. I curled up in my seat and closely analyzed my sensations. If I couldn't stop the suffering, I realized, I might as well enjoy it—try to copy that smiling old lady with her Buddhist secret.

❧

In Bangkok, I went straight to bed, and in the morning felt well enough to meet Diane and Leonard for breakfast. We boarded a Royal Nepal Airlines prop plane for the last leg of our journey, and were soon descending into the steep bowl of Kathmandu, set in a valley below high, snow-covered mountains. We swept down over bright green fields and brick buildings whose glassless windows made them look ancient and mysterious.

As promised, Peter was there to greet us, along with Mohan Rai, a short, Chinese-looking man in a brown checked shirt and khaki pants. Both held loops of chained marigolds.

"This is Mr. Rai," Peter said. He threw his flower necklace over Diane's head.

Mr. Rai smiled in welcome and lassoed me. He stepped back and pressed his hands together. "*Namaste.*"

"Namaste." I struggled with my purse, getting my hands free to copy his gesture.

He was smaller than I'd expected, but much more intense, like a hundred-watt bulb in a sixty-watt world. Tightly-knit, fine grained, energetic, barking orders right and left, he left no doubt about who was in charge. It made us feel secure. But now he was in a hurry, explaining that a group of German climbers bound for Annapurna would fly in later that day, and he still needed to locate hotel rooms and line up porters. His helper, Sandeep, a smooth-faced young Brahmin, would see us to the program house in a taxi.

We must have looked like easy marks, for the porters swarmed us. Diane, with her long, bushy hair and pink boom box, was typically American, as was I, hanging back and clutching my bulging purse. Leonard's eyes raked over the dark-skinned crowd as though looking for someone to bully.

Sandeep let out an exuberant yell and waved a taxi over. "You, you and you," Mr. Rai chose porters from among the crowd. "Quickly. No, the big bag first." He closed us into the taxi. "I will come by later to make sure you have what you need."

The steering wheel was on the right. Sandeep sat next to the driver up front, and we four westerners squeezed in back, bouncing against each other, as the taxi lurched over rutted roads, too narrow for one lane of traffic, but used for two. I cringed as a succession of cars and trucks swept straight down on us and our driver would wait until the last possible moment to swerve.

We drove past shacks and fields, until the dirt roads gave way to paved streets near the center of town. Our eyes began to itch, and the fumes made us cough. "Roll up your windows," Peter said. "It's the cheap Chinese gasoline they burn."

We slowed, sharing the road with ill-clad children, dogs, women in dingy T-shirts advertising American companies and wrap-around skirts called *lungis*, rich women in saris, dark-skinned men in white *dhotis* wrapped like diapers around their loins, or western suits, or shirts and slacks. Dark, half-naked peddlers sauntered along with huge, tray-like baskets on their heads, among a disorganized welter of carts, cars, trucks, buses, three-wheeled taxis, and motorcycles. Women and children squatted by the roadside picking trash.

"I had no idea conditions were so bad," I said.

"This is nothing like India," Peter answered. "At least they have food here."

Beyond the center of town, the paved roads stopped, giving way to a confusing network of dirt tracks. The pollution eased up. Green fields of rice, soybean and millet alternated with large imposing houses, small shacks, and temples scattered over the landscape in no apparent order. We bumped through the suburbs, pulling up finally before a fine two-story brick house near a large rice field. "This is the program house," Sandeep said. "The family lives upstairs. Your shaman school has the whole lower floor."

Four or five cooks and helpers came out to welcome us and take our bags. The front door of the program house opened onto a long living room, mostly empty, with a series of bedrooms off the side, and a hallway leading to an open bathroom door, where I caught a glimpse of six toilet paper rolls stacked in a pyramid atop the toilet tank. We Westerners got bedrooms to ourselves.

After we organized our things, we congregated in the main room, where a couch, several comfortable chairs, and a scattering of small rugs on the linoleum floor did little to relieve the bare, hollow feeling of the room. A table and chairs had been set up near the kitchen door. A large, brightly-colored poster of Lord Shiva, his long hair rounded in a topknot, effeminate despite the tiger skin and snakes that twined around his body, dominated the end wall.

Peter asked for whiskey and water as we waited for our meal. Leonard waved the drink away, but Diane reached eagerly for hers. So did I. Alcohol would be the perfect medicine for the raw, strained way I felt.

A succession of Nepalis no one bothered to introduce came and went, gathering in knots and filtering in and out of the kitchen, from which bursts of laughter and boisterous shouts were issuing, along with curry smells. Diane and Peter flirted. I kept quiet, ill at ease among so many strangers despite the soothing effect of the drink. Leonard, too, seemed tense, and hunched goggle-eyed behind his glasses. Nepalis stared at us from every corner of the room, their dark eyes unreadable, speaking a language we couldn't understand and laughing, probably at us. Leonard stood abruptly, marched off to his room, and shut the door. I knew how he felt, but made myself stay put.

I'd never been at ease with strangers, but from reading Jane Goodall's accounts of life with her chimpanzees, had found a way to deal with it. Outsider chimps gain entry into a group by hanging around the edges for long periods of time without trying to interact until the other chimps get used to them. I'd used the trick at parties and meetings. It ought to work here too. I eased back in my chair, non-threateningly sipping my Jack Daniels and water.

"Is this a party or what?" Diane waved her arms expansively toward a group of eight or ten Nepalis pushing through the door at once. Her ready laughter, beginning with a slightly constricted "ooh-hoo," and opening out into a generous cascade of "ho-ho-ho's," swept us up into her sense of how outlandish the whole thing really was. Peter smiled and scooted his chair close to hers.

"The Nepalis don't have our notions of privacy," he explained. "Anybody can come into your house any time and sit down and watch you."

Diane favored him with a wide, admiring look.

I gave them space, trying to sense, without staring, what was up with the Nepalis. They felt connected to each other in a way I hadn't experienced since early childhood, when the family would be gathered in Grandma's kitchen, laughing and teasing, accepting each other completely as veritable prototypes of what we were, without comparison to some other, better standard.

When had that sense of belonging disappeared? I tried to be cool, but couldn't help feeling exactly what I must appear, an American Gothic woman, stiff-faced and unresponsive to the sweetness all around. I didn't much like myself, but determined I would stick it out, stubborn and watchful, the outsider chimp.

THE DOLL

I could remember that sense of belonging from Grandma's house when I was four. That must have been when I lost it.

The wind raced over the Nebraska plains, across fields and pastures, flattening the grass, tearing at the cottonwoods, slamming dust, tiny rocks, and finger-sized sticks with leaves still attached, against the windows. Grandma had brushed my hair down with water and fastened it in place with bow-shaped plastic barrettes, but as soon as we stepped outside, the wind whipped it into a mess of tangles.

Pop, my grandfather, his long legs formal in sharp-creased suit trousers, brought the new humpbacked 1947 Dodge around from the garage so we wouldn't have to walk through the mud, and Grandma held onto her hat and dropped sideways into the passenger seat. I climbed onto her lap and wiggled against her stomach, corseted hard beneath her flowered Sunday dress.

I couldn't sit still. I loved the wind. It made me itch to run and shout. I kicked my legs against the floorboards, and clutched my hankie with the collection plate nickel tied into one corner.

Aunt Dorothy wouldn't be coming with us. She stomped around the car wearing an old pair of brown pants tucked into her boots, and headed toward the river. "Bye, Aunt Dorothy," I shouted. Grandma sucked her breath in through her teeth.

We bounced up the lane and picked up speed on the main gravel road. Grandma stared straight ahead, her lower lip moving up and down against the raised ball of flesh at the center of her upper lip, as though trying to blow bubbles without spit. Finally, she looked out the window at the rows of short corn in the fields, and said, "My, the crops look good this year."

"Yep." Pop slowed for the railroad bridge into town, and Grandma put on her social face as we parked by the white-frame Methodist church.

I sat between them in a blond wooden pew three rows from the back. The preacher's sharp voice sliced the air, dividing good from evil for the grownups. "Thou shalt *not*," I heard him say. A sparrow got in and fluttered, trapped, near the high, beamed ceiling. "Jesus loves me this I know," I hummed the Sunday school song. My legs and stomach kept sending pictures to my mind—jump, jump, jump, jump up. I kicked the pew in front. Grandma's big, knobby hand was jumping too, tapping the side of her leg. She gave me a scolding look and squeezed my knee hard. I stopped humming.

When we got home, Aunt Dorothy had just started dinner. She pushed back the stove lid from its round hole over the box of flames, and dangled a naked chicken Pop had killed earlier that morning over a burning rolled-up newspaper to singe off the pinfeathers. The kitchen smelled hard and angry, the way it did when Grandma cleaned out tangles from the brush she used to fix my hair and threw them into the stove. Aunt Dorothy cut up the chicken, dragged the pieces through a bowl of flour, and threw them into a skillet of melted lard, while Grandma peeled potatoes.

"I don't know why you won't ever come to church with us, Dorothy," Grandma said.

Aunt Dorothy jabbed a fork into the skillet and pried at the chicken, raising her voice above the frying noise. "There's more of God out there in the timber with the birds and animals than inside that church, with all those dressed-up *people*." She snapped the tablecloth over the table and let it float down smooth, then dealt out plates so hard they jarred around in a circle. Grandma kept quiet.

After dinner, I pestered Aunt Dorothy to take me to the sandbar at the river bend. Grandma, scared I would drown, never let me go alone.

The wind had died down. I stripped to my underpants and ran across the sloping beach, splashing forward until the force of the water against my skinny thighs made me stop. Water striders scattered in long smooth skates. I wasn't scared of them. When Mama was here to visit, she'd told me they wouldn't bite. She'd studied them in college. They spread their weight on the water with their long legs sticking out in all directions, but if they pulled their legs in, they would sink into the water and get wet.

The water was cool, so muddy it was yellow when you opened your eyes beneath the surface. It smelled of fish and the insides of rotting logs, like the chamber pot we kept under the bed in winter—shameful smells, but now that the sun had pulled them from their hiding places into the rippling light and fresh air, they were all right, so you didn't have to hold your nose and say *pyew*.

Once when the water was low, Aunt Dorothy had waded with me

all the way across, to the magic land of trees and uncut brush on the other side, where we met a groundhog standing on his hind legs like a little man, and came upon a tiny fawn under a tangle of low-hanging branches, so tender and new it lay curled in a circle as though still inside its mother.

The world was alive then, and part of me. Beyond the high bank, a border of hedge trees were somehow connected to my eyebrows; the weathered boards of the old hog house back toward the road prickled the inside of my nose; and my stomach lived with the cows in the barn. In the sky, where clouds piled soft and round and high, there was God—Grandma said—looking down and seeing everything we did. She said if you prayed, He would give you what you asked for. I had prayed to get a big toy car, the kind you could sit in and pedal around, but it never happened.

You were supposed to pray for others too, she said, and I did, saying, "God bless Daddy and Mama." But they were far away in California, Daddy doing war work as a chemist and Mama studying medicine.

My parents finally came when the corn was waist high. Daddy did magic tricks with chemicals to make green water in a glass turn clear, and change little pink strips of paper to blue. He said this was science, and because of science we know that people are animals too, just like dogs and cows and horses, and that long ago, people lived in trees and looked like apes. I liked to think about them, living in the forest with no houses. In my favorite daydream, I leapt through green treetops from branch to branch, swinging like a monkey, wearing a bright red dress and hiding from the people down below.

Now the corn stood higher than a man, and Daddy and Mama were gone again. I sat in Grandma's lap outside and watched a thunderstorm blow in. All was still. Then the wind began, a few small gusts at first, tickling the pit of my stomach, then more, and harder, ripping down small branches, sweeping me up in a crazy excitement. I stared at the thrashing branches, wanting to be up there among them. "We're animals. Daddy said so. We came from apes."

Grandma's arm tightened on my chest. "Your dad may be descended from apes, but I'm not." I looked up, ready to share the joke, but her face was set and angry.

I jumped from her lap and ran around like mad, turning cartwheels in the rising wind as shiny green leaves rained down. Thunder rolled across the sky like a farmer with a wheelbarrow full of loose potatoes, and the first big drops splashed hard on my bare arms and legs. I loved Grandma, but she was nowhere near as smart as Daddy.

Grandma, Pop and Ellen

Over the winter, I grew tall and difficult. Whenever I got ornery, Grandma would drop hints about the Easter Bunny—how much he liked good children. She didn't know Daddy had already told me he wasn't real.

Aunt Dorothy and I gathered eggs, tramping through the slushy snow, sticking our arms beneath the warm hens' bodies, and hoping they wouldn't peck. We carried the eggs to the kitchen in a straw-lined bucket and colored the white ones in cups of vinegar-smelling dye. The Easter Bunny was supposed to come and hide them.

After I went to bed, Grandma and Aunt Dorothy crept around the living room, poking eggs and candy down between the couch cushions, balancing them on the black piano keys and pedals underneath. I heard them whispering and laughing, and it struck me then that God was probably nothing but a big Easter Bunny for grownups like Grandma who didn't know better. I hated the thought, but it wouldn't go away. Everything changed for me after that. God wasn't real.

They're stupid. I hugged myself beneath the covers, feeling thin and small.

Far to the north, a pack of coyotes yipped at the stars, and then Grandma said, "Sh," and tiptoed past the bedroom door.

In the morning, when I looked for the eggs, I found a doll as well, a brand new pink baby with blue glass eyes and lids that closed when I laid it down. Grandma watched me pull it from its hiding place behind the couch. "That old Easter Bunny likes to make good children happy," she said.

I took the new doll out to the sandbox and dug my spoon through the sand to the hard dirt underneath. If you kept on digging, you would get to China. I picked up the doll, hating its round, blank eyes, and gouged them with the spoon. It skidded over the glass eye and caught on the pink plastic nose.

Aunt Dorothy opened the screen door, making its old spring stretch and twang. "Ellen, honey, *why* do you have to break things like that?"

"It's all right, Dorothy," Grandma said. "It's just a doll."

The plastic doll face buckled as I stabbed it with the spoon handle, scratching white lines on its fake pink cheeks. I dug a long groove down its arm. "It isn't real!" It couldn't have fooled a two-year-old. Was I supposed to believe it would sit up and talk, cry, reach out with its little rubber fingers and call me Mama?

I flung both doll and spoon beneath the porch, and ran around the side of the house, scattering a bunch of stupid, squawking chickens into a flapping panic, trying to lift their big hopeless bodies off the ground.

THE WILD SHAMAN

To be outside looking in had become so old and well-practiced a role for me, it almost felt comfortable. I sipped my drink. The Nepalis laughed and joked together. Peter and Diane conversed. At last a cook announced dinner. Peter sent a helper to knock on Leonard's door and fetch him. The cooks served us curried chicken and vegetables as the roomful of Nepalis looked on.

"*Chia, Memsa'b?*" A helper offered sweet milk tea.

Memsa'b? How embarrassing. But the others seemed to take it in stride. I nodded, and he set a cup by my plate.

"I thought it was called *chai*." Leonard sniffed and took a sip.

"It is, in India," Peter told him. "In Nepali, it's chia."

"Where did Mr. Rai go?" I asked.

"Probably home to his wives."

"His *wives?*" Diane protested, breaking into a grin.

"He has three wives, maybe four. It isn't legal but they do it here," Peter said.

"That little man? Ooh-hoo-ho-ho-ho."

Leonard forked rice and lentils into his mouth, chewing in stolid silence.

❧

Mr. Rai came in later with the shamans. Jebi Bhandari was dark-skinned, with a deeply lined simian face, wearing jeans and a tweed sport coat. He stuck his hand out western-style. Krishna Tamang, thinner, lighter-skinned and serious, wore a brown suit jacket over a traditional white Nepali dhoti. He bowed and said "Namaste."

"Jebi is from Jappa on Terai. That is plains of Eastern Nepal. He is not Rai. He is Chetri, warrior caste, but his guru was Rai," Mr. Rai said. Mr. Rai was shorter than the shamans, but clearly in charge. His speech made up in enthusiasm what it lacked in grammar. "You see, my father was famous *jhankri*—we say *dhami* or *jhankri*, means shaman in Nepali language—so I know everything, how it should be done. Jebi knows all proper way of ceremonies." Jebi beamed as though he understood. "Krishna too is very fine, of course, very powerful shaman, of Tamang tribe." Mr. Rai pulled up three more chairs, ordered whiskey for himself and us, and *rakshi,* distilled rice wine, for the shamans. The cooks rushed off to do his bidding.

"When I am setting up this shaman school with Peter, I have advertised in paper and interviewed more than twenty shamans from all over Nepal. I make them perform *chinta,* each in their own way, showing how they calls their gurus, with shaking, traveling, playing *massan* ghosts and other spirits. I have chosen Jebi and Krishna as two of the best. Even Jebi is not Rai, but has been taught by Rai guru. I have seen how he performs in true and correct *mudhum* way. He knows I can very easily find out when a shaman is lazy, and leaves out steps or shortcuts on proper way of ceremony. I am not a shaman. Of course. I cannot shake myself, but I know exactly everything." He faced us with the upright, confident stance of a small man who knows how to make his presence felt, filling his chest through open nostrils. His face was symmetrical and fine-featured, his straight dark hair cut western-style and combed back from his forehead. His eyes creased down to narrow slits, regarding us with canny intelligence.

"Our translator, Mr. Ganesh, will come in morning, and I have told these shamans to teach you all their shaman wisdom. Not hold back. Jebi is a very fine, best shaman. *Ramro manchhe,* good man." He patted Jebi's shoulder, making him smile. "And now, please give me your passports for safekeeping."

Diane and I went off to fetch our purses from our rooms.

Leonard stayed put. "What do you need our passports for?" he challenged.

"To keep safe," Mr. Rai said. "I have lock safe in my house to keep. You will get back at end of program, no problem."

"I have already given him mine," Peter said.

Diane and I brought ours and gave them up. Mr. Rai waited expectantly, and finally, Leonard pulled his from his breast pocket, flipped it open to his picture as though saying goodbye, and handed it over. Mr. Rai put it in his pocket, checked his watch, downed his drink in one gulp, and said he'd see us in the morning.

Mr. Rai arrived as we were finishing breakfast. Neither the shamans nor the translator had shown up, but as Peter seemed impatient, Mr. Rai told us to bring our pens and notebooks for class, and we gathered on the couch and chairs. Mr. Rai took the role of teacher and explained that Nepal was the only officially Hindu kingdom in the world, and for that reason it was illegal to sell hamburger or steaks. Still, he assured us, you could get beef in the expensive restaurants catering to Europeans and Americans.

I thought guiltily of the cans of beef stew and corned beef hash I'd brought through Customs—smuggled actually—glad the inspectors had been too lazy to open my bags.

"Didn't you say the Rais were Buddhist?" Diane asked Peter.

"Oh yes," Mr. Rai answered. "In Nepal we has many Buddhist monasteries, also Islamic mosques and Christian churches. Most people are religious, but they doesn't have arguments about it."

"There are thirty-two different ethnic groups in Nepal," Peter said.

"There are thirty-four different ethnic groups with different languages living side by side, respecting each other," Mr. Rai went on, apparently not noticing Peter had said thirty-two. "Even though Nepal is fourth poorest country in world, it might be it is happiest. Eighty percent of people are uneducated. We do not have so much science and technology as advanced countries. Most of Nepalese people believe in old ways. I would say that most Nepalis who live in remote areas have never seen a medical doctor. That's why shamans are not hard to find."

"Nepal has only been open to the West since 1950," Peter added.

"Late in 1950, King of Nepal and present Panchayat Government introduced public education. For previous hundred four years of Rana government, whole country was closed to West," Mr. Rai said. "There was no business or trade with foreigners, no educational system, no industry, but Nepalese people were allowed to go down to India to work as coolies while British Empire ruled there, 1789 to 1947." He paused as though expecting us to write down the dates, and Diane and I dutifully complied; but Leonard, scowling, made a point of keeping his notebook closed and consulted his watch.

"Our shamans are a little bit late," Mr. Rai said. "But they are coming, they are coming."

"We're on Nepali time," Peter said.

"In fact, I was captain in British Gurkha Army," Mr. Rai continued. He pulled out his wallet and showed us a picture of himself, much younger, in an army uniform. "Rai and Limbu tribes together—we calls Kirati—, mostly where Gurkha soldier recruited from. Very fierce, very honest and loyal, is why. Once Kirati ruled whole of Nepal. But first Ranas, then British, took over. Our language, *Ragdum—dum* means language—is dying, and our writing, *Thamdumling,* has been burned out by the Ranas, because they not wanting Kirati to be strong and have community. The Ranas were scared of men with bloods of Kirati."

We smelled onions cooking, and spices, our lunch, and still no sign of the shamans. Mr. Rai went on with his lecture. Leonard leaned back on the couch looking bored.

"How old would you say Kirati shamanism is?" Peter asked for our benefit.

"As far as I estimate, shamans were born about forty-nine thousand years ago, just after creation of world," Mr. Rai answered.

Lunch was called, and we ate. Peter told stories of his mountain-climbing adventures in Greenland, and when we gathered again in the teaching area, brought the subject back to shamanism. "You can be a shaman by being kidnapped by the Wild Shaman—like Mr. Rai's father, or, like Jebi, when a deity or the spirit of an ancestor comes on your body and makes you shake," he said.

Mr. Rai leaned back and lit a cigarette, holding it with his thumb and the tips of his fingers like a European. "Yes, my father was a *Banjhankri* shaman," he said. "Banjhankri means Wild Shaman. My father was kidnapped at age four, from garden just by house of my grandmom. She always told, when she was carrying in womb, he was shaking, especially during full moon time."

"Where did the Banjhankri take your father?" Peter asked.

"To his cave, all full of gold and jewels," Mr. Rai said. "He teaches children there, all shaman wisdom, drumming, mantras, and hides them from his terrible wife, Lemlemma, under a basket."

"She likes to eat children?" Peter prompted.

"Fee, fi, fo, fum," Diane said, entering into the spirit of the tale.

"Yes, she is terrible woman. Banjhankri kept my dad there, teaching, for two months, but when he is coming home, family thinks only few hours has passed."

"Did they miss him?" Diane asked. "Was he really gone?"

"Yes, of course, they has missed him," Mr. Rai said, as though surprised.

"What does Banjhankri look like?" Peter asked. "Tell our students."

Mr. Rai gestured one of the helpers to refill our glasses. "Yes, Banjhankri looks like small man, white beard, mustache, long white hair, and feets on backwards. With golden drum and beater."

"A sort of troll," Leonard said.

"Toll?" Mr. Rai repeated.

"A mythical being. From our fairy tales," Leonard explained.

"Not fairy tale, in our believeness," Mr. Rai said.

Mr. Ganesh, our translator, showed up then, a little man, with a large, serious face, and an upright bearing projecting an air of unshakeable dignity. Since the shamans still hadn't come, Mr. Rai directed him to take us sightseeing.

Our first stop was the National Museum. Mr. Ganesh halted us before a worn stone elephant-headed Ganesh. "He is the son of Shiva, called 'Remover of Obstacles.' I am most fond of this god, you understand." He smiled with lugubrious humor.

I tired quickly, overwhelmed with all the gods and artifacts, and wandered outside to the courtyard, as the others climbed to the upper floor. A light drizzle fell. The earth was dark and rich; birds flew every which way overhead. I missed my family. Thorne and Keri would be sleeping now; it was five in the morning there. Evans might still be awake, smoking, watching some old movie. I hoped he'd read Keri a story and not just parked her in front of the TV until she fell asleep. I felt the cool mist on my face. My family seemed so far away, from some other life a long, long time ago.

A little man in a peaked Nepali hat, one leg shorter than the other, smiled and nodded as he passed. I was alone, but the bricks of the building, irregular and separately handmade, had somehow made me feel at home. Tears welled up, spilled over, and ran down my cheeks with the rain.

JEBI

At twilight, people from the neighborhood began to filter into the program house in clusters and family groups—dark, reticent women with shawled heads leading small children and carrying babies, low-caste men, shy like the women, and a group of young Brahmins shouting boisterous comments with an air of license. Mr. Rai arrived with Jebi and Krishna and said Jebi would perform a shamanic ceremony, a chinta, he called it.

Jebi set right to work arranging an elaborate altar, first setting up a backdrop of fresh bamboo brushes laced with white string, porcupine quills, and then, on a bed of uncooked rice, an array of stones, bones, and tools, including, in a place of honor, a four-inch polished hollow bone, stained brown on one end as though scorched.

He retired to the kitchen to put on his costume, a white blouse lapped over in front and fastened with ties, and a long white skirt edged in red, with red and white strips of cloth around his waist. Draped on his shoulders were bandoleers of bells, a *mala* of shiny black *ritha* seeds, two malas of rough, round, *rudraksha* seeds, dull rose in color, and the backbone of a snake strung on a string. He had placed a crown of feathers on his head, but his bearing was more workmanlike than regal as he tipped the headdress back to wipe the sweat from his brow.

Mr. Rai led us to the front, where the crowd obligingly made space so we could sit cross-legged on the floor. Jebi lit a small oil lamp and lifted his two-sided drum by its long, carved handle in salute to us, his students. "Starting," he said in English.

He screwed his head down into his neck to free it up, and swallowed, betraying nervousness. Pressing the metal tip of his drum handle firmly against the floor, he took up his S-shaped drumstick and began to beat the drum on the side, painted with a red Shiva trident that faced the altar. He held a brass plate against the drum handle so that each stroke of the drumstick struck it as well, producing a compelling, clanging rhythm.

With a reverent expression, in total concentration, he bowed from his seated position and chanted to the objects on the altar, each in turn. Soon he began to tremble, and then to shake. His knees flapped upward from the floor like wings; and soon the shaking spread to his upper body, setting off the bells around his shoulders. He poured out liquid from a gourd in which he'd placed a bouquet of feathers, sparged plant gum around the room with a bamboo brush, and threw handfuls of uncooked rice grains toward the altar. No longer did he show signs of stage fright. In total control, he seemed to emanate a dark, powerful force. My stomach felt hollow, with a deep, waiting tension, as in the presence of something holy.

Mr. Rai's youngest sister and her husband, both tall and exceptionally good-looking, served as Jebi's helpers, keeping incense lit and taking over the drumming as Jebi danced. Mr. Rai stationed himself behind and to Jebi's left to supervise. The electric lights on the ceiling had been left full on, and the audience came and went, smoking, passing around glasses of rice wine, and talking and joking in normal tones. Despite the distractions, we students were spellbound, awed at this sight of a real shaman with feathers on his head performing an ancient tribal ceremony.

As Jebi danced, he held up a piece of ginger root to show it to the crowd, and then cut it with a feather. A nubbin rolled across the floor. Mr. Rai picked it up, examined the cut, and set it down. Jebi hopped and twirled, his long skirt flaring. Tucked into his armpits were two bamboo wands, tipped with brushes formed by peeling the stiff, fibrous strands part way down from the end and letting them curl backward. He brandished the wands in a series of symbolic gestures, and then, at last, called *"Ho ha!"* a signal to his helpers to stop drumming. He wiped the sweat from his face with a blue bandana and accepted a drink of clear liquid from someone in the crowd.

"Now he is ready to treat sick people," Mr. Rai said, taking charge and presenting the patients in prearranged order. The first was a slender, light brown woman with a two-year-old baby wrapped in one end of the shawl that covered her head. The child was thin and listless. Jebi examined it, stroked its arms and smiled into its face, speaking gently in his deep, kind voice to engage its attention and trust. Then he turned to the altar, drummed again, and chanted until his words began to come in short, forced grunts. "He is speaking for his guru," Mr. Rai explained. "Telling what is wrong with baby."

Diane leaned toward my ear and whispered, "A channeler."

The strange grunting stopped. Jebi shook violently, and then threw rice grains on the altar and set his drum down on its edge on the floor.

The shaking stopped, and he spoke to the mother in a normal voice about the baby's illness, asking questions and listening attentively to the answers. I heard her say "*Ho*," which means yes, and "ho," and "ho" again. He took a rudraksha mala from his altar, folded it in his hand, and passed it over the child's body as he whispered mantras punctuated with the kind of sharp, noisy in-breaths that, in most people, signal shocked surprise, and then blew out gently on the child.

Jebi

The baby and its mother had had the shaman's full and compassionate attention throughout, but the moment Jebi was finished, he waved them away with a gesture so abrupt it seemed rude. Diane, Leonard, and I exchanged surprised glances, but the woman got up without a word or sign to make room for the next patient.

This time it was a man, one of the boisterous Brahmins who'd been drinking in the doorway. He took a seat by Jebi and turned his head around to grin at his friends.

"He doesn't look like he believes in this," I whispered to Diane.

She nodded and agreed, "He's doing it for laughs."

Again, Jebi drummed and chanted, channeling his tutelary deity in rhythmic grunts, and then asked the man a series of questions. "Ho," the man said. "Ho. Ho." The patient turned to see how his friends were taking it, amazement showing on his face.

"What is he saying?" Leonard demanded loudly.

Mr. Rai held up his hand. "One moment. I will explain you later."

The Brahmin man got up, still laughing, as his friends shouted teasing remarks from the rear.

"Our shaman has told him about his house, where he lives. He asked if red flowers are growing in front of door. It was true. He asked if dark-faced woman lives to north. That man said yes. Jebi, of course, had no way of knowing. His guru told him in trance," Mr. Rai said.

"What was wrong with the man?" Leonard asked. "He didn't look sick."

"*Mohini*. That is love spell," Mr. Rai said. "Someone put love spell on him. Jebi will have to take it off, but not now. Later."

Jebi took a drink from the glass beside him, and Mr. Rai beckoned a heavy-set woman to come forward. Like the other patients, she laid a bit of money on Jebi's altar.

As the night wore on, Jebi treated many patients, all with the same grunting divinations, followed in many cases with attentive questions, compassionate looks and gestures, and mantras delivered with those strange sucking in-breaths, and outbreaths blown over their bodies.

Peter and Diane went to bed around eleven, followed shortly by Leonard. The crowd of Nepalis thinned out, but Jebi stayed fresh and full of energy. I didn't want to leave. I kept on watching, mesmerized, absorbing the energies and emotions, straining for meaning. I noticed how Jebi's fingers moved in odd patterns as he said the mantras—making mudras of magical significance, or simply counting repetitions? Mr. Rai was too busy for me to ask. He had told us Jebi would travel to the lower and upper worlds during the ceremony, but I couldn't tell when he did it, for he never sat quietly or lay down the way Harner taught his students to make spirit journeys. Instead, he stayed in constant motion, drumming, dancing, chanting, or channeling. The taut drum skin, crisscrossed with a network of tiny lines like the skin on the back of my hand, enclosed a dark, resounding space from which the beat went on and on, deep and compelling. I felt a like space forming in my soul.

When at last there were no more patients, Jebi sang a final song and drummed to release the spirits, while Mr. Rai's sister threw rice on the altar. I said goodnight and went to bed, my pulses still beating in time to the drumbeat's echoes. Through the closed door of my bedroom, I could hear Mr. Rai, Jebi, and the others talking and laughing, and fell asleep to the friendly sound as the first morning birds began to call.

DISPLAYS OF AFFECTION

Next morning, the shamans showed up on time with Mr. Rai, just as we finished our eggs and toast. Mr. Ganesh, the translator, bustled in and perched on a straight chair, accepting a cup of chia while we had our coffee. We sat on the floor for our lessons, on small carpets, using the furniture for backrests. Jebi, our teacher today, sat upright on a small Tibetan rug, his drum and bag of shamanic tools near to hand. Mr. Ganesh, dignified and serious, stationed himself to Jebi's left, his starched white dress shirt rising unassailably from the stable triangle of his short, brown-trousered legs. Mr. Rai smoked in the doorway, and Krishna turned a straight chair from the table to face the room. My knees and thighs began to ache from the unaccustomed cross-legged position.

"Jebi will tell how he got his massan bone, how he has to dig it up fresh from the grave in a cemetery at midnight," Mr. Rai said to start us off.

"Why don't you show us your bone, Jebi?" Mr. Ganesh asked politely, in English. Jebi's eyes were clear this morning, with no sign he'd been up most of the night drinking, drumming and channeling. He waited attentively for Mr. Ganesh to ask his question in a language he could understand. Jebi took his teaching role seriously.

"You see, I am going to ask him to show us the hollow bone he keeps on his altar, what it is used for, and where he got it, and how he uses it. This is very important for his ceremony, and he must explain to you thoroughly how he came to possess it, and about the spirits connected with it. There are many spirits recognized by our shamans, and many ways to call them," the translator nattered on, until, noticing he'd lost Jebi's attention, he spoke his name sharply, and asked a question in Nepali.

Jebi opened his bag and pulled out the short, polished bone he'd used in last night's ritual. "This is a human arm bone, you see," Mr. Ganesh said. "He blows it like a trumpet to call a helper spirit. He must take this bone himself from the grave of a man from the mustard oil caste who has been buried three days. He goes to the graveyard alone, naked, in secret, and says a mantra to make the bone come to the surface." Jebi twirled the bone between his fingers. "He was nineteen when he did this."

Jebi held up the bone and said, "Massan," in his deep voice.

"He must give offerings to his guru for protection. The massan are dead spirits, you see, of men of lower caste. Jal Massan, Bir Massan... these are ferocious. They are black and ugly, with piercing teeth. The shaman must cut his own arm and give an offering of his blood to the massan. Suke Massan is another type. Chanchal Massan. Raghu Masson—seven all together."

"Bir Massan." Jebi pointed to the bone.

"Bir Massan is supreme. He goes first in the massan procession. Suke Massan is at the rear," the translator continued.

"Bir," Jebi said.

"He is talking about Pir Baba," said Mr. Ganesh, having misunderstood. "There are Moslem holy men, you see, dead spirits that ride horses."

"Why does Jebi need the bone?" Peter brought him back.

Mr. Ganesh consulted Jebi. "Massans are only male," he continued, ignoring the question. "Suke Massan—means dried massan—makes a man waste away. Kali Massan turns a fair complexion black. Bir Massan makes your legs swell up. Chanchal Massan is fickle-minded, always moving. He can paralyze a person. Karabir Massan, he's second in command. He makes a person so he can't think. Like a nincompoop." The little translator paused proudly to give us a chance to admire the extent of his English vocabulary.

"There are sixteen massans in all," he continued, apparently forgetting he'd previously said seven.

Diane and I looked questioningly at Peter to see if he'd noticed, but he gave a slight shrug and let it pass.

"Karabir Massan and Bir Massan are deep red in color in the face. The rest of their bodies are black. Kali Massan is all black..."

"What does Jebi do with the bone?" Peter asked again.

After a lengthy discussion with Jebi, the translator said, "He calls the massan. He says, 'Why did you hurt this man?' He gives a sacrifice, you see."

I was gaining new respect for the anthropologist's task. Despite everyone's best efforts, it was clear it wouldn't be easy to learn the shamans' wisdom. "How do you ever make sense of all this?" I asked Peter. "So much contradictory information."

He frowned. "Lots of checking and cross-checking."

"I can imagine."

But I didn't see how any amount of cross-checking would ensure truth, when each person you talked to might say there was a different number of massans, or insist that the bone had to be dug up from the grave instead of being called to the surface with a mantra—and who was right? The majority? There was no Pope of shamanism, no encyclopedia with the final word. I'd been scribbling away, taking notes like a scientist or lawyer, looking for contradictions to expose the truth, becoming more and more frustrated. But it just didn't work that way.

I leaned back and gave my writing hand a rest. Maybe there wasn't any final truth, but so what? Diane and Peter still flirted, getting to know each other, sharing laughter and light, social touches to each other's safe parts—arms, shoulders, and knees. Mr. Ganesh presided in upright dignity. Jebi sorted through his bag, and Mr. Rai took a seat on the couch above us, offering Krishna a smoke. The cooks in the kitchen clattered and yelled, dropping spices into frying oil to release their odors. Leonard fidgeted and frowned. Truth or no truth, life was proceeding as usual.

I decided to keep an open mind and see if I could learn something useful.

ॐ

After lunch, we went on another sightseeing tour with Mr. Ganesh, this time to the Hanuman Dhoka, an ancient temple. He paused to lecture just inside the courtyard, waving his arms in a grand sweep toward the outside of the building. "These walls are carved with images of men and women having sexual relations in every imaginable position," he said in his high-pitched, tour guide voice.

The light was flat beneath a sky that threatened rain; the walls were grey, and the images worn down so that all I could make out were curlicues and bumps. If I tried really hard, I might resolve them into arms, legs, and bodies, but there was no way to tell what they might be up to with each other.

A statue of Hanuman, the monkey god, painted red and blue, stood before us, larger than life, splotched with red vermilion powder applied by worshipers. A brown paper grocery sack had been placed over his head. "That is so he cannot see the carvings on the walls and have his modesty shocked," Mr. Ganesh explained.

A land of contradictions.

ॐ

After dinner, even with no shamanic ceremony to draw them, curious Nepalis from the neighborhood gathered to watch us. Leonard went straight to his room. Peter and Diane bent their heads together in a corner, and I carried my cup of chia to the porch. Jebi followed and began a conversation, managing with gestures and smiles, despite our lack of a common language, to convey that he was forty-six, a year older than I, that his name was made up of the English letters J and B, which stood for Jhanga Bahadur, and that he was married and had three children.

I nodded attentively, as befit my stranger status in the chimpanzee troop. He knew a few words of English and I'd picked up a smattering of Nepali. I told him I, too, was married, had four children, and lived in Colorado where there were mountains: "*Pahad*," I said, raising my eyes and making high tent shapes with my hands.

He looked exactly as I'd always thought a shaman should, with a deeply wrinkled brown face, monkey-like energy, and dark, liquid eyes that could be both kind and ferocious—and as he'd shown last night while performing, could also express a fixed and determined intention. But now they were friendly, alight with a quick, humorous awareness he was eager to share. We might be friends, I thought, surprised.

At dark, we went inside, and Jebi disappeared into the kitchen. I joined Peter and Diane in their corner, and one of the cooks handed me a glass of Jack Daniels and water, what they were drinking. Peter was telling Diane about his pilgrimage up Mt. Kalinchok with Mr. Rai, how they'd been stuck in a rainstorm for three days on the side of the mountain and hatched their plot to start a shaman school, a story I'd already heard but was content to hear again, comfortable in the glow of the whiskey and the presence of these good friends.

Jebi, his dark eyes aswim with rakshi, came and sat beside me, draping an arm around my shoulder. I was pleased, sensing friendliness and a childlike desire for contact, but Peter frowned and motioned Diane and me to follow him at once to his room.

"You can't afford to get too close to the shamans," he warned. "Their dignity may be hurt—or yours."

"I like Jebi," I protested. "Nobody was thinking about dignity."

"That's just the point. They could get too familiar, and then be angry with us for letting them destroy the proper student-teacher relationship. I don't want that to happen."

"Really, Peter, I don't think Jebi had any idea of—."

"Men and women don't show affection to each other in public here.

Not even when they're married," he broke in sternly, and then softened, "although men can show affection to men. Or women to women."

"What about gay couples?" Diane asked the obvious.

"Never," Peter said. "If there are any, they hide it."

"Jebi was just being friendly," I pointed out.

"Sure, but you have to be careful. Pretty soon he'll be asking you to accept him as your guru. Then you're supposed to give him money and presents. Don't do it. Once you accept a guru, it's like having a new family member. His family becomes your family—and they're big families too, always needing money for weddings or *pujas*, or because someone's sick, or died and has to have a funeral. And they all want to come to America. You'd never hear the end of it."

I finished my drink and went to bed. Jebi was still in the main room, holding hands with Mr. Rai's young assistant, a Brahmin youth named Bhola Banstola. I wondered if Leonard had seen them, and if so, what he thought. I was sure they weren't gay. Their holding hands didn't mean that—any more than Jebi's arm around my shoulder had meant he was coming on to me. I bowed namaste.

Mohan Rai

A VOW TO LORD SHIVA

A cook's helper rapped on my bedroom door. "Coffee, Memsa'b." The day began, as usual, with a western-style breakfast of toast and scrambled eggs. None of us had much to say until the coffee cleared our heads. Mr. Rai arrived while we were eating and went to the kitchen to instruct the staff.

Peter was speaking of spirits we'd learned about in class, the *shikari* hunter spirits, Junglee, the Queen of the Forest, and Bhairab with the angry face, Shiva's younger brother. Apparently there were sixteen Bhairabs. The gods here seemed to multiply as fast as the population.

Leonard fidgeted, twisting his fork and looking more and more annoyed. Finally he broke into Peter's monologue. "This isn't what I thought it would be." His voice was low and gravelly. "You said we would be taught mantras. I didn't come here to be a spectator." He actually sounded choked, like someone near tears, his face dark with congested blood—but I knew he would shout before he'd weep.

"You have to understand," Peter said. "These men didn't learn to be shamans at a weekend seminar. They had to be chosen by the spirits. Their gurus give them their mantras as precious secrets. If they believe we're worthy, they may teach us—but it's their choice. This isn't something you can buy for money."

"Then maybe I should have a refund," Leonard challenged.

Mr. Rai appeared and planted himself behind a vacant chair with his hands on its back. "What is trouble here? We are here to teach you everything about our shamanism."

"I came to learn how to *do* something." Leonard turned to face him. "We've been here almost a week, and all we've done is take notes and watch. We were supposed to learn mantras."

Mr. Rai considered, looking grave. "Yes, yes, you will learn," he said. "I will talk to the shamans."

"Americans are too impatient," Peter said, his Danish accent making it clear he wasn't one. "You can't learn it just like that."

"Krishna will teach you protection mantra," Mr. Rai announced.

"The first thing a shaman must learn is protection for self from bad spirits, ghosts, witches. If not, then maybe he gets sick from spirits coming on his body." Still in English, for our benefit, he added, "Go ahead Krishna. Don't keep anything back."

Mr. Ganesh translated for Krishna, who frowned and answered something fast and angry. Mr. Rai barked a response.

"Now I am going to ask him to give you his mantra," Mr. Ganesh announced as though nothing were wrong. "Krishna—," he began in his schoolmasterish voice.

"*Hajur*," Krishna answered without looking up.

"It is a very long mantra," Mr. Ganesh told us. "Write it down."

Krishna spoke again, his face averted, with a quick glance at the translator.

"You must never tell anyone the mantra," Mr. Ganesh said. "It is very important. It can make the shaman sick if you reveal his mantra. You must not publish or tell it to anyone except your own students."

We nodded agreement—all but Leonard.

"Ho," Peter said directly to Krishna. "We promise."

After a long moment, the shaman began. "*Om.*"

"All mantras begin with "Om," Mr. Ganesh broke in. It is the name of Shiva, calling the Great God to witness. By the power of Shiva and by his promise...Krishna?"

Krishna recited in his native Tamang language, full of strange consonants hard to capture in writing—en's spoken far back in the throat, dees that were almost tees, sounds like ch or ts, and drawn-out vowels. He stressed some words more than others. I scribbled as fast as I could, filling a page and a half in my spiral notebook.

"Can you translate what it means?" Peter asked.

"I don't speak Tamang language," Mr. Ganesh said. "Krishna may tell us."

"*Angbannu*," Krishna answered shortly.

"It is angbannu," Mr. Ganesh repeated. "Means binding the body. He must say this mantra before he begins his ceremony, to avoid harm from spirits and ghosts, you see."

"Protection for shaman is most important," Mr. Rai added. "Without this, he might get sick. You must never reveal this mantra. Memorize it and tell no one, only your own students."

Krishna spoke again. "The next mantra is for asking his guru to sit on his head," Mr. Ganesh explained, "Come, sit on my head, be on my head, help me. Protect me. Make me not get sick." I marveled at how our translator could expand a scant few words from the shamans into paragraphs of monologue—and condense their longest explanations down to a single sentence.

"Guru means his tutelary deity," Peter explained.

"On his forehead, sun, moon, snake guru, on his mouth, his hand," Mr. Ganesh pronounced in a tone of dramatic awe.

Leonard had long since closed his notebook, and glared alternately at Peter and Mr. Rai. "Is he trying to trick us?" he demanded. "A mantra is supposed to be one word. He's given us a whole book. Was he telling some Tamang fairy tale? This is crazy."

"I told you it wasn't easy," Peter said. "We should be grateful for what he gave us and respect it. Maybe you're thinking of Transcendental Meditation or something like that, where they give you a single word as your own personal mantra—but that's not how these shamans work."

"It was obvious he didn't want to tell us anything," Leonard said. "I'm sure that wasn't a mantra."

❧

After lunch we were scheduled for more sightseeing with Mr. Ganesh, but Leonard declined. Peter made a show of urging him, but soon said, "Suit yourself," and came out on the porch to wait for the taxi with Diane and me.

"You're all laughing at me," Leonard said, following him outside. "I won't put up with it. I'm going to get what I came here for, or get my money back."

Peter ignored him.

The taxi arrived, a beat-up Chevrolet of mid-seventies vintage, and the four of us—Peter, Diane Mr. Ganesh, and I—crushed into the back seat. The driver had a friend in front. "Mr. Rai will calm Leonard down," Peter said. "I hope."

The taxi wound along the narrow dirt track and past the Japanese Teaching Hospital where the road began to widen. "People sometimes get weird when they come here," Peter said. "Everything seems strange, and they don't know how to control it. Not only is everyone around saying things you can't understand, but even the body language is different. If you're the least bit paranoid you start to think they're talking about you."

"The Nepalis meet each other's eyes," Diane remarked. "They don't look away when they see a stranger like we do."

"It's hard to get used to," Peter said. "You can feel very left out. I'm actually surprised Leonard's the only one with problems."

I kept quiet.

"I traveled all over the world when I worked for the airline," Diane said. "I'm used to it. I don't care what they think. I'm just a crazy American lady."

❧

Mr. Rai was gone when we returned, and Leonard had holed up in his room. Peter knocked and went in. Their voices rose, and Diane sneaked close and leaned her ear against the door. Fingers to her lips, she motioned me over.

"...passports," I heard Leonard say. "I told him to give back my passport. He refused."

Peter's answer was too soft to hear.

"I told him to go get it, and he just argued. He has no right to keep my passport. Am I a prisoner here or what?"

"...prisoner," Peter said. "...agreement you signed..."

"You breached our agreement." Leonard's voice was tight. "It's over. I demand a refund."

"What did you expect? This is Nepal. These are real shamans, not the kind of new age gurus you seem to want: 'Give me all your money and I'll sell you instant enlightenment.' If that's what you wanted, you should have stayed home."

"You misrepresented the program. Half the time the shamans don't even show up when they're supposed to, and when they do, they don't want to teach."

Diane caught my eye and mouthed *"Wo!"*

"They *are* teaching, if you cared to pay attention." We had no trouble hearing Peter now. "You think you can just sit there with your arms folded and have this fifty-thousand-year-old wisdom digested and served up like baby food?"

"I'm not—."

"This is an oral tradition, handed down only to carefully-chosen students. You have to win their confidence."

"This is fraud."

"I never led you to believe it was different than it is. I'm an anthropologist. You came with me to do what I do." His voice had gone cold.

"That's not what I paid for."

"You paid for what you're getting—a chance to show them you're serious and respectful, but you're not—."

"Fuck them. And fuck you. Why should I respect them? They're probably not even real shamans." Diane and I backed away from the door. "You could have pulled in anyone off the street and dressed them up in costumes to put on a show and trick us. What have these fakers done that anyone couldn't do?"

There was a moment of silence. Diane whispered, "Peter must be livid."

"They never give a straight answer to anything we ask. They hardly look at us. When they do say something, it's nonsense."

Mr. Rai came in then, and caught us listening. Diane beckoned him closer without a trace of embarrassment. "They're fighting," she whispered. "Leonard wants his money back."

Mr. Rai knocked and went in, leaving the door wide open. We drew back out of sight.

"If you don't like it, you don't have to stay," Mr. Rai said reasonably to Leonard. "Of course, you have to be satisfied with what you paid for."

"We had an agreement," Peter said. "He knew what he was getting into."

"Only don't give up too quickly, or you may regret later," Mr. Rai continued.

"Where's my passport?" Leonard demanded, refusing to be calmed.

"I have here, no problem. As I told you, I would get it. Only, I like to keep, to take to bank for changing money. That way you get special rates. If you don't mind."

"I'll take it now."

"Of course. Why not? It is yours."

"Do you think you could get the shamans to be a little more forthcoming?" Peter asked Mr. Rai. "Leonard thinks they're holding back, that they don't want to teach us their mantras."

"We'd like that too." Diane stepped into the doorway.

"We want to learn things we can use when we go home," I added, thinking that if Leonard felt we supported him, he might calm down. "I'd like to understand how the shamans think, how they feel when the deities come on them, what goes on inside."

"Not everything can be taught," Mr. Rai said.

"Then why did you tell us it could?" Leonard flared.

Peter made a disgusted noise and turned away.

"The shamans will test you," Mr. Rai said quickly. His forehead wrinkled in a complex pattern, as though each tiny muscle held the result of a separate calculation. "They will test you to see if you can become a shaman. They doesn't like to give their wisdom to someone if they don't know who *you* are, what kind of person, whether good person or not, unless and until they test you. You keep passport, then after tonight, you decide."

❧

Jebi and Krishna showed up after dinner. The word was out in the neighborhood that there'd be another ceremony, and the room was already full of spectators. "Another evening of drinking, smoking and shamanizing," Diane laughed, settling on the floor next to Peter to watch.

Krishna's costume was like Jebi's, with a red and white skirt, bells, and strings of seeds and snake bones. His performance got off to a slow start, with long songs and chants.

"Tamang mantras are very long," Mr. Rai explained.

Finally, Krishna began to shake, and then stood to dance. When he stopped and laid his drum down carefully on edge, Mr. Rai motioned Diane forward to the altar.

Krishna looked her over, took up his drum, and began to chant and shake again. He stopped momentarily, showered her with handfuls of rice grains, and blew mantras on her body.

"He is saying mantras to make her shake," Mr. Rai said. "If she shakes she can surely be shaman." But she remained unmoved, and Krishna stopped drumming. "Maybe another time," Mr. Rai said.

Diane shrugged and grinned, scooting back to make way for Leonard, who sat down seriously by the altar, his shoulder blades drawn together beneath his T-shirt.

"Open yourself," Mr. Rai shouted over the drumbeat. "Open yourself. Think of Lord Shiva."

The drumming and chanting went on a long time. Leonard sat with closed eyes as Krishna showered him with rice and blew mantras on him. The shaman danced a circle around Leonard, digging the point of his drum handle into the top of his head, but finally, when nothing happened, he stopped and looked at Mr. Rai.

"Again," Mr. Rai directed.

Krishna tried, but Leonard still didn't shake.

"If he doesn't shake, doesn't mean he won't be good healer," Mr. Rai said. "There is kind of healer that doesn't shake—heals by mantras only. If he doesn't shake, only it means he has to be different kind of healer."

Leonard pulled a face for our benefit, as though it didn't matter.

"Because you are American and you eat beef," Mr. Rai consoled.

"Lord Shiva doesn't like beef eating. If you didn't eat beef, I think you would all be shaking."

Now it was my turn. I sat by Krishna and closed my eyes, realizing I wanted very much to pass this test. The drumming began. "Think of Lord Shiva," Mr. Rai shouted.

I brought the image of Shiva to mind, not the effeminate, soft-faced god in mascara and lipstick depicted in the poster on our wall, but a stronger god made up from the words that described him: Destroyer, Master of Beasts, Great God. I visualized the ashes on his body, the tiger skin he wore, his three-pronged weapon, the live snakes winding up and down his arms, the top of his head wide open, pouring forth clear water. My stomach felt shaky, but my legs didn't move.

"*Lo paramaswara!*" Mr. Rai shouted the traditional greeting to the god who comes on a shaman's body. "*Concentrate!* You must concentrate yourself," he ordered, surprising me with his intensity. I felt the force of his strong will focused on me, bringing the whole scene into present time, heightening my awareness like a drug.

I prayed silently to the god, Lord Shiva: *"I promise never again to eat beef."* A light trembling swept over my body, not the large, muscular twitching of the shamans, and probably not even visible to the others. The drumming stopped.

"I think she can be a shaman," Mr. Rai said. "It was starting. For sure she would be shaking if she doesn't eat beef."

Diane smiled and mimed applause. Leonard's gaze was fixed and unreadable, but I could sense the tumblers whirling back behind his eyes, looking for a way to devalue my experience so he could live with it. But I didn't mind. I'd rather have that than his envy.

THE WITCHES AND THE SHAMANS

We had a long, leisurely time to drink our coffee on the porch, waiting for Mr. Rai and the shamans to show up. A steady stream of people walked along the road beyond the rice field, or rode past on bicycles, a blend of races. The men wore western suits, or jeans, or Gandhi-style dhotis; the women were in saris or long wrap-around skirts. Nepali women didn't wear slacks. An occasional Westerner passed in shorts, or the red and blue patchwork pantsuits sold only to tourists.

Mr. Ganesh arrived and had his coffee, and finally, Jebi and Mr. Rai showed up. Mr. Rai watched from the doorway, a twist of smoke from the cigarette dangling from his mouth turning his eyes to unreadable slits. Jebi was talking about witches, who were often blamed for illness and misfortune. "They control massans and other bad spirits, and send them into the bodies of those they wish harm," he said.

Diane, who had attended full-moon Wiccan ceremonies back home, with men and women who called themselves white witches, asked, "Are all witches bad?"

"There are no good witches," Jebi assured us. "Besides using massan ghosts to do her work, the witch can send her own spirit into someone else's body to make her sick, or angry and rude to her family."

"They are called *bokshies*, these witches," Mr. Ganesh translated. "Their wisdom comes from Parvati, Shiva's wife. Shiva has more wisdom than Parvati, but Parvati is the one who gives her wisdom to the witches." He was going off again, displaying his own knowledge instead of translating, but neither Peter nor Mr. Rai tried to stop him.

"One day Parvati got bored because her husband was always drinking, smoking hashish, and sleeping. So she looked for nine women with black tongues and evil eyes. She started teaching them, and when she finished, sent them out in eight directions to do bad things.

"Then down on earth, all the people began to get sick. They called Naradmuni, messenger of the gods, and asked him to wake up Lord Shiva. Naradmuni got everyone to come to the foot of Mt. Kailash with musical instruments, cymbals, drums, and horns, to make a big noise. Shiva finally woke up. He opened his third eye and realized the women were *heinous*."

I grinned and Diane raised her eyebrows at Mr. Ganesh's impressive command of English.

"So Shiva decided he would have to teach some men to be shamans to fight the witches. He chose seven men with solid, clean bodies, and no cuts from metals or accidental wounds, to be his shaman disciples. He gave them mantras, altars, oil lamps, drums, malas, and words of power, and promised to come and help when they called.

"The witches got worried and went to ask Mother Parvati what they should do about these shamans. 'Don't worry,' the goddess said. 'This will be good for you. You'll get more offerings.'

"'We want to kill the shamans,' the witches said. They used ashes to make boils on the shamans' bodies, but the shamans healed themselves with holy water. Then the shamans sent fire against the witches. Witches can only use fire of animal or human fat, not butter or mustard oil, and they had no fire, but they sent clouds and shadows the shamans could not dispel.

"Then the shamans brought three different sizes of metal boxes, one inside the other, and three keys. They hid a sick person inside the innermost box, locked the second around it, and the third around that. 'You must open the boxes without touching them,' they challenged the witches. The witches circled the boxes three times counterclockwise and whistled, and the locks opened. The shamans had lost again.

"Then the shamans asked permission from Naradmuni to speak to Shiva. 'Now the age of *kali yuga* has come,' Shiva said. 'Parvati and I have many names in these days, and we have to travel to kill monsters on earth. Ordinary people can no longer speak to us. Only shamans.' He gave the men *amliso*, a plant with long leaves like maize, and his trident, and told them his plan for defeating the witches."

Jebi removed a long leaf, like a giant blade of grass, from his pack. We passed it around. It was like a corn leaf, only thicker, and a lighter shade of green. A row of dents crossed it halfway along its length.

"'Call *Om Namo Shivaya* seven times,' Lord Shiva told the shamans. 'Bite the amliso leaf in two, and then challenge the witches to do the same. They won't be able to. The leaves will be like metal plates against their teeth.' After Lord Shiva had spoken, the shamans went back down to earth taking the tridents and amliso leaves with them."

Diane and I, cross-legged on the floor, furiously took notes, but

Leonard had long-since closed his notebook, and sat on the couch looking bored.

"The shamans practiced biting the leaves in two with the help of their mantras for seven days and nights, and then set a full moon night for the contest with the witches. Each side would build their altars and call their powers. 'No one can leave until we're finished, and none can use *liso*,' the shamans said, referring to the sacred plant gum embodying the god, Sharma. 'And the loser must swear seven times to live underground in the daytime and never see the sun. A boundary will be fixed between the middle world and the lower world, and the loser cannot cross without permission.'

"The witches clapped their hands and laughed, 'Why are you going to so much trouble?'

"The contest began. The shamans chopped cauliflower with feathers, but the witches chopped it with air. The shamans produced thousands of honey bees, but the witches produced bumble bees. The shamans called Hanuman, the monkey god, upon their bodies and climbed the trees, but the witches jumped up to the treetops in one bound.

"Then the shamans said to the witches, 'You are really great and powerful. No doubt you will win. But just do one more little thing. Watch how easily we bite these amliso leaves in two. You try and do it too. Then we will concede that you have won.'

The shamans said their mantra seven times, and each took a long leaf from the pile they'd laid out on a table, stuck it far down his throat, and bit it in two. 'Go ahead,' they challenged the witches. 'It's easy.'

"The witches laughed. They put the ends of the leaves in their mouths and pushed them in as far as they could. When they were halfway in, the witches bit down hard, but the leaves were like metal. Their teeth could only make a row of dents. Even to this day you can see the dents of the witches' teeth across the middle of amliso leaves." Mr. Ganesh took the leaf from Jebi and pointed out the row of shallow impressions that crossed the middle of the leaf.

"So the witches lost, and the shamans banished them to the lower world." Mr. Ganesh paused, and Diane took a breath, as though about to speak.

"Then the people had no one to bother them or make them sick," Mr. Ganesh continued, with relish. "The shamans had nothing to do. No one came with chickens for healing.

"Meanwhile the witches were drowning and freezing in the water down there in the lower world. They begged to come up, and the shamans realized they had to let them back into the middle world. But before they did, they made an agreement. The witches would cast spells, and the shamans would heal. The witches would work only at night, but the shamans could work both day and night. And whenever a shaman has to fight a witch, the shaman always wins."

Diane gave me a significant look. I thought it was because she'd been struck, as I had, by the story's message that both good and evil must be present for the world to exist at all. But instead she asked, "So witches are women and shamans are men?"

"No, no." The translator hastened to set her straight. "There are male witches and women shamans. We call witches bokshies, but if they are men, they are called bokshas. They do not have to be women, but the wisdom of the witches is Parvati's wisdom, you see, and the wisdom of Shiva, which is greater, was given only to the shamans. Shiva has armed his shamans with one more mantra than the witches. That is why they always win, you see."

"What is that mantra," Leonard asked. "Are you going to tell us?"

After a brief conversation in Nepali with Jebi, Mr. Ganesh said, "Of course, why not. It is Om." He looked significantly at each of us in turn, and Jebi nodded. "The shamans call upon the name of God."

"It is by the promise of Lord Shiva that they heal," Mr. Rai added.

"Lord Shiva," said Leonard flatly.

"It's very simple—," Mr. Rai said.

"Om," said Leonard in that same expressionless way. "I suppose the witches never heard of Om."

"Of course, everyone knows Om," Mr. Rai said. "Only witches doesn't say it."

"You have to understand—," Peter began.

"I don't *have* to understand anything, Peter," Leonard said with cold dignity, "but I understand I have learned what I need to know, and now *you* must understand I want my money refunded so I can go home and stop wasting my time."

Peter slapped his notebook on the couch and rose to his feet.

"No, no, is no need to argue," Mr. Rai broke in, hurrying between them. "If you has to go, Peter will give back money. Only, I have asked my shamans to do divination for you tonight, for path of your soul, to see what is getting in *your* way and what you need to do." Without giving Leonard time to protest, he motioned the cooks to bring out lunch.

"I'll be here tonight in any event," Leonard grumbled, pulling out his chair with a scraping noise and allowed his elbows to spread on the table into Peter's space.

"Peter, do you know of any women shamans," Diane asked brightly.

"I have seen one or two. They are not so common."

"Oh, yes, some women are shamans," Mr. Rai assured us.

"Do you think we could see one?" Diane looked to me for support.

"We'd really like to," I seconded.

"As a matter of fact, there is one woman shaman living nearby here," Mr. Rai said. "I will try and get her."

A SPIRIT IN MY BEDROOM

That night, both shamans performed, divining for Leonard as he sat between them, still and reverent, with lowered eyes. Both shamans spoke from their trances, saying he must leave the program and make a pilgrimage to Mt. Kalinchok, sacred to Lord Shiva.

"Lord Shiva," Leonard repeated, when Mr. Rai translated the shamans' findings, but more in speculation than protest.

"You have to understand," Peter explained, "Lord Shiva is God to these people. *Mahadeo*, the *Great God.*" This time Leonard let him finish.

"Yes, it is the same God everywhere," Mr. Rai said, "only we call by different names."

"It is only God who heals," Mr. Rai's young assistant, Bhola, added.

Surprisingly, Leonard seemed more pleased than not with the shamans' prescription, and said, "This must be the reason I came here."

Mr. Rai arranged Leonard's trip, hiring porters and buying supplies, and as it turned out, Leonard ended up paying more money—which allowed Mr. Rai to refund some of his tuition to Peter. All this got worked out in a closed-door session in Leonard's bedroom while Diane and I joked with Jebi outside and tried to converse with Krishna. The men came out smiling. Leonard would leave in the morning to pursue his own special destiny.

Jovial at having the problem resolved, Mr. Rai asked if we were comfortable with our beds, warm enough at night, and was the food to our liking? "Anything not right, just tell me." He shouted for the cooks to bring us drinks.

"He's one hell of a business man," Diane remarked.

"A genius at figuring out how to give Westerners whatever they want," Peter agreed.

"And get Mr. Rai what *he* wants too," Diane added, rubbing

her thumb and finger together in the universal gesture of testing an imaginary gold coin.

Even the shamans seemed relieved. Jebi laughed a lot. We all stayed up late enjoying the atmosphere of tensions eased, except, of course, for Leonard, who'd gone straight to his room to pack. Diane laughed her bubbling, incredulous laugh, and tossed her full head of curls, and we got high on the rakshi we insisted on trying, though Mr. Rai warned it was bad for our health. "I drink only good bottled whiskey," he said, dragging on his cigarette and blowing smoke. "That's why I never get sick."

❧

Before we went to bed, Jebi went outside to circle the house, on shaman patrol to be sure no evil spirits were lurking. I thought it was a joke. I wanted to accept the reality of gods and spirits. I was here to be convinced, but all my early training worked against it. My parents had told me there were no such things, at a time when I desperately needed to believe them.

❧

My mother had finished medical school when I was nearly five, and my parents took me to Ames Iowa, where we lived in a corrugated metal house with a curved roof—married student housing, because Daddy was a graduate student at Iowa State. I had my own room for the first time, sleeping by myself instead of with Grandma, and I missed the reassuring warmth of her body, the *puh* sounds she made with her lips when she fell asleep.

Now things came in the night, floating in the dark over my bed. Once it was great big bare butts. People weren't supposed to show their butts, but here they were—fat ladies' butts, big men's butts with hair, and little boy butts that floated away when I tried to get a closer look.

Daddy and Mama came to tuck me in, and I went cold with embarrassment thinking now they'd see my shameful thoughts. But Mama pulled the covers around my neck, Daddy kissed me on the forehead, and they left as though nothing was wrong. They never even saw those butts.

After that came mean, scary faces. I screamed. Daddy's footsteps pounded toward my room. He burst through the door and turned on the light. "Honey what's wrong?"

"Mean monsters." I put into my voice how awful they were, so he'd do something to chase them away. The last of them, no more than a featureless dark blob now that the light was on, floated past Daddy's head and disappeared.

"No such thing as monsters," he said. "It's just your imagination. Go to sleep." He turned off the light, but left the door open. "See, we'll leave the light on in the hall."

A few nights later, at bedtime, I asked if there was such a thing as ghosts. "*No-ho-ho*," Daddy said, making a pretend surprised face. "How much does a ghost weigh? If you want *me* to believe in ghosts, you'll have to show me one."

There's no such thing as ghosts, I repeated when he'd gone. But that didn't stop them from coming—angry faces, scared faces, visions of gravestones, skeletons, bodies rotting underground, stink, and softened flesh. My own body rotting in a cold, damp, narrow coffin. Rigid with fear, I scarcely breathed. If only Grandma had been right about God and going to heaven when you died.

I believed Daddy that the monsters were only thoughts, and thoughts weren't real, but they still showed up to scare me. I couldn't call for help, because Daddy had already said they didn't exist. Wide-eyed in the darkness, I prayed, "Oh God, if there is a God, *please* give me faith."

A prayer that was never answered. God, if there was a God, had given me doubts instead.

❧

That night, in bed in the program house, I was buzzed and happy from the rakshi—but not impaired. I knew my senses were intact. And, I knew I wasn't dreaming.

Jebi had long since finished his shaman patrol. The house was dark and quiet. I'd been asleep an hour or two with the door closed when I suddenly woke with a sense of someone in the room. My eyes shot open. The air held a strange tension, a sense of space, an energy that pulled on my ribs and stomach. Halfway between my bed and the doorway, I saw the outline of a short man, no more than three and a half feet tall, transparent and slightly shimmering, as though made of heat waves. His large round head was well-defined, almost solid.

"This can't be real," I thought.

And at that, he disappeared.

I groaned aloud from a keen sense of loss. There *had* been someone there—a spirit—and I'd let him get away. Why? *Why* had I doubted? I should have tried to communicate.

Next morning, in the bright light of day, I remembered him clearly.

He had seemed as real as the air I breathed; he was no dream. But the odd feeling of his presence was gone, and I couldn't bring it back.

Several days passed, with classes after breakfast, sightseeing junkets in the afternoons and ceremonies at night. Our notebooks filled with lists of gods and spirits—*nagas, bhairabs, sharmas*, ghosts—how they looked, their powers, what kind of harm they did, what offerings of food or drink or incense they required, what rituals would make them go away. I told no one what I'd seen in my bedroom that night. It would sound like bragging, or the others might say it was a dream.

I understood now why the shamans insisted we keep their mantras secret. Exposed to other people's doubts, they'd surely lose their power, just as I felt the spirit's reality would disappear if I mentioned having seen him.

WE'RE WITCHES!

True to his word, Mr. Rai brought a woman shaman to the program house, introducing her as Maile Lama, a Tamang shaman who lived in the neighborhood. Her light brown skin was clear and smooth, her forehead high and marked near the hairline with a deep scar, her thickened body setting her age at late thirties or early forties. Her husband, a thin old man, was with her, along with a younger woman carrying a baby.

Maile bowed namaste and kept her head down, smiling shyly. I knew that *maile* was the word used within families for second daughter, and wondered what her real name was. "Mr. Lama is a Buddhist lama," Mr. Rai told us as the old man bowed.

Maile took the baby from the other woman as we all sat down. "Dorje," she said, her face lighting up to speak her son's name. She held him beneath her shawl to nurse.

Mr. Ganesh appeared and seated himself on a straight chair, his spine upright and well away from the chair back. He accepted coffee from one of the cooks and announced, "Now, this morning, Maile will tell us who she is and how she got to be a shaman. She is of the Tamang tribe. That is a tribe from the mountains on the border of Tibet. So her name is Maile Tamangni."

"Maile *Lama*," she corrected, but so quietly he seemed not to hear.

"She is a Banjhankri shaman."

Maile smiled, recognizing the name of her guru.

"When she was a child, it happened she was playing outdoors, and the Wild Shaman, Banjhankri, captured her. I will ask her to tell us how it happened." They conversed in Nepali, Mr. Ganesh taking a condescending tone, like a father speaking to a child.

"Maile has been a shaman since she was seven years old, when she was kidnapped by the Banjhankri. He took her to his cave, filled with gold and jewels, and taught her healing mantras and how to drum.

"She grew up in the mountain village of Okaldhunga. Her family was neither poor nor very rich, though they owned several fields and had servants to help with the work. Her uncle was a shaman. It was rare, but sometimes happened, that women of her tribe would become shamans. Her great-grandmother had been a shaman, and before that there were others. That's why she was chosen by the gods and ancestors to be a woman shaman in her generation.

"One night, the servant who usually stayed in the cowshed to look after the cattle got sick, and while Maile's mother and elder sister cared for him in the house, her father took the servant's place in the cowshed to guard the cattle. Maile begged to come along, and her father let her bring her blanket and stay with him. He built a little fire with charcoal and a few sticks, and when it was completely dark, wrapped her in her blanket and put her to bed in the straw. The family had called a shaman for the servant, and when her father heard his footsteps coming slowly up the hill, he went outside to lead him to the house."

Mr. Ganesh consulted with Maile. She spoke with animation, and made motions of covering her face, acting out her story.

Mr. Ganesh continued, "She woke in the cowshed to find her father gone. It was nearly midnight. She sat up and watched the red coals of the fire. A little man, no taller than a child, came in without a sound and went over to the fire. He picked up a stick and dug among the coals until they glowed, and then sat beside the fire and started to shake. He looked at Maile with bright eyes under thick eyebrows that hung down, and she hid her face in her shawl. She peeked out while he was poking the fire, and the little man suddenly raised his head and caught her looking. She hid her face again.

"Then she heard her father cough outside. The little man spread his hands wide open, and with a joking look, picked up a bunch burning coals and small sticks, and threw them everywhere, toward the cows and calves, and all over the cowshed, in every direction except toward Maile. But when her father opened the door, the little man was gone.

"'Dad, Dad, a little man was here,' she said. 'Just now, throwing fire with his bare hands.'

"'Shush,' her father said. 'Just go to sleep.' He rolled up in his blanket and began to snore. But the next morning he noticed the bits of charcoal and sticks all over the cowshed, and knew something had happened. He went looking for the most important shaman in the village to ask what it was.

"The shaman asked his spirits, and told Maile's father, 'The Banjhankri came to your daughter to protect her.'

"A few days later, Maile and her father were still sleeping in the cowshed, and the Banjhankri came back and carried her away, hooking his little finger in hers and flying through the air. He took her to his cave, where everything was made of gold, and fed her on tadpoles, worms and eggs. When his terrible wife, Lemlemma, came in with her long, flat breasts hanging down to her feet, looking for children to eat, he hid Maile under a basket. He taught her drumbeats and a special mantra, and told her, 'If you say this mantra, you can cure the world.'

"Then he took her home, flying to the cowshed where her father was still asleep. After that she began to shake when the moon was full, and a human guru had to be found to teach her to control the spirit that came on her. Her uncle, the shaman, agreed to take her as his student. He brought her along whenever he did healings."

The translator stopped, and Maile spoke again. Her husband, the old lama, looked on, proudly nodding.

"The next time she saw the Banjhankri, she was nine years old. She and her mother had gone to a nearby meadow to cut grass for the cows. It was Maile's job to gather the grass into a pile so they could bundle it up and carry it home. The Banjhankri came, dressed in old, torn clothes, and stepped over her pile three times. She didn't see him right away, but then he came straight up to her, put his hand on her forehead and led her away.

They walked near the river, and he held her hand and pulled her sideways up a cliff. He carried her under a waterfall, and she saw a broad road leading into the distance. They followed the road to his cave, a great room furnished with golden drums and beaters, a golden sword, and plates and spoons all made of gold. She fell down unconscious. When she came to, the Banjhankri put his hand on her forehead and brought her back to the meadow.

"She heard her mother scolding, 'Not much grass. That's all the grass you've gathered?' They tied it up and went home. The next day Maile tried to go back to the cave by herself. She went to the cliff and climbed up. There were lots of rocks, and she had to hold on to the bushes and small trees to pull herself up. When she got to the waterfall, she looked underneath. All she could see were slick, shiny rocks, and thorns and nettles.

"The Banjhankri came again when she was eleven. She was asleep in her own bed at home. Her sister-in-law saw the little man come in, and heard his steps as he climbed to the upper floor. He carried Maile out through an upstairs window, flying so fast no one could follow. He kept her in his cave three hours, and then brought her back to bed. 'Don't watch me leave,' he warned. 'If you do I'll take you for good.' She hid her face under the blanket. 'Don't think of meeting me again,' he told her.

"After that, she grew strong and stubborn, and began to argue with her parents, demanding special things to eat and choosing her own place to sleep. When she went with her uncle to the home of a sick person, as soon as she saw the patient, she began to shake, even before the drumming started. She used the mantras Banjhankri had taught her. Sometimes when her uncle drummed, she could hear Banjhankri circling the house outside, blowing a conch shell, drumming, and speaking mantras. Others heard him too. At night, in dreams, he taught her rituals and mantras. When she stayed in the cowshed overnight, he called her from the dark outside, but she remembered his warning, and didn't go out to meet him."

Mr. Ganesh asked Maile a short question and she shook her head. "She doesn't like to be a shaman," he told us.

"Why not?" I asked.

"If someone is sick she has to go," he said. "Even if she's tired. People are coming to her house all day for healing. But she was taken by Banjhankri, so she has to do it."

Maile appraised Diane and me with long, steady looks as he spoke. I gave her my warmest smile. But before we could question her, Mr. Ganesh abruptly dismissed the little family. Mr. Rai said he had to go to meet his German climbers, and left without a word to Maile and her husband.

Maile handed the baby to the younger woman and bowed namaste to each of us in turn. I'd been shocked at what I took as the men's rudeness, and she'd noticed my startled reaction. I hoped she understood I didn't share their hurry to banish her. "*Pheri aunuhos*," please come back, I said as I bowed goodbye.

That afternoon Mr. Ganesh took us to see the temple of Kumari, the living virgin goddess, where a long line of devotees waited with offerings, hoping for a glimpse of the prepubescent girl who'd been chosen to be the goddess. Her reign would end as soon as her menses began, and a new girl-child would be chosen to live in the temple and be fed and worshiped and closely guarded. We waited with the others, and at last the goddess appeared on a balcony, a wide-faced girl obviously near the end of her deification. "They usually make a good marriage when they leave the temple," Mr. Ganesh told us.

Back at the program house, Diane and I took Star beers to the porch. "Can you believe how Mr. Ganesh told us that whole story about the Banjhankri out of no more than a few sentences from Maile?" She snorted. "She seems demure and proper, doesn't she, but I'll bet she knows a thing or two."

"What makes you think so?" I agreed but wanted to hear her opinion.

"You saw how everyone tried to run all over her, but it wasn't because they thought she was unimportant. They're scared."

"Scared? If they're scared, they do a good job hiding it."

"They probably don't even realize they're scared. They tell themselves women don't matter, and that's how they act. The fact that she's a shaman makes it worse. They *have* to put her down."

Mr. Rai had offered to buy gifts for us to bring home, and I took him up on it at once. I hated the haggling at the market. That afternoon, he interrupted our class with Jebi to show me what he'd bought, a fine selection of Buddhist bells, a colorful backpack, strings of rudraksha beads, two excellent wool shawls, and a large two-sided shaman's drum with a finely-carved wooden handle. The drum was black from years of hanging in the smoke of a chimneyless house, and had a small tear in one side. I picked up the beater, a hardened, curved vine, and tested the sound. It was deep and resonant, and when I tilted it sideways, the crystals sealed inside slid and rattled, murmuring portentously. It seemed a thing of power, so much so that I dared not embrace it at once as my own.

Also among the purchases was a necklace of small white skulls Mr. Rai said were carved from bone, a Kali mala.

"The skulls are the severed heads of monsters," Mr. Ganesh explained. "The black goddess, Kali, wears them for a necklace. She is our very powerful goddess. We must give only uncastrated males for sacrifice to Mother Kali. She is Shiva's consort Parvati in her anger." He raised his chin and made a serious face.

"She got angry about the demons hurting people on earth and started warring on them. She cut off their heads and hung them around her neck. That's why, in all the pictures of Kali, she is wearing necklaces of skulls. She thought she was the most powerful lady in the world. She became proud of herself." Mr. Ganesh's high-pitched voice had taken on a preacher's rhythm.

"She decided to go to Pashupati Temple. Lord Shiva was there. He was addicted to drugs, you know, and intoxicated, lying in the temple.

Kali was so proud of her power, she said, 'There are no other gods and goddesses. I am supreme.' She put her foot on Lord Shiva." Mr. Ganesh's falling tone and slow, deliberate cadence warned us that Kali was sure to be punished for touching her husband with her foot.

Diane and I exchanged glances.

"You know, this is a heinous sin in Hinduism," Mr. Ganesh explained.

We wiped the smiles from our faces, taking care not to catch each other's eyes.

"When she realized it was her husband she was stepping on, she stuck her tongue all the way out in shame. She began to pray to her husband in repentance, and said, 'If you ask anything of me, I will do it all my life.'

"'You will do everything for me,' Shiva said, 'and I will take away your power.'

Mr. Ganesh held up my new drum. "Shiva's drum had a tear on one side, just like this one. Kali asked if she could make him a new one, but Shiva said, 'No! It will never be so! I will never give you that power!'

"Then she said, 'Forgive me. I'll wash your leg and drink the water, but please don't take my power.'"

"Shiva said, 'I will never pardon you. You may not create me a new drum. I can create it myself. If you really want pardon, get me a tiger skin—from any part of the universe.'

"So Kali brought Lord Shiva a tiger skin." Mr. Ganesh pointed to the brightly-colored poster taped to the far wall that showed Lord Shiva with the skin draped over one shoulder. "He put it on, sat down, and called for drugs—marijuana and hashish. He said, 'I will give you back your power if you're not afraid, but if you are afraid, I may not be able to.'" The translator stopped, his story at an end.

I fingered the shiny skull beads. They had a slick, plastic feel.

"Why don't we see if those 'genuine bone' beads melt," Peter said. He pulled out a lighter and snapped it into flame.

"That's okay." I gathered the mala to my chest. "I want them anyway."

I took the new drum to my room and set it carefully upright in the corner on its curved edge, and then emptied my duffel bag of canned food to make room for the gifts, embarrassed that Mr. Rai would see I'd brought beef. But I didn't want to waste it. I brought out the cans and piled them on the table, and Mr. Rai said, "Thanks, I can use," sweeping them away to the kitchen.

၏

After dinner, Mr. Rai said we'd been invited to a ceremony Jebi was to perform at another house. We set out at dusk. I'd been thinking the patient must be too sick to come to the program house, but instead, she looked quite healthy, a pretty young woman with a delicate gold ring in the side of her nose.

We crowded into the house along with forty or fifty neighbors. Jebi had arrived before us and set up his altar in a doorway between two rooms. Now he entered from somewhere in the back, striding through the crowd in full costume, looking fierce.

He began to drum and simultaneously beat his brass plate. I felt the familiar excitement gather in the pit of my stomach. Two strong men hustled the patient to the altar and made her sit there by the shaman.

"He is asking to see, is a witch on her," Mr. Rai explained.

The young woman sat silently, head down, and began to shake. Jebi shot questions at her with increasing rudeness. "Bokshi ho?" I knew that bokshi meant witch. "Ko ho? Bhut ho? Pret ho? Deota ho?"

"Now he is asking about ghosts and spirits, and is it deity or bad spirit that is on her," Mr. Rai said.

She didn't respond.

Jebi turned to face the altar and drummed with renewed fervor. He dipped the tip of his drum handle into the oil of his lamp and touched it to his forehead, asking for more help from the gods. He shouted again at the woman, but she only sat and shook. Then he directed his assistant to heat up a long metal spoon in the kitchen. When the red-hot spoon was brought, he brandished it toward the young woman. "Bokshi ho?" he shouted.

"He will make her speak," Mr. Rai said. "This is for sure. What is on her, he will make it tell who it is, where it lives, why it has come to bother her."

"He isn't really going to burn her, is he?" Diane cringed.

"No, no, of course not. That is only to scare witch that is on her body and make her talk."

Half an hour later, the patient still refused to speak. It had become a contest of wills, and she was resisting the only way she could, with silence. Jebi set his drum aside, and someone handed him a drink.

"We take break," Mr. Rai explained, passing us cups of rakshi that, I noted with embarrassment, had been brought out only for himself and his American guests.

Jebi drummed again, alternately shouting and speaking in a soft, cajoling tone, trying to break the patient down. The night wore on.

Finally, as nothing seemed to be happening, Peter and Diane went home. Soon afterward, Mr. Rai left as well, assigning Bhola to guide me back.

I didn't want to leave. By now I was definitely rooting for the witch. Bhola explained that the young woman lived in this house with her brother, Sandeep, Mr. Rai's assistant who'd helped us at the airport, a large young man with a well-fed, spoiled expression.

"What's wrong with her?" I asked.

"Maybe it is witch," Bhola said. "Sometimes she shakes for no reason. Sometimes she shouts, and her brother beats her."

"Oh."

Peter had explained that once a witch begins to speak, she usually curses and shouts at her family members, taking the opportunity to air a host of pent-up grievances. Then, after the shaman has expelled the witch from her body, the family is reconciled. But this witch wasn't to be easily appeased.

As the hours passed, Jebi threatened to whip the woman with stinging nettles, but didn't actually do so, beating himself instead of the patient. Then he tried to bribe her with gifts of whatever she wanted. But the patient maintained her stubborn silence.

At three in the morning, Jebi took a break, lay down, and began to snore. She has won! I thought.

Most of the audience was gone, but after a few minutes, Jebi woke and started in again. The pretty young woman endured it all with her head submissively bowed, but I could sense her inner steel, and knew Jebi would fail.

It was dawn when he finally gave up. Bhola led me out to the dirt road toward the program house. "She is not talking," he said. "Jebi will have to try again, or some other shaman has to come—a stronger shaman." I felt bad for Jebi, but fiercely happy that he'd failed to break the woman's will.

"Good," Diane said next evening when I told her. We were lounging on the porch, waiting for Peter and Mr. Rai to finish their business talk so we could have dinner. "They act like women don't matter, but if that's true, why are they so terrified of witches? The men are scared all right. They know their power is mostly puff and blow."

"Maybe it's the women's fault." I leaned forward. "No, listen, really. Maybe women screwed up a long time ago, letting the men think they were more powerful—maybe they noticed how much better the men were in bed when they thought they had the upper hand."

Diane giggled, hiding her mouth with her hand.

"Those first women knew it was only an act, pretending to be weak and submissive," I went on. "But they forgot to let their daughters in on the secret. The daughters thought it was true. That's what I was raised to think, weren't you? It makes me mad."

"Honey, Ah was raised in Texas. I'm mad as hell," she said.

After dinner she brought her pink boom box to the porch, inserted a rock and roll tape and began to dance. I joined her, twisting and rocking in a free-form celebration of female freedom. We twirled and writhed and raised our arms, hair loose and flying, letting our bodies move in ways that had to be illegal.

"You shouldn't do that," Peter cautioned. "The Nepalis will be embarrassed."

"*Let* them be." Diane was fearless.

"Bokshies," I said, but not too loud. "We're bokshies."

MAILE

I wanted to see how Maile worked as a shaman in her natural setting, and asked Mr. Rai if I could visit her.

"Of course you can," he said. "Bhola will take you."

We walked along the dirt lane, past a long rice field, around three corners of a square, to Maile's home on the second floor of a ramshackle building. The stairs were on the outside. Maile and old Mr. Lama welcomed us into their small, single room with cordial namastes, and seated us on the bed, a double-sized mattress on a wooden platform.

Though the floor of the upstairs room was covered with a layer of dirt, Maile was housecleaning, dipping water from a bucket with her hand to make mud, and smoothing it down on the few square feet of floor space, where it was drying to a high, red-brown gloss. "She makes it shiny like that with cow dung," Bhola told me, obviously enjoying his chance to shock an American.

She offered us chia, Nepali milk tea, kept warm in a thermos. Peter had warned us never to drink anything that hadn't been boiled in the program house kitchen, but I accepted anyway. The baby woke and Maile took him in her arms to nurse. Before she finished, a patient arrived, a mother with a small child wrapped in her rust-colored, red and dark-brown striped shawl. Mother and child waited quietly on the dry, shiny floor as we finished our tea.

Maile moved to the floor beside them, and the woman handed her a blue plastic bag containing a bit of rice and two eggs. They had a friendly conversation, mother to mother, Maile asking how the child had been eating and sleeping, and the color of its stools. She smelled its breath, then lit her tiny oil lamp, placed her hands together in a gesture of prayer, and bowed forward. Holding her brass altar plate on her lap, she spread rice grains from the mother's offering on its surface and blew mantras on single pinches which she took up one by one and laid in a clear spot on the plate. She separated the grains into pairs and counted, whispering mantras with a rapturous expression, her eyes rolled up and focused inward.

"She is speaking to Mahadeo, the Great God," Bhola said.

She set the brass plate on the floor. "Now she has found out what is bothering the patient."

She lit a twist of hemp incense at the oil lamp's flame and passed it repeatedly over the child's body, breathing in with that same shocked-sounding gasp that Jebi used, and blowing out on the child with breath made holy by her mantras. Then she snapped her fingers, moving her hand down and away from the little patient, as though leading the spirit of illness out.

During the next several hours, she treated a succession of patients with varied rituals, some longer than others. "How do you know when you've done enough?" I asked.

"I watch their faces."

"She can see their faces change when the bad spirits go away," Bhola said.

⌘

After that I began to skip the afternoon sightseeing and shopping sessions to watch Maile work. She never failed to welcome me with that radiant, toothy smile of hers, and offer tea and food. I accepted a scrambled egg cooked on her kerosene burner, and didn't get sick. Sometimes she would use her long upper lip in the Tamang way to point at a patient as she explained his problem.

Meanwhile, Peter and Diane had picked up severe eye infections. Their eyes were raw and puffy, oozing yellow pus, and painful to the point of distraction. Peter had suffered for a week; the tissue around his eyes was fiercely red, as though turned inside out.

After I'd been showing up for several days, Maile said she would do a divination to see if I had the ability to become a shaman. "Bring your shaman's drum and a small jar of rakshi and some flowers," she said.

Bhola stopped me as I brought my drum out from my room. "Don't go out with your drum like that in the daytime where people can see." He fetched a towel and wrapped it. I didn't see why, but his expression was earnest. He was obviously trying to protect me. I realized I'd been treating him like another American because his English was so good and he seemed such a progressive young man, interested in Western ways. But of course, he had the sensibilities of his culture, feelings I hadn't even tried to be aware of. I suddenly regretted our wild bokshi dance and wished I were wearing a skirt instead of jeans.

But Bhola shouldered the covered drum with good cheer, and picked a bouquet of marigolds and red flowers from the borders around the yard for Maile. We set off around the rice field. Laborers were hard at work harvesting, gathering great armloads of stalks. A foreman watched like a thuggish Buddha from one corner, his bare brown belly hanging out above his pants. The dirt paths, left rutted by taxis and rare private cars during the rainy season, were lined with flowers, and the soft air smelled of gasoline and blossoms. Children played and shouted hello.

We stopped at a vendor's stall beside the road and bought a jar of rakshi for ten rupees, about thirty cents, then climbed the stairs to Maile's room. She laid out mats on the floor, and placing me beside her, lit a small oil lamp in an altar arranged on her brass plate, with piles of uncooked rice and flower petals. Bhola handed me a ten rupee note and told me to put it in the plate. She poured a bit of rakshi from the jar into a juice glass and set it beside the rice, then took down her drum from its place on the wall and told me to watch and follow her rhythm. Bhola unwrapped my drum and passed it over.

As soon as she began her ritual, little Dorje started to cry. She put him on her lap and let him nurse, then handed him off to the old lama, who rocked him, softly crooning. The baby kept crying, but Maile took up her drum and turned her whole attention to the altar.

I noted how high her forehead was, and the large scar near the hairline, where she said a tree had fallen and cut her head open, a punishment from Banjhankri for some childish infraction. Her long dark hair was shiny and neat, gathered in a knot behind her head. A red *tika* marked her third eye. She lowered her head to pray, and a stream of energy ran up the center of her forehead to the top of the scar. I didn't see it with my eyes, but when I closed them, a river of white light showed on the after-image of her face. Dorje was snuffling now, making little sobs, but no longer screaming.

I paid careful attention, copying Maile's every move, resting my drum handle on the floor and gripping it as she did, thumb behind the handle and fingers spread in front. She whispered a mantra and blew on the drum, then tapped it on each side with her beater, a piece of curved, hardened vine wood. She said another mantra, aloud this time so that I could repeat it, and then began to beat—two regular taps, and then a sliding, longer stroke—as she chanted. I picked up the rhythm.

Her voice gathered power. From time to time she glanced toward me, her eyes dark and full of intent. Little Dorje was silent. Maile's song, in Tamang, touched on a universe of gods, great forms who bodied forth in the sounds of her chant, so that their presence in the room was almost palpable. Triumph and authority transformed her from the shy village woman she'd been to someone strong and confident. Her knees began to shake; the shaking intensified and spread to the rest of her body as she invited the deities to come and sit in their places in the doorway, on the house beam, the altar, and her body. With her chant, she bound all evil spirits and called for assistance from the deities of the streams and mountains of her home in Okaldhunga, eastern Nepal. She asked also for help and blessings for this foreign woman beside her.

All at once she cried out *"Hut!"* and jumped straight into the air from her seated position, landing cross-legged. Violently shaking, *"Hut!"* she cried again, and then once more, because the shaking was too much.

I gripped my beater, hesitating as she broke her rhythm. All my doubts and fears had assembled in a knot in the pit of my stomach. Strong forces seemed to surge around us, like many people shouting.

Her chanting quieted, and then swelled again, and the drum beat changed to a portentous, four-stroke rhythm with the second stroke stressed. I faltered, caught the beat, and forgot my cramped legs, folded under.

Maile leaned forward, her left hand gripping the handle of her drum as she sang to her guiding deity. Then she leaned back, hands open, as though to receive his answer, holding the drum handle with her thumb and forefinger, and spreading the other fingers. As she violently shook, she gasped out a series of words from deep in her throat, her eyes rolled up beneath closed lids. Again and again, she leaned forward, chanted, trembled, leaned back, opened her hands, and let the words and shouts pour through her. I listened rapt, unable to understand, and so imbuing her words with extra mystery and power.

At last she set down the drum, but kept on shaking in spasms. She gathered a handful of rice from her altar plate, swept it close past her heart and forehead and threw it forward to the altar with a prodigal gesture, not minding how it scattered on the floor. She did this twice more. "That is how we stop the shaking," she said.

I too felt shaky. Coming back to herself, Maile smiled, shy yet proud of this special thing she'd showed me she could do. She spoke, and as Bhola translated, regarded me expectantly.

"She saw you in the woods," he said. "When you were a child, the shadow of the Banjhankri fell across you. He is the one who makes shamans."

I looked from his face to hers. "You can be a shaman, she says." His accent intensified, enhanced by excitement, loud and almost overbearing. Maile smiled, and I felt the force of her personality, very sure, yet gentle and incredibly sensitive, hoping I'd be pleased.

I smiled back, receiving the sweetness of her meaning through Bhola's harsh translation, and believing. As a child, I'd often been alone in fields and woods, when Banjhankri, making his nightly tour of the world on the rays of the setting sun, might have cast his shadow on me. Once in a swing beneath a cottonwood in Grandma's yard, in a bright red dress...or had I only dreamed it?

"He would have taken you away if you had been here in Nepal," Bhola said. "But because you lived in America where no one knows or understands about him, his shadow fell on you instead." Maile continued talking as he spoke, as though he could both translate and listen at once, and now he stopped, not bothering with the rest. After all, he was a Brahmin with knowledge of the West, and she but a village woman whose words couldn't mean much.

She hoisted herself from the floor, took four small glasses from a cabinet against the wall and poured a small amount of liquid from the jar into each. "Rakshi *khanne?*" She offered the drink with her right hand, her left hand holding her right wrist, as though to participate in the gesture of giving and prevent the gift from returning to herself, a gesture used in making an offering to a deity.

"*Dhanyabad*," thank you. I bowed namaste and accepted the glass, but didn't go so far as to hold it to my forehead as I'd seen her do with gifts. She gave Bhola and her husband their drinks in that same formal way. The old man beamed and let little Dorje free to crawl into his mother's lap.

❧

"Do you believe in this—shamanism?" Bhola asked as we walked back toward the program house.

"I don't know," I said. "I think so, maybe."

After dinner I sought solitude on the porch and probed myself for signs of vocation as I watched the harvest workers lay down their bundled stalks and leave the field. Could I really be called to be a shaman? It was an exciting thought, fluttering among the familiar collection of self-doubts, anxieties, and small vanities resting on their beds of ashes in my soul.

In a lull between patients the next afternoon, Maile said, "I have many people who believe in me. They come all day and late into the evening. Sometimes I have to go to them and do big ceremonies. No matter if I'm tired, I have to go." Her eyes searched mine. "Why do you want to be a shaman?"

I thought quickly. I want your firsthand experience of God, I could have said. You seem so sure He exists. But I didn't dare let her see the abject depths of my loneliness and doubt, the selfishness that drove me. "I want to help people. It makes me feel good when the spirits use me for healing," I said instead. This, too, was truth.

She considered, and then greeted another patient, a thin old man who moved with difficulty. As she treated him, I watched the pain lines in his face smooth out. When she finished, he rose, his movements discernibly easier, and bowed his namaste.

After he'd gone, Bhola said, translating, "She wants to teach you a mantra. You must promise not to tell the others. Only if they take you as their guru."

I laughed at the idea of anyone taking me as a guru, but Maile was waiting for my answer.

"You must promise," Bhola repeated. "And she wants you to accept her as your guru."

Peter had warned that taking her as my guru would make me responsible for her and her family the rest of my life. But as I looked on her happy, questioning face and Mr. Lama's silvery, benevolent smile, I felt how much I liked them both. What burden could it be to have her for a life-long friend?

"I *will* accept her as my guru," I said seriously. "And I promise."

"We must make a little ceremony," Bhola said. He went out for another jar of rakshi and some flowers. While he was gone, Maile and I sat and smiled at each other, not needing to converse.

Bhola returned and handed me the rakshi and a few white flowers, along with another ten rupee note. "Put this in her altar," he directed.

She held out the brass plate to receive the money, then sprinkled me with water, said several mantras, and stepped back. Now she was officially my guru. Old Mr. Lama beamed down from his perch on a corner of the bed.

Then she dictated a mantra, instructing me to write it in my notebook. Bhola helped with spelling and translation. It was sixteen lines long, and bound the directions and called on helping deities. "You must memorize it," she said. "Say it three times for protection, and blow on your own chest. Think of me when you say it, because you don't yet have a spirit teacher."

I knew the first thing the Wild Shaman taught children he

kidnapped was a protection mantra, and asked her if Banjhankri had given her this mantra.

She laughed and said that Banjhankri's mantras were shorter.

The old lama stood before me. "You must not tell anyone the mantra," he warned. "If you tell the mantra to others who don't understand it or value it, it will lose its power. Or you may get sick."

I kept the mantra secret, even kept secret the fact that Maile had given it to me. Mr. Rai knew, of course, for Bhola reported to him daily. But I got sick anyway. The very next morning I woke with my right eye swollen shut. It was harshly painful. Diane lent me some antibiotic eye drops she'd bought at the pharmacy for her own eye infection, but the drops did little to halt it, and nothing for the pain. I tried to ignore the burning during morning lessons, but by afternoon it reached such a crescendo I wanted only to curl up on my bed. The next afternoon, the other eye felt scratchy too. I steeled myself to endure it. The time of our stay was running out; I wanted to be with Maile as much as I could, and forced myself to walk down to her house.

I'd been watching her work for an hour, trying to behave normally through the red haze of pain, when she asked with her usual diffidence, "Do you want me to heal your eyes?"

I nodded, amazed I hadn't thought of it sooner—and that Peter and Diane hadn't either.

She spread rice grains on her brass plate, sorted them into pairs and singles, and then lit a twist of hemp incense and passed it over me, whispering and half-singing her mantras as she blew them on me. With each pass of the smoking incense, she dropped a bit of rice on the floor. At last, she snapped her fingers three times as she pulled her hand away and downward. "*Dolo, dolo, dolo,*" be well, be well, be well. She laced a piece of red string through the fingers of my right hand and told me to sleep with it that night.

By morning, the pain was gone. I'd suffered only two days, while Peter and Diane had endured their infections for a week.

REARRANGING PLANETS

Mr. Rai asked Maile to perform at the program house. A crowd began to gather at dusk, the largest yet. Her altar, less elaborate than Jebi's, was set with *tormas,* cones molded from sticky rice to represent deities. A short torma, she told us, was Banjhankri, and next to it, taller, his dreadful wife, Lemlemma. Others, larger still, represented Mahadeo, Kali, and a number of Tamang deities.

Mr. Rai supervised from his position by the altar, explaining, "She is dancing for Kali," as Maile bent above her drum in serious concentration, moving her feet in a careful, studied pattern and singing *"koho koho-oh, koho."*

"You can feel the power," Diane said, showing me goose bumps on her arms.

After the ritual of her dance, Maile sat and drummed, shaking and setting up a cacophony of ringing from the bells on bandoleers around her shoulders. Mr. Rai watched intently as she chanted and spoke for her deity.

"What is she saying?" I asked Bhola.

"It's about Mr. Rai. She is doing *jokhanna* for him, telling what will happen in his life."

"He doesn't look too happy," Diane said. "What is she telling him?"

"It's about his family gods. He must set up his altar and worship. She is saying he has neglected to honor his ancestors in the Rai way, and so they are going to punish him."

Mr. Rai listened to Maile's words. "Lo paramaswara," he said quietly, acknowledging the god on her body, and agreeing, "Ho, ho...ho."

The three-hour ceremony included jokhannas for many of those present, and ended with the sacrifice of a chicken. Maile had brought her cousin, Nima Dawa, a handsome young trekking guide, as a helper to twist off the chicken's head and pour its blood on the altar, explaining that because she was Buddhist, it would be a sin to kill it herself.

"This is her *guru puja* ceremony," Mr. Rai said. "Once each year she has to make sacrifice to her gurus and all spirit helpers."

"To Kali?" I asked, because she'd danced for the black goddess.

"Ye-e-es, Kali. And others too."

༄

After Maile's altar had been taken down and she and her family had gone home, Mr. Rai poured out a drink for Jebi and the two of them sat in a corner talking seriously. "What's going on?" Peter asked.

"Mr. Rai is talking about the bad luck he is having since a few years. Jebi says he has to worship his *pitri*, that is ancestors, at *chula*," Bhola said.

"Chula is the fireplace, made of three stones, in every Rai house," Peter explained. "It is so sacred that no one outside the family can touch it."

"Not even wife, if person marries outside the tribe." Mr. Rai had overheard, and broke off his conversation with Jebi, beckoning us over with all the fingers of one hand, held downward, palm facing in. "In my case, I have married first a Mughur woman, and then a Gurungi. Only new wife is Rai. So I have hard time with keeping up twice-year ceremonies, *Udhauli* and *Ubhauli*, for worshipping family gods."

Jebi spoke seriously in Nepali, giving Mr. Rai instructions, punctuating each phrase by dropping his hand, very lightly, on Mr. Rai's leg.

"You see, my father was a shaman," Mr. Rai told us. "I was supposed to follow after him. So it could be very bad for me. Now Jebi is saying, and Maile has said too, I have to set up my special *mangchhamma* room for worship, keep clean, do all things as is required by our mudhum."

"Mudhum means the rules and mantras and ceremonies for the Rai," Peter said.

"All things has to be done according to mudhum. Jebi knows," Mr. Rai said, bringing Jebi up to date on the conversation in Nepali and asking him to confirm what he said.

Jebi nodded seriously.

"Even, every head of Rai family has to know mantras for taking care and keeping family gods," Mr. Rai continued. "I have let go too long."

"Why *didn't* you become a shaman?" Diane asked.

"Is long story, as they say." Mr. Rai took a big gulp of the light brown liquid in his glass, and studied the rest, tipping it this way and that. "Is not right time." He firmed up his mouth. "But someday, I am sure on it, all will come to know who *I* am."

He repeated what he'd said in Nepali, and Jebi said, "Ho," namasted, bowing over his hands, and called Mr. Rai "guru."

On the last night of our stay, Krishna performed a final ceremony, a traditional ritual to rearrange a patient's planets and change her luck. "You be our sick person tonight," Mr. Rai instructed, waving me to a special seat on a large banana leaf in the center of the room, beneath which coins, rice and other objects had been hidden.

"Why not you?" I suggested. "Maile said you were having bad luck."

"Oh, yes, with trekking business, so much competition now coming," he said. "At first, when I am just starting, only few trekking companies was here. But I have under control. I know what has to be done, and I am doing it."

"Worshipping your family gods?"

"I am doing. Is not your worry. But now you must let Krishna find out what is bothering *you*. We calls *khadco kattne*—cutting your bad stars, as we say."

I sat on the large, slick, green leaf, facing the doorway as directed, and Krishna tied a string from the top of my head to a banana stem that had been pounded upright into the dirt outside, where it stood like a small tree with broad spears of leaves flared out in all directions. Behind me, under the poster of Lord Shiva, Krishna chanted his long Tamang chant of invocation, and then a helper brought in a black rooster, squawking and flapping, and carried it around in back of me to Krishna at his altar.

Forbidden to turn, I listened to the shaman chant and drum, and thought he must be dancing too, in his deliberate, bookkeeperish way. I looked along the white cotton string to where it was tied to the banana stem. A diagram of nine concentric circles representing the nine planets, and symbols of the Sun, Moon, and Lord Shiva had been drawn on the ground around the stem with white flour. A seven-squared symbol represented the lower world. Nine offering piles of rice, flower petals, and copper coins lay beside it, for nine was the number of stories of the upper world.

I'd been keyed up to begin with, scattered and anxious as the drumming started, but calmed as it went on and on in monotonous cadence, with only minor crescendos and no change in rhythm, until at last I felt only boredom. Seven hours went by. My bladder was full, but tethered as I was to the banana stem, I couldn't leave.

Krishna came around in front of me and passed the rooster over my body again and again until the bird was completely hypnotized. Then he took it outside and laid it, stupefied, on the diagram, its long neck flopped out sideways. His helper lit nine wicks and hung them on the banana leaves, then placed an egg on the ground by the nine concentric circles. At one and the same moment, Krishna stepped on the egg and smashed it, one helper poured a handful of water on the rooster's head to make it shake and then cut off its head, another helper severed the string connecting me to the stem, and Krishna slashed the banana stem clear through with a single blow of his long, curved *kukhuri* knife.

Bhola's thumb pressed grittily into the skin of my forehead, smudging a tika of black ash, and then he grasped my shoulders, turned me around to face the altar, and wiped the tika off.

Krishna drummed, thanked the deities and spirits, fed them with rice grains he threw on the altar, and sent them away. I was free.

It was long past midnight. The audience had dispersed, and Jebi and the cooks were asleep on their mats. Peter and Diane had stayed up out of politeness, and leaned against each other, looking tired.

"How do you feel?" Mr. Rai asked.

"Fine." I managed to thank the shaman and his helpers, then ran for the toilet.

"My shaman has rearranged your planets," Mr. Rai said. "You may not feel anything now, but in two months, it is definite you will know."

BOOK TWO

THOUGHTS IN THE MIND OF GOD

It was Kali's own fear that kept her from recovering her full power from Lord Shiva, according to Mr. Ganesh's story. High above the Pacific, flying home, I fingered the many skulls of my Kali mala like a rosary and wondered why the goddess demanded the sacrifice of *uncastrated* animals. Did she want to overpower all males, or was it their life force she was after, to fuel Lord Shiva's potency? With all that smoking and drinking, not to mention his resentment that she'd touched him with her foot, he probably needed help in that department. It had been at least three years since Evans and I had made love.

A pretty Thai stewardess came around with a tray of wine glasses, but remembering how bad I'd felt on the flight over after drinking, I asked for coke instead. I'd never meant to put my foot on Evans' head, but when I went to law school, and got ahead of him, he took it that way. He'd lost energy then, like an electron dropping into a lower orbit, sinking into a kind of shadow life, sleeping all day and staying up at night to drink and play with his friends at medieval court life.

"Take back your power," Diane had cheered me on, "Remember Kali." She pronounced it Kal-*lee*, coming down hard on the last syllable with a kind of fierce joy.

༅

Thorne met me at the Denver airport, thin and looking as though he'd grown an inch. Calm and kind, he was fast turning into the kind of man I wanted him to be. He'd brought Keri with him, and she hugged me tight and refused to let go, snuggling in my lap as we drove home. Thorne brought me up to date on what they'd been through in the three weeks I'd been gone. Evans had hurt his back again, and Thorne had had to get him to the hospital by himself. Meanwhile, Keri had come down with a fever and missed the last two weeks of school. They were glad I was home.

Evans came to the door, hugged me, and sank onto the couch with a groan. I gave him his gift, a curved kukhuri knife in a leather scabbard equipped with pockets holding fire-making tools. He carefully drew out the blade. "A fine tool," he said, replacing it in its sheath and setting it aside. "I suppose you're a shaman now."

"Not yet. They said I could be, though."

"Well, what did you learn?"

I pulled out my blue spiral notebook and flipped through the pages where I'd recorded different types of spirits and the mantras Krishna and Maile had given me. But Evans didn't really care.

"I hope it was worth it." He focused toward the far wall where it met the ceiling, and sighed as if it were all too heavy.

"I'm drawn to shamanism—to healing. Why do you find that so wrong?"

"As in any religion, you have to lie to people," he said.

"It's not a..." I started to say it was a technology, not a religion, but realized that for the Rai and Tamang tribes it *was* a form of worship— before Buddhism, it had been the only form.

"Lying is evil," he went on, glancing around to make sure Keri and Thorne were listening. "Every species has its own means of survival. Tigers have sharp claws and teeth, tortoises make shells, cactuses have thorns—but for humans, the brain is the organ of survival. We act from the picture of reality in our brains. We use our brains to hunt our prey, escape danger, find shelter. But if our brains can't form an accurate picture of what's real, things go wrong, and we die. Lying to someone gives him a wrong picture of reality and messes up his survival mechanism. Lying to yourself is suicide."

"People lie to themselves all the time," I said. "Why do you smoke? Do you tell yourself it won't hurt you?"

"I know it *will* hurt me, but I enjoy it. Maybe I'll lose some time at the end of my life, when I'm too old to care, but that's the choice I'm making."

"Don't die, Daddy," Keri said, leaning into him.

"It's all right honey, that's not what we're talking about. We're talking about lying and how it can hurt people." He put an arm around her. "Let's say there was an earthquake. Would you run into an old stone building that was likely to collapse?"

"Huh-uh," Keri said.

"What if it was a church and the priest said you'd be safe—that God would protect you inside?"

"You'd be a fool," Thorne said.

"The priest would be guilty of murder if you believed him and the church fell down on you," Evans said.

I had to agree. That kind of respect for truth was bred in the bone of our northern European stock. An experienced policeman had once said of the Scots-Irish hill men of Kentucky: "They might rape or steal or murder, and try to run, but if you ask them straight out if they did it, they have to confess, because they never lie."

The only spanking my father ever gave me was for lying. I was five, and we lived next door to the Slippy boys, Ronnie and Jimmy. Jimmy was a big boy, nine or ten, and could hop on one foot and balance a broomstick on one bare big toe. Mama had cooked hamburgers and we were having a picnic in the back yard, swatting mosquitoes and watching the Slippy boys show off in their yard. Jimmy leaned down and picked a silver dime from the grass. He held it out across the fence. "Who lost a dime?"

"I did." I ran to take it.

"Here you go." He flipped the dime high, so it twirled and caught the light, landing at my feet. I scooped it up.

"Wait a minute." Daddy grabbed my arm. "Did you really lose a dime?"

"I—."

"You mustn't say things that aren't true."

"I didn't lose it," I admitted, squeezing it so hard that its thin, valuable edge made grooves in my thumb and finger.

"Why did you lie?"

"I wanted it." The breath left my chest and wouldn't come back.

"Well, Ellen, that's very wrong. I'm afraid Daddy's going to have to spank you." He swatted my bottom just hard enough to hurt my feelings.

Sobbing, I shuffled slowly to the fence to give back the dime.

"Aw, she can have it." Jimmy bounced the upright broomstick on his palm. "I don't need it."

Daddy shook his head, warning me not to keep it.

I dropped it in the grass.

Inside, Daddy put me on his lap and explained, "It's very important to tell the truth. That's what scientists do. If people just made up anything they liked, we'd never know what was true or what was real. But when we do know what's true, we can do so many good things, make medicines to help sick people, invent electric lights and cars—."

"And refrigerators," I said.

"That's right, honey." He talked more about science, telling me how big the sun was, that it took eight minutes for its light to reach us, that the moon was just a great big rock, and that the stars were far-away suns. "It looks like a face on the moon," he said, "but it's only mountains and valleys on a giant stone that goes around the earth." He said the stars went on to infinity and that once there had been a big explosion, and everything was still flying apart. It was scary, but you had to believe what was true.

&

"Your Dad's right about telling the truth," I said to Thorne and Keri. "But shamans aren't liars. When they talk about gods and spirits, they're reporting what they experience."

"Do shamans ever tell people gods and spirits exist?" Evans asked.

"Of course."

He raised an eyebrow as though that proved his point.

"What if I told you I saw a spirit?" I ventured.

"I'd have to say you were lying—or crazy."

&

Back at the office next morning, eager to catch up, I telephoned my client for evidence to prove that the corn regeneration process worked, and got passed around from research director to project manager, and finally to a bench scientist who told me the original inventor had gone and they hadn't been able to reproduce his results. I fed the appeal brief to the shredder, feeling disappointed, wondering why science had to insist on reproducible results.

When I was little, I'd taken it for granted that science and truth were the same.

I was ten when we moved to Kentucky. Daddy taught Chemistry at the University, and Mama worked as a psychiatrist at the state insane asylum, so we got to live in one of the doctors' cottages on the hospital farm. Patients well enough to work were let out during the day. They did our laundry and mowed our yard, and worked on the hospital farm. On Sundays, in the doctors' dining room, at a long table spread with a thick white linen tablecloth, washed and ironed by patients, we ate dinners of roast beef or chicken, mashed potatoes, and green beans or carrots from the gardens, planted, weeded, cooked, and served by patients; and patients cleaned up afterward.

"It must have been like this in the old slave days," Mama said. But the patients were white as well as black.

At school I was an outcast, my crisp, Midwestern accent too sharp against my classmates' negligent drawls. Being brainy wasn't cool. Two grades ahead of my age, I was still skinny, sensitive, knobby-kneed, and flat-chested, when the rest of the girls were getting their periods and giggling about boys. I wore glasses and my feet turned in. The kids called me "freak" and "four eyes" to make me cry. Mama said to ignore them, and I did. I could look right through them as though they didn't exist, and for all I could tell, bumping around like great big stupid walking dolls, they didn't. I had my books and piano for company and long bike rides around the hospital grounds to get me through the days.

But the nights were bad. I cracked my bedroom door open to let in the flickering, otherworldly light from the living room where Daddy and Mama were watching Ed Sullivan on TV, and made up rhymes to keep from thinking. But no matter what I did, I knew someday I'd die. Years from now, perhaps, but still the moment would arrive. Nothing could stop it. A heavy weight sat on my chest and stopped my breath, as it would in the coffin, closed in the dark and buried underground. *The worms crawl in, the worms crawl out, the worms play pinochle on your snout.* Rigid as a corpse, I prayed, but no one answered.

⌁

That spring, my hyperactive legs and itchy knees propelled me outside, into the warming sunshine to ride my bike around the one-lane gravel roads of the hospital farm. The patients were mostly well-behaved. If they talked to themselves, they did no harm. If they shouted or got excited, they were locked up in the violent ward, whose awful smell I knew. Mama had taken me down the hallway outside its heavy metal doors. It smelled as old and foul as ancient stables floored with decomposing straw, forgotten ages of urine, feces, vomit, sweat, old cigarette butts, phlegm and chaw, never turned or cleaned, a stench that solidified, coating the nostrils like rock, to make a prison of despair. It was the fifties, before there were drugs to control the patients. Mama said they were tied up in straitjackets, wrapped in heavy sheets and held down inside tubs of warm running water, or hooked to electric wires and shocked into convulsions.

I wasn't scared of the patients on the grounds. They were harmless, or they wouldn't have been let out. Their faces had odd ways of wrinkling up; and most of their teeth were missing. They knew I was Dr. Plucknett's daughter and called out in the ingratiating way of good patients, "Hi, there." "Hello." "Come over here." I knew how to ignore them.

But one old woman, squatting in the dirt by a wall of rough, dark-red bricks, watched me as though we shared a secret. "Hey, girl!" she called as I rode by on my bicycle. An old man hunkered down beside her, prune-wrinkled as herself, and handed her an unfiltered butt. She took a drag. Her black, mussy hair bushed out around her crumpled face. Thick dark eyebrows crawled like caterpillars above a pair of eyes that snapped with unexpected life. I was so startled to recognize another living soul in this wasteland of life-size dolls and dead things, that I stopped and stared, my hand lifting from the handlebar in an involuntary half wave.

"She knows," the old woman said in her long-time patient's voice that fit right into the air without disturbing anything, as matter-of-fact as leaves stirred by the wind, or bike tires crunching over new-laid cinders.

The old man reached for the butt. "She don't know nothin'." He turned his head and spat.

I rode on, circling the building and heading toward the fields. So there *was* something to know. A secret though—taboo. The old man was right; I didn't know what it was. But the look the old woman had passed me, those eyes alight with awareness in the crazy wrinkled face—it had to do with *that. That* was real.

No one else had ever looked at me that way, really seeing. Certainly no schoolmate or teacher, nor even my parents. Not even my little brother Albert, eighteen months old, with great round, clear, blue eyes, who didn't yet know a single bad thing about me.

The summer heat brought us out of the house after supper to spread a blanket on the bluegrass and lie in the cool beneath the stars— Daddy, Mama, me, and little Al. Across the main road, in a vacant field beyond the hospital grounds, a giant tent revival was underway. Only black people went. Al crawled around the blanket as we listened to the singing and shouting. *"Yes, Lord!" "Amen!" "I'm comin' Lord!"*

Daddy showed me the North star, in line with the side stars of the big dipper, and Mama pointed out the seven sisters. "The light we're seeing left some of those stars millions of years ago," Daddy said. "When you think of it, we're awfully small—just specks in a very big universe."

I shivered as the breeze turned cool.

"Lord, Lord, Lord. Oh Jesus!"

"Help me Lord." The voices floated toward us from the tent.

"There's lots of really ignorant belief," Mama said. "Quite a few patients have religious delusions. And it's amazing how many people believe in astrology. Not only the paranoids and schizophrenics, but people on the staff—nurses and aides. People who ought to know better."

"What's paranoid and schizophrenic?" I asked.

Mama laughed. "If only we knew. Paranoids think they're the center of the universe. Everyone's out to get them. Or they have delusions of grandeur and think they're the king of the world. Schizophrenics hear voices—God or evil spirits telling them to do things."

"Once you realize how small we are in the scheme of things," Daddy said, spreading his arms toward the distant stars, "I don't know how anyone could think that way."

Generalized shouting came from across the road, organizing itself finally into the rhythm of a song, *"Amazing Grace, how sweet the sound, to save a wretch like me..."*

"Daddy," I ventured, struggling to keep my voice neutral. "Do you think there's a God?" He didn't know about my nightly terrors—no one did, and I hoped he wouldn't guess.

"We can't really know," he said. "It can't be proved scientifically. Philosophers have wondered for centuries. Some of our best scientists believed in God—Francis Bacon, Newton, Pascal—."

"What about Einstein?" Mama said. "Didn't he say, 'God doesn't play dice with the universe'?"

"Yes, but he was wrong. God does play dice with the universe. Anyway it was just an expression. He may have had a sort of religious feeling, because there's so much that our minds can't grasp, but I don't think he really believed in a personal god."

"There isn't any evidence for it," Mama said.

"That's right. But there's lots we don't know," Daddy said. "Maybe, like the philosopher Berkeley said, we're all just thoughts in the mind of God." He laughed.

"Ha, ha," Mama said in a plain voice, not laughing. "I think I'll stick to science. Look at that. Little Albert's asleep." She picked up the baby.

"An' He bring fire, I say a *flame* of fire," the preacher preached.

"Amen! Amen! Oh, yes He does."

"Tell it!" Scattered shouts rang out.

"An' He bring *light*. He shines it on they faces, an' he *knows* his people, yes he does."

"He does, he surely does."

"Hallelujah, yes he does!"

We went inside. Mama dished out ice cream. Then it was bedtime. It was dark in my room except for the TV light reflected from the hallway and the green glow of the owl clock on my night stand. Science, religion, superstition, madness. Those were the choices. I watched the second hand go round and round, rolling away the seconds, minutes, and hours of my finite life.

CONSCIOUSNESS

Of course I studied science, majoring in chemistry. If you're a scientist, you don't say a thing is true unless you can prove it, and proof is when you can make something happen over and over, the same way every time.

I couldn't make that little man made out of transparent heat waves appear in my bedroom in America to prove to Evans he was real. But neither could I dismiss him as hallucination. I was willing to entertain the idea that he could be real because when I was fourteen, something had happened to crack my mind open and make me question the reality of solid things everyone else seemed to take for granted.

Adolescence brought a new set of fantasies—romantic love scenes to crowd out the old death visions. But the boys at school were nowhere near as good-looking—or romantically inclined—as the ones I fantasized. And since I was still just a flat-chested, skinny little kid, they'd double over and gag out loud when Mrs. Dobbs, our teacher, made them dance with me at school dances. She said I ought to be making straight A's, but it wasn't true. I had a flickering, unreliable kind of intelligence, not strong and steady like the kids who could tell you the Latin name for any plant or bug, or mix up explosions in chem lab.

In those days, I was always cold. One Saturday morning, I was crouched in my favorite spot over the heat vent in the corner of our living room, reading a Nancy Drew mystery, while little Albert sat on a beach ball, bouncing and watching cartoons. A perky teenager came on, gushing through bright pink, bow-shaped lips, "Be nice to your parents, kids. Don't monopolize the phone." It made me sick. Our phone hunched black and silent in its wall niche, ready to ring for anyone but me. I only wished I had the guts to kill myself.

Mama bustled down the hallway, said what a nice day it was, clicked off the furnace, and threw the front door open. A blast of cold air swirled into my corner.

I shivered, and hugging my book to my stomach, scuttled to the bathroom for a hot bath, opening the taps full blast. A pale spring sun shone in through Mama's ironed white curtains. The bath was so hot it raised goose bumps.

When the tub was full, I turned off the faucet, and in the roaring silence, considered my skinny arms beneath the surface. Tiny bubbles caught among the pale hairs broke loose and floated upward one by one. These arms, I thought, invoking a familiar sweet dread, these little arms so dear to me, will someday die, be shoveled underground, and rot. I visualized my body going still, flesh soft and sagging, falling from the bones to make a home for worms and little bugs. My stomach turned hollow, a void surrounded by my thin, stiff carcass.

Then suddenly, I sensed a golden light above my head, and a word came into my mind: *Consciousness!* That was its name. I'm *consciousness.* That's what I *am.* It's all there is. *It* never dies! I understood. I *knew.*

This was salvation, a knowing that erased all my fears, resolved all my doubts, made everything all right. But at once, my intellect rose up to fight, mercilessly efficient, permitting not one moment of relief. In my father's gruff, dismissive voice, it said, "Don't kid yourself into believing something just because you want to." Then, my own dry tone: "Just because there's such a word as "consciousness" doesn't mean it's real. You can't hang everything on a word."

"Consciousness" *was* just a word, a sound made up by men, not as it had seemed for that one brief moment, something separate, with a glorious existence of its own outside our mortal brains. I jumped from the bath and toweled myself with short, jerky motions, as my mind issued frantic orders to repair the breach in its walls: "Don't think that way. Think only what's true."

But my soul had recognized a sacred understanding, wall it off though I might. That golden light. *Consciousness is all!* I wanted another taste.

ACID

I was grown up and married to Bob Denberg in 1966, when Bob's friend, Jon Glazer, offered us a hit of Blue Cheer, guaranteed pure LSD. Tommy was two and Aaron just a baby.

I loved LSD. Nothing really changed on acid—except that you suddenly understood the way things really were, that everything is one. I felt love for every living thing. The dog was thirsty, and I felt his need as my own and filled his bowl with water. I could even love Jon and his girlfriend, Sara, in spite of their neurotic New York mannerisms—forever touching their own faces, stroking their arms, smoothing their hair, making sure they still existed. I shared the childish joy that bounced in Jon's ample stomach, knew the ancient sadness behind Sara's dark, hooded eyes, weary of cycles that saw each rising hope whole with its own death. But, ah, it was beautiful. The Consciousness in everything. Right here, right now, shining from the eyes of every living creature, rejoicing in its own myriad viewpoints.

Only Bob was closed to me, walled off by anger. He'd never expected, so young, to be tied down with babies. He fell asleep near dawn, and lay half covered by the tangled sheet. I straightened it and pinched up a twist of the cloth in my fingers to form a loose bubble—a symbol of the oneness I felt.

I wanted to wake him and explain: we're all one, all of us together like a big, connected piece of cloth. Only, see, we twist ourselves up, like this. It's what we do. I kept on twisting the pinch of sheet, screwing the bubble so tight it stood up on the base of its own coils. See how the twist comes back on itself. It can see itself now. One turn of cloth touches the next, and says that's me. And then we twist again, and again. Tighter and tighter. Pretty soon we're twisted up so tight we forget we were ever part of the sheet. We think we're just this little bubble, separate and alone. But it isn't true. We're all just twisted-up bubbles on the same big sheet. That's all we ever were. I opened my fingers and let the fabric unwind as the sheet flattened out.

"There's nothing but the sheet," I said out loud. The words sounded ordinary on the quiet morning air.

Bob woke up. "Nothing but the sheet?" He frowned and rolled his eyes, and turned his back, pulling the sheet around him.

It didn't matter. I was beginning to suspect he didn't even exist outside my own mind anyway. Maybe no one did.

There *was* only the one consciousness. I told myself to remember the twisted sheet so I wouldn't forget this oneness when the acid wore off.

The boys woke up and wanted breakfast. "All one," I whispered, snatching at the fading realization as I dumped a cup of dry oatmeal in a pot, but the word I heard was "alone," for the laws of normal consciousness imprison, even as they protect us in our cozy world of objects.

I was sure I'd take acid again.

◈

The tutoring school Bob started failed, and our friend Ray Peat invited us to Eugene, Oregon to stay with him until we found a place of our own. His large bachelor's house was dusty but neat. I taped a Mona Lisa print to the bare board wall in the bedroom he gave us for the boys to sleep in, pleased with the colors of the landscape behind the smiling woman, all peace and beauty. I loved how the painting revealed the man who'd made it, the breadth and *thereness* of his being, that fine attention to detail, the woman's smile that hinted knowing to be shared. A conscious man had painted this, had lived on earth as master of his world. Someone *else*.

Bob had a stash of LSD dissolved in water in a round-bottom flask. He'd buried it in Ray's yard, planning to mix it with pond water and watch the one-celled creatures get high through his microscope. One night, as he and Ray were engaged in one of their long-winded philosophical arguments in the kitchen, I put the boys to bed and wandered outside in the cool, humid darkness, following Bob's flattened trail across the uncut grass. He didn't think I knew where it was.

I dug down, feeling the rounded surface of the flask under loose, grassy clods. The world in gentle darkness held its breath. Calm and fated, I raised the vessel and drank deep.

With no idea how much acid I'd drunk, I reburied the flask. Wanting to be alone, I headed to the basement, and sank onto the floor against a stack of cardboard boxes beneath a square, metal heating duct that ran along the ceiling. Before long, my sense of reality began to separate into hundreds of closely-spaced folds like a Chinese fan, straddling many timelines. A sparkling, sharp-edged vision of Colorado snow peaks capped by a great white wolf face appeared, replaced as it faded by a ruined shack, canted sideways and sinking into a misty, pastel swamp. The wolf was good; the shack could mean disintegration—but by now I was far beyond the personal; the images spoke of great, opposing universal forces rather than choices on my own life's path.

I made my way upstairs to our bedroom. My body arched and heaved on the bed, birthing spheres of clear energy that floated toward the ceiling. In a state of emotionless clarity, I understood that these were babies I'd never have.

It didn't get bad until Bob came in and looked down on me, the right side of his lip climbing toward his nose.

"Why do you do that?" I said.

"Do what?" The sneer inched upward.

"Your lip."

"You're paranoid." His face became an empty mask, his skin loose and hanging from his skull as proof of the existence of gravity.

"You're not real," I remarked. "There's nothing inside you."

"What's wrong with you, Ellen?"

"You're just an empty bag."

His vacant eyes got wide, a parody of shock.

"I drank your acid."

He turned his pupils toward me, meaningless black circles with nothing inside.

❧

"Blocks your knock off, blocks your knock off." The sign was a gasoline advertisement, I knew, but what could it mean? It was so funny. It had to do with the inside of my nose, high up where the hard boogers lodged. I laughed. Bob was driving, hunched over the steering wheel, as the grey triangle of highway in our headlights swooshed endlessly inward, swallowed under the car and constantly reborn from darkness. "Blocks your knock off," I said, and laughed again, but he didn't respond. Maybe I hadn't spoken. The boys were asleep in the back seat.

Tommy whimpered. I lifted him over the seat. His skin was burning hot. I held him, trying to absorb and dissipate his fever.

❧

It was still night. Tall brick walls, purporting to represent a hospital building, sheared off the view to the right. Baby Aaron slept in back. Bob and Tommy were inside the building. I didn't remember them leaving the car, but I knew that's where they were. I stared at the pocked vinyl surface of the dashboard, lit and shadowed by a nearby street light. The sense of unreality had been zeroing in for hours, and now it arrived. None of this was real. It was all a lie—the highway, the crazy "Blocks your knock off" signs, the brick façade of the hospital, the car, the fake leather pattern on the pitted dashboard, these hands, these arms and legs, these muscle tensions here, and here—illusion, clumsily contrived. Not even worthy of attention.

I, I, *I*, a spark. Only *this*. Alight and burning in an empty universe.

Everything collapsed, but *I* persisted. That which never dies. Dawn light came up and made the dust on the grey-green dashboard sparkle. I, whatever that was, was here.

❧

Tommy lay sweating in my lap, fever broken. The sun was high. Bob was driving again, a bottle of erythromycin bulging in his shirt pocket.

"I know what it is," I croaked, my voice rusty from hours of silence. The universe swam into place. "People try to close off their gestalts too soon—roof them over. The Jews, especially."

He threw me an angry look, resenting the attack on his race.

"Look at their arches. They should have kept reaching up toward God, but they wanted to capture him, put him in an ark. The Catholics were better. They made their gothic arches taller, but they still closed off too soon. Every form is a lie, don't you see?"

He pressed his lips tight shut.

Tightness gathered in my chest. I knew I was coming down—talking *about* it now, not experiencing it—feeling the old frustration because he didn't understand and never would. But it didn't matter. I knew what I knew.

We passed St. Louis, then Louisville. He must be taking me home to my parents. By the time we got there, I was down from the acid.

After that, we quit doing drugs, but I could never stop searching for what was real.

RESCUE

After the shaman class, Diane and Peter had traveled through India building their relationship, but in the end Peter went back to his wife. Diane came to Boulder to visit. "I don't know why I always do this to myself," she mourned.

We ate dinner in Evans' "great hall" in the garage. The weather had turned cold. Evans poured wine. He brought out his jewelry to show Diane, and she charmed him, exclaiming at how good it was. "You should have been there in Nepal," she said. "We had a great time drinking, smoking and shamanizing. You've got the drinking and smoking part down, anyway, hoo hoo hoo."

She turned to me. "Do you think you'll ever go back to Nepal?"

"I'd love to, but how can I?"

"Why not? You'd let her go, wouldn't you, Evans?"

He took a short, sharp puff.

Later, Diane and I walked off our dinner through the neighborhood, still slightly buzzed. "Wo, he didn't like it at all when I mentioned you going back to Nepal, did he?" Diane said. "Are things any better since you got home?"

"Worse, if anything."

"I can see his attraction," she generously offered. "How did you two get hooked up in the first place?"

"He was my first love. Not my first husband, though."

"He's got charisma, but what a narcissist."

Narcissus was the Greek youth who fell so in love with his reflection in a pool that he got stuck there forever admiring it. Evans was like that—but I'd carried it even further. I'd fallen into the pool. It had been Evans who saved me from drowning. This was my guilty secret.

"I think I deserved him," I said dismissively. "How about you? What made you get married?"

"Youthful folly." She waved a hand and laughed. "Are you trying to change the subject? Why did you deserve him?"

"Well...he grounds me in a way."

"Grounds you? Who needs to be grounded?" She spread her arms. "Be free!"

We cut across an open field and took a faint path by the irrigation ditch, exchanging reminiscences, and then turned back toward the house. Evans' friends were beginning to show up in their medieval costumes. Diane followed them into the great hall, with her usual enthusiastic interest.

Before long, she joined me upstairs with a pewter wine glass. I put down my book.

"What it with these men?" She wandered to the window, pulled back the drapes, and looked out onto the street. "What did you ever see in him?"

"I was only nineteen. He was thirty. He was just so smart, so sure of himself. I was a premed student, sweating my grades. I still thought that someday, when I grew up, everything would make sense, or at least I'd find someone to explain it all."

"Yeah, right," Diane said.

"You'll appreciate this. He was married when we met," I told her.

"The best kind."

"He came to Boulder for the rock climbing. His wife was pushing for open marriage—so he tried it out on me. He seduced me with his brains. He was really smart. He was in charge of a government decoding section before he was twenty, and after that, he was an artist." Remembering the magic of those times, I fell silent. Evans had told me all there was to know about everything—art, evolution, anthropology, the nature of time, the pyramids, politics, religion, social theory, tectonic plates.

"Watch out for that kind."

"I thought he was the one who could explain life to me. I started skipping classes."

"Did you flunk out?"

"Almost. I screwed up my chances for med school, but it only lasted two months, and then he moved on to his next conquest."

"Bastard."

"Then Bob showed up. He was smart too. I'm a sucker for brains—and when I got pregnant with Tom, he did the honorable thing."

Diane sipped her wine. "So how did you end up with Evans?"

"I never fell out of love with him. That's all. When his wife finally left him, I pounced."

"Be careful what you ask for."

"Pounced" wasn't the right word, but sometimes when you explain your life to another person, without meaning to, you tailor it to suit their views. It was true that I'd never fallen out of love with Evans, but there was no way I could explain how he'd rescued me from madness.

After I overdosed on acid, Bob and I found a house in Eldorado Springs just south of Boulder. We hadn't seen Evans in two years. It was 1969. Tommy was four and Aaron two. Our old friends had left town or drifted away, and we didn't make new ones. There was no one to save us from each other, or ourselves.

That winter, with the active little boys, our life turned to chaos—children's toys and games, and books and dishes and pans—everything we owned ending up as broken playthings on the floor.

The floor was tiled with squares of dull, brown linoleum, and always cold. The bedrooms were freezing. As winter deepened, the oversized gas heater in the big, bare living room became my dearest friend.

The sun rose late and set early beyond the steep canyon walls, veined on climbing maps with famous routes that Bob was determined to master. Across the dirt road, South Boulder Creek roared out of the mountains with the power of a superhighway. I lived in a cold paralysis of watchfulness, afraid the boys would wander off and fall in, to be hurled away and bashed against the rocks. They caught one cold after another from playing on the floor too far from my friend, the heater. Bob tried to start his tutoring school again, but as it failed, he took refuge in his books of philosophy and a growing stack of spiral notebooks he kept by his bed and slowly filled with thickets of incomprehensible paragraphs.

We hadn't dropped acid for a year. We didn't drink. We didn't smoke pot. We were young, strong, bright, and full of health, though poor. But we were lost. As Bob disengaged more and more from the struggle to put food on the table, find money for the mortgage, clothes and coats and shoes and doctors for the boys, I knew I'd have to find a job.

Yet I continued to sit, day after short, dark day, night after shivering, drafty night, in my rocker, frozen with inertia, watching the blue flames burn through the scaly, mica windows of the heater. When the boys' demands got loud enough, I energized to meet them and felt better for it, but always, the rocker awaited, and my mind's obsessive work there, trying to think its way to salvation.

My head ached; my thoughts pressed on the inside of my skull like the deeper currents beneath the whirling surface of the creek—stubborn, heavy flows determined to push their way through solid rock.

Bob, too, was thinking day and night. But, alone in our private worlds, we couldn't reach each other. He spoke in looming abstractions: phenomenology, existentialism, physical teleology. My forehead strained open to receive his words, but they spread in my brain like clouds, lacking weight or form. And seeing how I tried and failed to understand, his lip would curl into a sneer.

The certain paths of my childhood, the Methodist religion of my grandparents, the objective certainties of my scientist parents, eroded away in the battering onslaught of my thoughts. All I knew for sure was that I had a mind. I forced my way backward to first principles, demanding proof that anything at all existed. My senses brought messages to my brain, but for all I knew, the world—so-called by those who fondly believed it was real—might be no thicker than the outer surface of my eyeballs; sounds, though seeming to come through space from all directions, no more than jangling nerves inside my ears.

"How do I know you're not just a figment of my imagination?" I challenged Bob.

"If you don't know that," he said with ill-disguised contempt, "you're denying an existent of any sort of embodying free will—negating freedom as idea." He meant I was wrong.

Aaron gave up playing and climbed into my lap. I tucked my blanket around him and rocked as Tommy built a tower of books, shouted with delight, and pushed it over.

"I think, therefore I am," Descartes had said. I'd never had a class in philosophy, preferring the certainties of hard science, but everyone knew that quotation. It was a place to start. Consciousness exists. If it didn't, how could I even be thinking about it?

And I knew a secret about consciousness, one that should never be spoken, though it might be hinted at. I'd been given such hints—that old woman in the mental hospital, a knowing glance from a stranger, crude letters on the side of a building that spelled, "I AM," a picture drawn with crayons and taped to a light pole, of a long, segmented worm with an intelligent face, captioned, "The Worm Ourselves" in bold black letters—hints no one would understand unless they already knew.

The secret was this: *there is only one consciousness in the universe.* Since I knew *I* was conscious, it followed that this consciousness could only be mine. And this one consciousness—mine—must be solely responsible for all that existed. For all the pain and suffering of creation.

Tommy stopped playing and leaned against me. "I have a headache," he announced. I carried the sleeping Aaron to the bathroom and stood him up. The cold against his bare feet woke him enough to pee.

I shook two baby aspirins from the bottle, feeling both helpless and guilty. "Chew them up," I told Tommy. "We'll see if you're better in the morning."

I tucked the boys in bed, left the doorway open to their room, and returned to my rocker to take up my burden once again—guilt for Tommy's pain, for Aaron's rash from wetting his bed, for the cold, the darkness, the fragile deer that froze to death on the mountainsides each winter, their unmarked carcasses emerging with the snow melt, the spiders I scalded down the bathroom drain, for the suffering, nameless, groaning millions of the earth.

Some time, in a past beyond recall, this consciousness, that was mine and all there was, must have made a wrong turn, committed some unknown sin for which no remedy was known. It had forgotten its own nature, and couldn't go back, could never know if the sin of forgetting had been deliberate, or merely some stupid, irretrievable mistake. It only knew it was trapped, caught here in this dark and silent crack in the rocks of Eldorado Canyon, stupid, powerless, and raw from the constant jangling messages of its own distant suffering. I rocked and rocked, and thought and thought, with no way out. If only I could withdraw myself completely from this spoiled illusion of a world I'd created. But I couldn't, because it held my children. Having brought them into this suffering world, the guilt was mine. I couldn't desert them now.

Spring came at last, and I ran into Evans by chance on a day of occasional sunshine and chinook winds in late March. I spotted him striding down the hill from the University, the open sides of his orange Mountain Rescue jacket flapping in the wind like the wings of some giant grounded bird. I pulled to the curb and yelled, "Hey stranger, want a ride?"

"It's you." He poked an elbow through the open window and leaned in. "Long time no see. How's married life these days?"

"Probably better than yours." I'd heard his wife had left him.

"Let's have a cup of coffee."

We took a table at the front of a student café directly beneath a plate glass window that shuddered in the wind. A long, smooth cloud covered the sun, and Evans' orange jacket glowed in the flat light as I played my new game of wondering if he had a separate consciousness of his own.

His elegant thinness hadn't changed, nor the dramatic way he raised his arm to light his cigarette. His fine, dark hair, full of static electricity, stuck out in a cowlick at the crown of his head and tufted over his forehead as he pulled off his hat, contrasting with his sophisticated gestures in a way that made him even more likeable than I remembered.

He leaned back, squinting through his smoke. "What a shame you're married now."

That's how it started.

"Are you real?" I asked then, knowing he'd hear in my voice what I meant, that it wasn't just some sort of coy attempt to flirt. He was Anna Kennedy's son, after all.

He reached across the table and pinched my arm, a sharp, welcome pain.

"You're not just a figment of my imagination?"

"I could pinch you again," he said. "Did you think you imagined it?"

"I might have." I smiled as the waitress set thick white mugs of coffee before us.

"Well, you didn't. Though maybe you're a figment of *my* imagination." He tore open two packs of sugar and stirred them into his cup. "You know you have a really lovely smile." The setting sun moved down below the cloud, and his eyes in the slanting light turned to green jewels. "You may have made up everything else, but you didn't make up me."

"Maybe we're the only two real people in the world," I suggested, for he *was* undeniably *there*.

"I've had that thought." He'd raised his cup as in a toast, an invitation to play.

❧

"I needed him at the time," was all I could say as Diane drained her glass.

Evans had saved me from the hell of solipsism, pulled me up and lashed me like a broken body to the mountain rescue litter of his certainties. And I'd learned to survive, to act "as if" the life of the senses were real and all there was, and never, ever to look back. But in the end, it hadn't worked for either of us.

FAITH

I got up early the next morning to see Diane off. "I'm giving you a hard time about Evans," she said, as she poured cornflakes into a bowl, "but he really is a good artist. I was impressed with the stuff in his workroom."

"He let you see it?"

"We all trooped down there last night. He had this brooch he was copying from an ancient Celtic design in a coffee table book. Come on, I'll show you."

I hadn't been in Evans' workroom since Keri was a baby. I followed her downstairs. The brooch was beautiful.

"Who's that?" She craned around a corner and pointed to two photos mounted side by side on a single dark brown matte board on the wall.

"Why, that's me and Evans, right after we were married."

"You looked happy then."

"I was." I squeezed around the table for a closer look. "I had no idea he had these pictures up." We'd snapped each other on a train in Europe on our honeymoon journey. "He was working then."

☙

Evans had been running an outdoor program, funded by the City of Los Angeles and held in the mountains of New Mexico, for troubled inner-city youth, when I left Bob to join him. I remembered how, in those first glowing months, he'd awed me with his mastery of physical reality. He could patch a VW engine with rubber bands, change a washer in a faucet, stop a toilet from running, seal windows with layers of plastic to keep out winter winds.

In the evenings we'd light a fire in the fireplace, and once the boys were asleep, nestle in each other's arms and watch the flames. In bed, we took our time. He was slow and gentle, and most of all, *there*, as we abandoned ourselves to our tenderest feelings, our bodies moving of themselves to gently kiss and draw back, tasting the delicate sensation of merging energy fields, more beautiful than touch, as we slowly drew together. And touch itself, the culmination that sent us whirling beyond our bodies to states of rapture, my cries mingling with his murmured Celtic syllables, encoded in his genes, closer than lovers in the dear intimacy of skin against skin, as close as siblings, as twins in the womb, two lobes of the same beating heart.

He *was* real, more evolved than anyone I knew, a twist of the universal stuff wound tight and sharpened to a fine, aristocratic point of living intelligence, his thoughts of unimaginable complexity, rich in color and detail like the Mona Lisa print on our bedroom wall—Master of Forms, an artist of life and of love.

I studied him covertly, watching with admiration as he planned and perfectly carried out his projects, from a three-week trip with the juvenile delinquents to an oil change for the car. I marveled at the way he organized his books, and his music, and camping gear, everything assigned its own right place. I copied what I could. I'd never been good at crafts, but now I took up calligraphy and made hand-lettered cards to send our friends, and embroidered a tablecloth with fine attention to detail, marveling at my new-found skills, safe in his presence, the world no longer my own personal burden, but a playground, an artist's workshop from which to create our shared lives.

One night, in the tender aftermath of love, he told me he wanted a son.

I froze, whirled back into that old dark mother's guilt. "You...do you ever feel there might be something wrong with bringing children into the world?"

"Why ever should I think that?"

I lay on his chest and he stroked my hair. "Because they suffer."

"Everyone suffers," he pointed out, "but obviously, most people enjoy life more than they suffer. They're free to off themselves if they want, but most people don't."

"I guess I mean the pain of being separate..." I raised my head and looked into his face.

He pulled his arm from beneath my shoulders and sat up, stimulated and ready for a good discussion. "Separate from whom?" He raised an eyebrow, definitively tapped off an ash.

I pulled the covers to my chin. "I'm just trying to tell you how I feel. Sometimes I feel like I made some cosmic mistake to be alive on this earth. Like maybe once I had a choice, but chose wrong, and for some reason it's no longer possible to go back to the choice point and do it right. Like an original sin I can't even remember." I didn't know whether he understood or not, but at least he was listening. "Then I made it even worse by bringing innocent children into the world to suffer the same pain and ignorance — to struggle and die. And for what?"

"That's silly," he said. "Ask Tom and Aaron if they're glad to be alive — if they'd want it any other way. Anyway, any child of mine — yours too — would be an asset to the world. He'd have a place."

I did want his child, brilliant, artistic, musical, with long fingers like his, coaxing beauty from whatever they touched, his silver flute, his oboe with its dark, wry voice...my body. "You're right." I lowered my head to his chest and ran my cheek along his fine, long chest hairs.

"I'm always right."

The funding for Evans' program ran out, and we moved to Los Angeles, where our son, Evans Hawthorne Winner III, was born. A calm, undemanding baby, he would lie contented in his crib for hours, thinking his own long, quiet thoughts while I was at work. With Evans jobless, I had to take temporary secretarial assignments.

Anna Kennedy phoned, as she did each week, to find out how we were. Baby Thorne was teething, fussing on my shoulder. "Evans is waiting for his friends to write another grant," I told her.

"I know it's hard for you, but have faith. Things will work out. He *is* an old soul."

But his mother made Evans angry, with her talk of higher truths. "You're an intelligent woman," he scolded her. "People look up to you and believe what you say. You shouldn't be talking such nonsense about astral bodies and life after death. It's immoral to promote superstition in people who can't think for themselves. Mother, Mother...are you crying?" He handed me the phone.

One night, I drove home from work in a rainstorm that washed the dust from the air and made it smell alive, and entered our upstairs apartment to find it full of cigarette smoke, as usual. Staticky canned laughter and snappy sitcom dialog polluted the room as well. Dirty diapers in the hamper stank. The table wobbled, the counters were sticky, the stove burners were clogged, and a light smell of rot seeped out from the under the refrigerator. Evans could have fixed all this if he weren't so depressed.

I wiped the raindrops from my glasses and picked up the baby. The zipper on his sleeper was stuck half open, and his chest was black with a spot of sticky dirt. "I figured out your problem," I said.

"Hold on a sec." I waited until a commercial came on. Evans turned down the sound, but kept on staring at the screen.

"You have no faith," I told him. "If you can't see the end of a project you won't even start."

He cast me a sideways look.

"Don't you see, all you have to do is begin, and things will fall into place. Just take the first step."

"What first step? I don't know what you're talking about." At least I had his attention.

"I'm talking about getting a job. Doing something useful."

"I am doing something useful."

"What?"

"Taking care of the baby for one thing. Don't nag."

"I'm not. I'm trying to tell you something." On the TV screen, the camera panned a row of shiny new cars on a lot. Sensing my annoyance, baby Thorne began to cry. I yanked his zipper over the stuck spot and changed his diaper and set him in his highchair, handing him a cracker. I slapped hamburger meat into patties, threw them into the hot skillet where they landed with a gasp, and dumped a sack of frozen vegetables into a pan.

"I would have done that," Evans said.

I slammed around, wiping surfaces, throwing dishes in the sink.

I could tell Evans was angry by the way he snapped his lighter, but he waited until Thorne was in his crib asleep to confront me. "I want to know *why* you said I'm not doing something useful."

I got into bed beside him, moving stiffly, careful not to let our bodies touch.

"You're obviously not."

"Someone has to take care of our son. What else *should* I be doing?"

"Working, or...writing a grant proposal." I leaned up on an elbow and faced him, excited at the idea.

"I don't have the credentials."

"So what? Yes you do."

"All right, if you're so sure. You guarantee it'll get funded, and I'll write one."

"Jesus. You don't have any faith in yourself at all, do you?"

"*You* don't have faith in me. If I say it won't work, it won't work." His anger drove him on. "You still haven't answered my question. What makes you think I'm not already doing something worth while?"

I pressed my hands against my ears and curled away from him.

"Are you going to answer?"

I clamped my teeth and willed him to leave me be.

"I said—answer me." He jerked my hand from my ear, trapping my wrist in an aching grip.

"Leave. Me. Alone."

"You leave *me* alone. You're the one that started this. Now finish it. Tell me what you mean."

"All right, I will." Fury overcame all care. "You never do anything that takes effort or vision. You just lie here day after day, doing nothing but watching TV. Does that answer your question?" I hadn't known how much contempt I felt until I heard it in my voice.

"That's a lie." He hit my cheek hard with his fist. "That's a *lie*."

I jumped up, shaking. "I'll call the police. I'm leaving." I pulled on my jeans but he yanked me off balance, and I fell back on the bed. He held me down.

I squeezed my eyes tight shut and waited until he reached for a cigarette, then tried to jerk free. He tightened his grip. "Tell me what you mean," he said from time to time. "You're not making sense. Baby, Babe? I can keep this up as long as you can."

My thoughts churned angry red. After a long time I started to cry.

"I love you, Babe. I don't want to hurt you." He loosened his grip and stroked my hair. "Promise you won't leave."

"Oh God," I said. "Oh God, oh God."

WINNING

Evans and I had returned to Colorado when it became apparent he would never find work in L. A. He had big plans at first, and tried to start a business making outdoor gear. He sewed up a few down jackets and half a sleeping bag before he lost heart and let things slide. I worked hard to help him set up, but he blamed me anyway when the effort failed. I wasn't giving him enough support, he said. Maybe if I stopped nagging and acted sweet like a proper wife, he'd feel more like working.

I found a job with a patent law firm where I could use my chemistry degree. Determined to excel and amazed at how fast I could progress when I used my energies for my own career instead of pushing him, I soon passed the patent bar and got a raise. The next logical step was law school. I could keep my job and attend class at night, and if I spent every spare minute studying, it would work.

Evans still organized occasional climbing trips with friends, and once in a while, I let my studies go and went along, pacing up and up the long, steep trails to the top of one of the Collegiate Peaks, or Gray's and Torreys, or Flattop, all for the thrill of that singular moment when there was nowhere higher left to go; nothing to see but sky and the jagged blue landscape below. There were raft trips too, but my grades began to suffer, and I had to give them up.

Jealous of my studies, Evans picked a fight as I pored over a hornbook of patent law. He hated me getting ahead of him. "What are you reading?"

"It's an old case about a guy who lost his patent on a corset design because his wife had worn it on the street more than a year before he applied for his patent. The court said it was a public use."

"Was that all she was wearing?"

"Of course not. It was under her clothes."

"And that's the law?"

"That's court-made law."

"That's theft," he barked, as though personally offended. "They ought to be shot."

I ran my eyes to the bottom of the page and turned it, trying not to react.

"People have deep-seated convictions about theft, especially theft of ideas. That's *natural* law," he said, competing for my attention. "If courts don't uphold it, they'll take matters into their own hands."

"You're right," I said, my stomach knotting. "Patent laws are ridiculous. People are so proud and protective when an idea happens to pop into their heads. They don't realize it was already floating around in the collective consciousness and all they did was catch it. They think they made it up out of their own genius." I pretended to study, clicked my four-color pen to blue, and whispered, "*Dictum.*"

A long moment passed. "You don't believe that."

"Sure I do." I did, though I'd said it to annoy him.

"That's nonsense." He puffed at his cigarette, arms rigid, close in to his body.

"Name one original thought *you've* had in the past ten years."

"I *said,* that's nonsense." He grabbed the hornbook and forced the covers backward, breaking the spine, and then ripped it down the crack. Glossy pages scattered on the floor.

I was shocked. Evans respected books. He must be really angry. Some sections were still holding together by their white mesh backing. I knelt to gather them, but he scooped them up and tore off pages by the handful, crumpling and throwing them across the room.

I scuttled backward on the floor. "Stop it! You're crazy." He dropped the pages and stood above me, his hands balled into fists.

"Mom?" Tom was in the doorway. "What's wrong?" At sixteen, he was strong and wiry.

I took his arm and turned him back. "Nothing honey, we're just having a little argument. Everything's all right."

"Are you sure?"

"I'm sure. Thanks for asking." I squeezed the tight bulge of muscle on his arm to let him know he'd done right.

Evans crouched on the floor, smoothing and sorting pages. "I'm sorry," he said. "You're wrong, but I shouldn't have torn the book. I'll fix it."

He never tried to argue law with me again, retreating instead to his own pursuits: genealogy, history, metalwork, and making jewelry. That's when he joined the Society for Creative Anachronism. He gave up climbing and rafting, and still refused to work.

When I graduated, I told myself, things would improve. Midway through the last semester, I found I was pregnant. I chewed soda crackers through the bar exam to keep from throwing up, and Keri was born, healthy and beautiful, on the coldest night of the year, with eyes of metallic, newborn blue under long, dark lashes. Even the whites were blue. After six weeks of maternity leave, I went back to work. My name moved higher on the letterhead; my salary climbed.

I loved being a patent attorney, making money to buy the house, a car, a stereo, a TV, and tools for Evans' workshop. I'd worked hard to earn it. But in the back of my mind, I still couldn't forget there was no proof it was real. I had decided to act "as if" it were. But how could I be sure the whole thing wasn't just my own projection, something I'd made up? It was my own mind and will, after all, that had created this new and better life. Waking in the early morning hours, following the logic to its end, my body would go cold with dread. I still needed Evans to say, "Nonsense, life is what you see around you, nothing more." Yet I knew his way didn't work.

Looking for answers, I took up serious reading: *The Science of Yoga, Gurdjieff and Ouspensky, The Bhagavad Gita*. Something was wrong with how I understood the world, that much was clear. It began to dawn that I'd have to actually *do* something different if I wanted to change how I saw things. That's when I found *The Way of the Shaman*, Michael Harner's guide to shamanic practice. It described the shaman's spirit journey, making it sound as though anyone could do it.

Harner was an American anthropologist who'd been initiated into shamanism by an old Conibo shaman of Peru, who fed him a sacred drink the Indians called "the little death." He experienced visions, revelations, and journeys through the galaxy, meeting monstrous, bat-like spirits who claimed supreme power. To his amazement, when he recovered from the frightening, near-fatal experience, the old shaman told him he was already acquainted with those bat-like spirits. "They always say that," the shaman dismissed the bat things' dire warnings, convincing Harner his visions had been part of shared reality rather than mere products of his personal imagination.

After that, he studied shamanic practices of other cultures the same way, from the inside, identifying common themes and techniques, and abstracting a set of effective methods he called core shamanism he could teach to Westerners.

I fashioned a drum from an empty oatmeal box and recorded half an hour of steady drumming, four beats per second, to entrain my alpha waves. On an afternoon when no one else was home, I rewound the tape to try the journey to the lower world in search of a Power Animal, a protecting spirit to act as personal guardian, helper, and teacher.

This wasn't religion, as I saw it, but simply a set of techniques others had found useful. The instructions in the book were clear. I didn't particularly believe it would work, but as an experiment, descended, in my mind, through a fissure in the earth, working my way through loose, dark soil, studded here and there with sparkling crystals. At length, I seemed to enter a tunnel of alternating rings of bright and dark. At the end of the tunnel, an animal waited—a graceful deer. I held him to my heart and returned, retracing my steps; and still following instructions, danced in Deer's honor, letting him guide the movements of my limbs.

It was a daydream but somehow more. I recognized a new vibration.

I got in touch with Harner's Foundation for Shamanic Studies, and received a brochure for a beginners' workshop at Joy Lake, Nevada.

Evans was in his great hall, enthroned on the heavy wooden chair he'd built. Its high, peaked, carved back rose behind his head as he sipped wine and waited for his friends at the long board table.

"I want to go to this." I handed him the flyer and slid onto the side bench, pushing it over the flagstones with a loud, yelping sound.

"You want to be a witch doctor?" His eye fell on the price. "You *are* joking, aren't you?"

"No, I'm not."

"Superstition." He pushed the folder back. A cylinder of ash fell across it. "You want to waste your time—and money—on things that aren't real?"

"Oh, right. What do *you* think is real? All this? These fake shields and swords? These hokey coats of arms? Your stupid friends and parties? Your cigarettes? Is that what you think we should spend money on?"

He stared off toward the far end of the room. It still looked like a garage door, despite all the flags and jeweled drinking horns.

"My money, I might add."

"Look," he said, "This is silly. You can't be serious. It's a con game."

"What makes you think so?"

"I know so. Pay *me* the money. *I'll* show you spirits—and if you can't see them, well, I guess you just aren't ready." He cast me a humorous look.

I could have stopped right then and let it go. "You think you're so logical. But you can't prove your so-called real world even exists. All you know for sure is what your senses tell you. Face it. You can't even prove *this* is real," I smacked my hand on the boards, sticky with spilt wine, "or even your own body." I shoved his elbow, angered somehow at the sight of the fine, dark hairs on his wrists, those sensitive hands with their long, aristocratic fingers.

He cupped his elbow, pretending hurt. "I thought we got through this a long time ago. Use your brain."

"You make fun of people for having blind faith, but you're the one with blind faith, thinking *this* is real," I waved my arms, dismissing his world. "Use your own brain."

"You want to know what's real? How about if I hit you? I guarantee you'll know *that's* real."

"That's your answer to everything, isn't it? You bully. You...baby."

He narrowed his eyes. They shone with resentment and something else I didn't want to admit—thwarted passion, thwarted love masquerading as anger. I knew then he was finished, that I'd won—and I didn't care what I'd lost. I picked up the brochure. "I'm going," I said, cold as stone.

BOOK THREE

INITIATION

I set up my tent near the Joy Lake Lodge in the dry Nevada hills near Reno and wandered down to the main building. A burly Native American, his hair gathered in a pony tail, lounged by a rail fence beside a white man in a wheelchair. I felt shy, but forced myself to join them. The white man, who called himself Red Elk, introduced the Indian as Running Water, a recognized Mojave medicine man. They, too, were here for Harner's workshop.

Overawed, I leaned on the fence and gazed across the coarse meadow grass toward a set of low hills, purple on the horizon. Running Water's solid, quiet presence reminded me of my mother in certain moods. She'd told me once we had a Native American ancestor. I stood in silence, trying to tune in. Soon more students came up, and conversation started.

That night, in my tent, I heard a deer pound past. I fell asleep and dreamed that Running Water was telling me something important: "For what you are about to learn, have proper reverence." I woke in deep night, the desert air crisp and cold against my face, grasping at the message before it slipped away.

Proper reverence.

I scooted to the door, keeping my legs inside the sleeping bag, and opened the tent flap. The sky was clear, but the stars kept their distance. A truck rumbled low a long way off. Proper reverence. From taking drugs, I'd learned all forms are lies—gestalts made up in our brains. We need these forms to think with, like toys for children, but that doesn't mean they're real. I shifted and lay down. Electric sparks shot from the nylon bag.

I had no fear of spirits. How could I believe in spirits when I didn't even believe in solid objects? If all forms are lies, what good is proper reverence—when everything we see and feel and hear and think is only form? Lies and illusion, in other words. But I'd come here to learn about spirits. I decided to try as hard as I could to experience what the others did, to honor these teachings no matter how much I doubted. My head began to ache with contradiction.

Morning came. I downed a megadose of Tylenol and took a seat by Running Water in the circle of thirty students. Harner, balding and powerfully-built, with a salt-and-pepper beard, lit a short stick of pine incense, placed it upright in a tuna can, and set it beside a single candle in the center of the room. He began to lecture on indigenous shamanic practices, making terrible puns and checking our faces to make sure we got them, his eyes twinkling, small and sharp, behind his scholar's glasses. We groaned and laughed.

The first thing he taught was the spirit journey to the Lower World, down the shamanic tunnel to contact our Power Animals. He described it the same way he had in the book. "Don't worry if you think it's only your imagination," he added, grinning and wiggling his eyebrows like thick black caterpillars. "Whose imagination is it, anyway?"

He knows, I thought. He *knows!*

Still in the grip of the worst headache I could remember, I followed instructions and found a new Power Animal. This time, I not only saw it, but also felt a sense of love as Eagle's wings folded around me. But journeying didn't come easily. Most of the visions and feelings rushed by at high speed, too fast to catch or understand.

"Just keep doing it," Harner reassured. "It'll come."

It was true. Little by little, the journeys slowed and sharpened.

After we learned the basic techniques, he said we'd journey for each other, "because it makes the spirits happy when we work to serve others." He asked us all to rattle.

I hadn't thought to bring a rattle, but Running Water lent me his spare, fashioned from a gourd grown into a perfect sphere, cleaned and filled with tiny stones and crystals. I shook it, suspecting it was meant for peyote ceremonies where a good, clear sound was supposed to be essential.

Running Water followed Harner's instructions like any other student. I was surprised at how willing he was to learn from an American anthropologist, but Harner had had powerful experiences in the spirit world, and approached it with respect that showed. It was clear he had much to teach. He asked Running Water about his own ways of contacting spirits and wasn't above learning from us all, questioning us closely about what we were experiencing, acting the part of a fellow seeker.

We danced the Power Animals we'd found. Running Water, a big man with little physical grace, danced Quail, circling the room in small hops, his fingers spread behind his back to form its tail. Tears marked his cheeks, and all of us were moved. At the end, he thanked each helping spirit, surprising me again by naming Jesus among a list that included Bear, Deer, Grandmother Moon, and Grandfather Sky.

Next Harner assigned us to look for a plant spirit helper. A weed with a single tall stalk and fuzzy leaves stood out, and I sat with it a while, then journeyed to meet its spirit. It showed me how its leaves could be used as a poultice. Later, a classmate said it was mullein, and indeed was used that way.

We danced outdoors to honor our plant spirits. My body flowed as I let the spirit take it over, becoming mullein, with strong, flexible leaves stretching upward to the sun, fearlessly opening to the unknown.

"It's a whole new world," a classmate marveled, throwing off his shirt to dance bare-chested in the sun.

The resistance headache was gone.

Near the end of the second week, Harner announced a Power Dance he'd learned from northwestern American Indians. We would sit and drum in a circle until one, then another, would be overcome with spirit and forced to rise and dance.

Three pairs of drummers paced the circle in solemn dignity, their heads faced forward like Egyptian gods. The dark, massive drum sounds transported us into a space so deep and timeless I sought in panic for something to hold onto, fixing finally on a glint of light from someone's modern wire frame glasses.

Many students were overcome by a spirit and compelled to dance that night, though I wasn't one of them. A small round woman, her short blonde curls flaming outward from a wide, freckled face, leapt into the circle and ran around and around, accelerating wildly. Stolid and graceless in ordinary life, now she was transformed, whirling, turning, propelled by a spirit demanding release of her long-pent life force. She danced with abandon, redeeming years of childhood taunts, boring hours of study, hopeless longings and despair, and beyond that, centuries of joyless ancestors, harsh winters, war, slaughter, duty, and endurance. But that was all behind her now, for the path of her life had finally brought her here—to this, her time to flower. She danced for herself, and for her race. Tears filled my eyes. She danced for me.

I was high without drugs, gifted with a second chance at childhood, free. The world was moving and alive, the way it had been when I was four, before I decided God wasn't real and smashed my new doll's face.

"You have learned a little," Harner said. "If it serves you to help others, I'm glad. But don't go around telling people you're shamans. That's for them to say."

I thanked Running Water for the loan of his rattle and gave it back, but he hugged me and said to keep it. I caressed its smooth, hard surface, round like a newborn baby's head, a close-to-perfect sphere of golden tan, a form to treasure with proper reverence.

POSITIONAL LIFE

I had been home from Nepal a month. Winter clamped down, cold and dark. Tom and Aaron were away at college and Thorne moved out to share an apartment with friends. Keri looked after herself when she came home from school until her dad woke up. When I came in from work, we'd eat together in silence, and then Evans would go off to his workroom.

Maile had said I could be a shaman, that the Banjhankri's shadow had fallen on me, and I'd thought that meant something. But here at home it seemed impossible. After my initiation into core shamanism by Michael Harner, I'd been excited for a while. Shamans could bring down rain from the skies, turn sticks into snakes, cause rattles to fly by themselves through the air of a sweat lodge, call ghosts to appear and speak. I'd experienced none of these miracles first hand, but if the tales were true, if I could learn such powers, it would be proof of an unseen world of spirits, forces, and powers — of God himself.

But shamanism had long been lost to our culture, persecuted out of existence by the Church. If I suddenly started talking about gods and spirits and shaking like a Nepali shaman, people would think I was crazy. I wouldn't get any clients for my patent work, and we'd starve.

Still, I thought, if the spirit world were real, over the centuries, people in our own Western tradition must have found it. I scoured the library for books on Christian mystics: Theresa of Avila, Joan of Arc, Emanuel Swedenborg, William Blake, saints and mystics who spoke from the far side of the rift that separates intellect from faith, a chasm I still dared not leap. But I fastened on the words of George Bernard Shaw's Saint Joan at the suggestion she had imagined her Voices, "Of course. That is how the messages of God come to us." Maybe my father had been wrong, and thoughts *were* real.

Emanuel Swedenborg's writings affected me most. A Swedish scientist two and half centuries ago, at age sixty he had begun having visions, journeys into Heaven and Hell that he meticulously recorded, describing his conversations with angels and devils, the houses they lived in, the clothes they wore, the landscapes and skies of the three levels of heaven. We are all surrounded by spirits in normal life, he wrote, and our thoughts, whether good or evil, flow into us from the spirit world. It's not our fault when evil spirits slip bad thoughts into our heads, but it's up to us to push them away. The good thoughts are given into our minds by angels and we should act on these "as if from ourselves," but without taking credit, for they come from God, not us. Swedenborg had been a Christian, and I decided to start attending church. It would probably be good for Keri to go to Sunday school.

Evans objected. He didn't want his daughter exposed to "that evil nonsense."

"She's not an idiot," I pointed out. "She's your daughter after all. Could you have been brainwashed at that age?"

He gave in, grumbling, "It *is* evil. Haven't you ever heard of the Crusades—or the Inquisition?"

The trouble was, I had. Church was still all about good and evil, and that felt wrong. If nothing else, it was bad grammar, a sign of sloppy thinking, like using a transitive verb without an object, as though you could make a complete sentence out of, "I heard," or "She touched," or "I need." Heard what? Touched what? Need what?

A thing couldn't be good or evil in a vacuum. You had to say what it was good *for*, who got hurt by the evil. Otherwise, it left you hanging, wasn't a complete thought. A hawk swooping overhead would be evil for chickens, but goodness itself for her babies when she brought home fresh meat. Conversion by the sword had been good for the power of Christian kings, but evil for those who resisted. Adultery, theft, covetousness, bearing false witness, failing to honor the elders—evil for the peace and stability of human communities, but what did the animal kingdom care?

It was obvious to me that if those church people would just take the trouble to finish their sentences, they could quit worrying about the nebulous "evil" they all seemed so afraid of.

I kept on going to church though, mostly for the music. It bypassed my mind and made me feel uplifted. One Sunday morning, I brought two new friends home after services for coffee, a kind, broad-faced couple in their late forties who sold real estate for a living. Evans was just waking up, smoking and drinking his coffee on the couch. His hair was uncombed and he looked as though he'd slept in his clothes, which he had. "This is Harry and Carol," I introduced my friends. "My husband, Evans."

Evans raised one eyebrow and fixed them with a disapproving

look. "Oh, your God people." He turned and stared out the window, and blew smoke.

Carol hugged her arms.

"We can't stay," Harry said.

Safely outside, Carol whispered, "I don't mean to offend you, but it seems to me like he's dark and you're light—like he's evil and you're good."

Harry nodded.

"I know what you mean." I basked in their sympathy. "But evil for what? Good for what?"

They nodded encouragingly. Their big round eyes searched my face, trying to understand.

"You can't just say 'evil' in a vacuum," I felt constrained to say. "Who is it evil for?"

"For you?" Carol ventured.

"Evil is evil," Harry said.

Evans had never been evil. It annoyed me that they said so. Part of the problem, of course, was his pain. He wouldn't let me try to heal his back using shamanism, and Harner cautioned his students not to ask the spirits to work on anyone against their will. But I could pray. I still had doubts that God was real, but as I closed my eyes and silently asked for Evans' pain to leave, I sensed a peaceful, white vibration.

Now that he had safely escaped, Thorne didn't mind turning up now and again for a meal and a game of chess with his dad. Wanting to cook him something special, and missing Nepal, I decided on a chicken curry. I chopped up onions and threw them in the skillet with a bit of hot oil, then added spices, a pinch of crescent-shaped cumin seeds, coriander, small round mustard seeds, a tablespoon of chili powder.

"What's burning?" Evans squinted through the acrid chili fumes. "I thought you didn't like smoke."

Thorne turned on the stereo and they set up the chess board in the living room. Keri helped arrange the pieces.

I diced tomatoes on the cutting board, scraped them into the skillet, and tore up lettuce for a salad, arranging it in a large glass bowl and laying thin circles of cucumber around the edges for decoration, a festive touch.

A little milk for the curry, the secret ingredient, sugar, and it bubbled orange-white, giving off a sweet, exotic fragrance like incense. I added the chicken and let it simmer, lifting a spoonful to my mouth.

Delicious. Light on the tongue, delicate at first, slightly sweet, slightly tangy; then a growing awareness of deeper, full-bodied flavors of chicken and curry spices. Good, nourishing food that made you want more.

"You're going to like this," I called out over the stereo. I started the oven and whacked the tube rolls open on the counter, enjoying the small explosion, and then drifted in to watch the chess game. "Dinner's almost ready."

Evans moved his queen diagonally from Thorne's knight. "I'll leave you to ponder that, while I take a whiz." He pushed himself sideways from the couch to spare his back.

Thorne stared at the board, working something out, and looked questioningly after his father. "I don't see how he can just break off in the middle of the game," he said. "I have to keep concentrating."

Evans leaned in from the hallway. "Positional chess. It's how I used to win tournaments." He came back, zipping his fly, and stood over the board. "In tournaments, you have to go around from one game to another and play a whole roomful of competitors at once. Some people try to keep all the games in their heads, but it's easier to play positional chess."

"Yeah?" Thorne prompted.

"You look at the layout of each game when you come to it, and decide on the best move you could make right then. You make that move and go on to the next game. You don't even think about that one again until you get back to it. Make the best move you can, and go on to the next game. Statistically you come out ahead."

The meal was ready, and I set it on the table. "I hope you like it."

Evans dropped into his chair with a groan. "I'm glad you learned *something* useful in Nepal."

I smiled at Thorne, happy the family was together, determined that Evans wouldn't spoil it.

☙

I tried to keep my spirits up, but it was December, each day darker than the one before. Evans and his friends observed the solstice with a party. I didn't feel like making the effort, but the kids expected Christmas. "Positional life," I told myself. "Don't look ahead. Just do the most loving thing you can in the moment and trust it will work out. I bought a tree, wrapped presents, and cooked a turkey. Evans woke in time to share the meal.

"It would be nice if you did *something* around here to help," I muttered as he went off to his workroom leaving the dirty dishes on the table.

"This is *your* celebration," he shot back from the stairs. "I don't see the point. Since you wanted it, fine, but don't ask me to believe in your dead god."

His friends showed up later, and as I brought a load of clothes from the dryer in the basement past the door to the great hall/garage, I heard someone say, "She'll have to pay alimony."

I dropped the clothesbasket right there, and stalked into the study to the far wall, wrapping my arms around my body to contain my fury. The game was over; the only move left was to knock down my pieces and concede.

I put Keri to bed, unloaded the dishwasher, and kept busy scrubbing the sink and bathtub, waiting until I heard the front door close behind Evans' friends. It was two in the morning.

I caught him in the kitchen, stirring up his tap water coffee. He looked up surprised. "What are you doing up so late?"

"I can't live this way any more." I followed him to the living room. "I want a separation."

He eased onto the couch and raised his hand to his forehead so I couldn't see his eyes. "I don't suppose you'd change your mind."

"No."

It had been exactly two months since Krishna rearranged my planets.

SHAKING IN AMERICA

Keri and I moved to a clean, rented house two blocks from the old one, where she could walk over any time and see her dad. I was overjoyed at the smoke-free air, and spread out my clothes in the closet. We hung pink, ruffled curtains in Keri's room, and loose-weave, off-white drapes in mine, pulling them back to let in light. Evans' application for disability payments was denied, but two of his friends moved in with him and paid enough rent to cover the mortgage.

Peter had set up seminars on shamanism in Santa Barbara and Boulder that spring, and brought Mr. Rai and Jebi over to teach. They arrived at my house on a Sunday evening, having driven from California through miles of open country—mountains, deserts, and vast prairie vistas empty of people, eating in cafes that smelled of cooked beef, served by leathery waitresses, outspoken as men.

Jebi wore a nappy, American-style sports coat and blue polyester slacks. He'd had a few drinks, and his eyes were big and glazy. He was exhausted. His dark face, so humorous when animated, was heavily lined, almost frightening, in repose.

I made tea, and Mr. Rai performed a hilarious reenactment of Jebi's encounter with Customs when they opened his bag and found his shaman's things—drum, necklaces of brown rudraksha and black ritha seeds, the sheaf of green *kauli* leaves. Mr. Rai mimed how the Customs man had gingerly lifted Jebi's massan bone with two fingers.

He chuckled. "Luckily, I was there. 'This man is a shaman,' I told them."

He had offered the Customs man a smoke and pulled out photos of Jebi in full costume, dancing with his feather headdress and drum. "These are all things he needs to do his work. University of California have called us do seminar with famous anthropologist, Dr. Peter Skafte. I can guarantee you, these things are not against the law."

Mr. Rai's whole body took part in the telling, acting out the scene. It made me trust him. We Americans tend to hold our bodies still—so they won't betray us when we lie about our feelings. I thought the officials must have warmed to him too, as he worked so hard, with such good cheer, to persuade them.

We opened the hide-a-bed in the living room for Jebi and cleared the toys from Keri's room for Mr. Rai. She would sleep with me. Peter left to stay with other friends. I cooked at first, American-style fried chicken and rice—no beef, of course. But after a few days, Mr. Rai took over, making *dhalbhat,* the Nepali lentil and rice dish they were used to. He was as confident and full of energy here as in Nepal, never afraid to ask for what he needed, riveting my attention by the way he sharpened my name to Allen. "*Allen,* do you have such thing as curry powder and chilies? *Allen,* you have coffee?"

I lifted a can of coffee from a high shelf and began to show him how the percolator worked. He waved me aside. He already knew, of course.

Rested, Jebi was his old self, alert and commenting on everything in his deep, unstrained voice. The sympathy that had started between us in Kathmandu, and been quashed by Peter's concern for dignity and distance, now flourished. Jebi worked hard at communicating. An exquisite mimic with quick emotional responses, he kept us laughing as he imitated people's walks and gestures. His stories got funnier, at least to him, with every repetition. Again and again we got to witness how, with increasing shock, the Customs official had pulled strange objects from his bag. "This mala," he said in English, holding up an imaginary string of seeds, dropping his jaw and pulling down the corners of his mouth. "This kauli. This bone." We couldn't help laughing every time.

My landlord came by, bustling about to check the plumbing, but really to get a good look at our unusual house guests. Jebi namasted with respect but, no more taken in by self-importance here than in Nepal, caught my eye for a moment of shared amusement.

Keri, at seven, didn't need language to make friends. She and Jebi spent hours on the floor playing cards. War was their game. Jebi's broad, work-hardened hand would slap down a matching card, and they'd both roar with laughter because of the special high cards she knew he had hidden behind his back. He'd taught her to cheat. She had her own secret pile too. He called her *bhaihini,* little sister, which meant he called me *ama,* mother, though he was actually my elder by a year.

Jebi was never still except to sleep, and even then, tossed and muttered, or shouted, fighting with dreams. I would have liked to serve him, bring him tea and snacks, fetch his clothes, wash his dishes like a dutiful student, but he was always right there beside me, anticipating the work and doing it himself. There wasn't a lazy bone in his body.

I wasn't officially his student anyway. It wasn't clear he thought I could become a shaman.

Each morning, Peter drove Jebi and Mr. Rai to the Spiritual Emergence Network in North Boulder for their seminar. I asked Jebi one evening if he liked being a shaman. He'd been teaching all day and seemed tired. He made a stern face. "No. This shaman work is no good. When sick people call, you have to go. You might have to walk for miles. You have to set up an altar, put on your healing dress, and shake." He acted out his words, jumping up to show how he struggled into his costume. "Even if they have no money to give, you do it anyway. You have to do it."

I had to work and so didn't join their daytime classes. After dropping Keri off at school, I would go on to my office. I was partner in my own firm now, and half believed this success was due to the plant spirit helper I'd found at Michael Harner's initiatory workshop in core shamanism.

ॐ

On the plane back to Denver from Joy Lake where the class had been held, Emily Bornstein and I had decided to start a regular drumming circle. Others joined, and soon a core group of Emily, Joe Goldberg, Howard Schiff and I, were meeting every week in Emily's psychotherapy office to drum, try out healing techniques, and journey to the spirits for help and advice. All our lives were changing.

Emily apprenticed herself to Black Elk, a Lakota medicine man, and gradually gave up her therapy practice. Black Elk invited our group to several sweats in his lodge of willow withes overlaid with tarps and blankets, with a doorway closed with hanging skins. An aging, big man, he groaned as he folded his legs and took his seat inside, to the right of the doorway.

A great buffalo skull kept guard on a pile of rocks outside, as we crawled past Black Elk into the dark, round space. A helper brought glowing hot stones on a pitchfork from a fire outside and laid them in the central pit. Black Elk threw green leaves on the stones and called for water. As he poured it on the heated stones, great clouds of searing, pungent steam rolled over us, weakening our muscles and vaporizing all our pride.

The Lakotas prayed with fervor, begging God for pity. I sensed how deeply their souls were moved, far deeper than the mothlike fluttering of my own thoughts. The sound of a rattle seemed to circle above us near the dome of the ceiling, too high for anyone to be holding it. But I was angry at the darkness that wouldn't let me see, and wouldn't believe anything without proof.

Nevertheless, my life began to change. My first vision, always when we drummed, was the plant. It spoke no words, but swayed and bloomed open, inviting me to rest in its center, a void where forms took shape, flowed outward and away. Whenever I closed my eyes, even for a moment—in the sun, at stoplights, pauses at work between tasks—the plant vision was there.

I began to feel uncomfortable at my old firm, as though I didn't belong. I sent my resume around, and six months after meeting the plant spirit, had a new job at Agrigenetics, a company recently formed to improve crop plants. I toured the labs, passing row on row of culture plates, each growing a dark lump of cauliflower-like, tumorous tissue. In the successful experiments, fresh green shoots pushed up through the mass of undifferentiated cells, and the sight of them set off tiny explosions of joy in my veins.

The company was sold and moved soon after I began working there, but we in the Patent Department didn't want to leave Boulder, and instead set up an independent law firm. I loved my work, on the borderland between law and science. Respect for science was in my blood, but I could no longer take it as seriously as I once had. I was beginning to suspect a big joke behind its search for truth, like looking for a box within a box within a box within a box, smaller and smaller and smaller, and never an end to the boxes—never that last box with a gift.

❧

While Mr. Rai and Jebi were staying with us, every evening after work, I would take Keri to the healing ceremonies, which were open to the public. My son Aaron, home for spring break, joined us.

We found seats on the right side of the auditorium near the back. Up front, there was a stage and backstage area where Jebi got into his shaman's dress.

Peter gave a scholarly introduction, and then Mr. Rai, his compact energy intensified by the large audience, explained his translator's role in a voice sharp-edged with excitement, reaching every corner of the room. "I am not shaman," he said, "For I cannot shake myself. But my father was great shaman in Bhutan."

I felt a shiver as Jebi came on stage, transformed by his red and white costume and crown of peacock feathers from our friend to a man of power. The room fell silent. His face took on a serious, forbidding look as he reached to adjust his headdress and seated himself at his traditional Rai altar.

In Nepal, people laughed and chattered and moved around as the shaman performed, but the American audience kept silent, respectfully attentive. Some sat in meditative postures, eyes closed, hands open on their thighs.

Jebi lit the oil lamp on his altar and bowed three times before it, hands pressed together. His adam's apple moved convulsively as he swallowed, nervous as always before he began, unable to take it for granted the deities would come.

Mr. Rai lit incense. The holy smell drifted out among the audience, and Jebi took up his drum and brass plate and beat a jangling rhythm. His chant named a myriad of deities and spirits, called them his gurus, and asked them to come onto his body. Finally, when he called his *kuldeota*, the *mashta* spirits of his Chetri ancestors, his body began to shake. His knees jerked off the floor and the bells around his shoulders rang. The audience watched intently, awed and aware of the power that filled the room. No one still pretended to meditate.

Jebi handed off the drum and plate to Mr. Rai, who wedged the drum handle into the crook of his folded leg and began beating a complicated Rai rhythm with two straight drumsticks of bamboo. Jebi danced, dipped a bamboo brush into a bowl of liso plant gum and sprinkled it about the altar, the stage, and into the audience for protection, then threw back his head and let a string of the viscous liquid drip into his mouth. Peter brought the first patient forward, a woman in her forties, and seated her near the altar.

Jebi sprinkled an offering of vodka from his gourd onto the altar as he danced, and then sent his spirit traveling to the three worlds of the shaman, first to the lower world to visit Sessnag, the seven-headed snake, to ask for power and knowledge. As the rhythm changed and Jebi came back to the middle world, he chose a long, curved feather from the gourd, took a piece of ginger, and circled the patient, humming a mantra. He held the feather to her head until it moved, curling in the opposite direction; and then, whistling his mantra, he raised the feather high, shouted *"Ho, ha,"* and sliced it completely through. The cut piece skittered across the floor. Peter picked it up, saw that it had fallen cut side down, and placed it near the altar.

Again the rhythm changed, and Jebi's dance became a series of hops, as he climbed toward the upper world. Then Mr. Rai began a fast and furious drumbeat, hands flying, elbows arcing up and down as he beat a different rhythm with each drumstick. Jebi whirled, his long white skirt with its red border flaring. He was dancing in the upper world. Yet wild as he appeared, his feet never varied from their set pattern, as he enlisted the aid of Lord Shiva himself and the thirty thousand deities among the stars.

Mr. Rai stopped drumming, and Jebi sank down by his altar, wiped the sweat from his face with a hand towel, and dug the back of his head into its socket, rocking it to ease his neck. He pushed back his headdress and drank clear liquid from a water glass. Mr. Rai explained that the shaman was taking a rest after going on his way and finding that he could indeed do something to help the patient.

Again Jebi drummed and went into trance, this time speaking for the god in odd, rhythmic grunts. He paused, and Mr. Rai questioned the patient, "You live in house that faces east?" She seemed confused. "You must answer yes or no," he urged. "If no, he will have to go back to his gurus and ask again."

"There is a white fence near your door?"

"Yes."

"You have son or daughter who is giving you trouble?"

"I have a son," she said. "He's seventeen."

"He comes in, eats, goes out. Mother doesn't know where son is. He doesn't study lessons. Yes or no?"

"That's true." She took a sharp breath in.

"Our shaman will give you something to make your son obedient," Mr. Rai told her. Jebi placed a little rice and charcoal on a small piece of paper and ground his thumb into it, blowing a whispered mantra. He folded the paper and tied it with a crossed string like a Christmas present, and then smoked it with incense.

"Give this to your son to wear—or if he doesn't like to wear it, put it under his pillow," Mr. Rai instructed, handing her the amulet.

"Finished," Jebi said in Nepali. He turned from the patient and waved dismissively. Mr. Rai, more diplomatic, helped her to her feet. "You will see, at the end your son will be with you. He will take care of you and respect you."

"You don't have to be a shaman to figure that out," Aaron whispered.

"What about the house facing east and the white fence?" I whispered back.

"A lucky guess."

A woman with an oxygen tank came forward, tall and swaying with her burden, suffering on her face. Jebi took her hand in both of his and said something compassionate in Nepali. He drank from the water glass and began again, dancing, traveling to the three worlds, cutting ginger with a feather. The omens were good, and he called an intermission.

After resting, he sifted red vermilion powder through his fingers onto a piece of white paper to form sixteen squares, and placed offerings in each square—uncooked rice, vermilion, flower petals, copper coins, betel nuts, and betel leaves. Then, as Mr. Rai kept up a middle world rhythm, Jebi passed his massan bone over the woman's body, blowing mantras, and at the end of the passes, dropped a bit of rice into each of the sixteen squares in turn. After sixteen passes, he folded the paper and handed it to Peter to dispose of, taking it for granted, as usual, that when he was shamanizing, others would serve him.

The patient bent with willowy grace to retrieve her tank, and returned to her seat in the audience.

"Why doesn't she just throw the oxygen away right now?" Aaron whispered with a grin.

"It takes time," Mr. Rai said to the audience. "I can tell you, she will be better, but it takes time."

He conferred with Jebi and Peter. "When a new shaman is being made, he or she must be someone who hears drumming and starts to shake," he explained to the audience. "Then the shaman has to find out what deity or spirit is on them. Shaman will ask, 'Are you deity, or witch or bad spirit?' Maybe he will threaten the spirit with a red-hot spoon, or beating with nettles, to scare and make it speak."

Jebi drummed again; the audience fell silent as the power came up. This time there was no patient. Shaking, Jebi left the stage and came down into the audience, sniffing the air with nostrils flared like an animal's, his eyes wide and glazed, as he circled the back of the room and up the center aisle. "He is possessed by Hanuman, the monkey god," Mr. Rai explained. Jebi stopped beside me, still sniffing, and pawed at my arm.

"He wants you up here," Mr. Rai called.

I followed Jebi to the stage. I'd come straight from work and wore a black dress, pantyhose, and uncomfortable high heels. My hair was done up in a French roll. I slipped out of my shoes and sat cross-legged facing the audience, tugging at my dress to cover my knees. A man in the front row pointed a video camera toward us and began to film.

Jebi placed a rudraksha seed mala over my head, reassuring me with his touch that everything would be all right, and handed me a drum and beater. I concentrated on following his rhythm as he drummed and shook, and gathered in my attention until the videotape, the audience, even the fact that my children were watching, became irrelevant. My focus narrowed solely to Jebi, as he blew mantras and threw grains of rice around my head and shoulders. I felt his breath, and the rice landed gently in my hair, each grain large and full of blessing.

"Concentrate yourself!" Mr. Rai shouted, and I remembered Nepal and pictured Lord Shiva, powerful in the upper world, dressed in tiger skin, with long locks coiled on his head and living cobras writhing on his arms. My solar plexus began to tremble. Each time Jebi showered me with rice grains, my stomach shook harder. Then something loosened where my legs joined my hips, and my knees escaped control and rose and fell of themselves as Jebi chanted and shouted in Nepali.

I felt a powerful magnetic energy within me—the same as I'd sensed watching Jebi travel to the lower world, and wondered briefly if I could stop the shaking. But this was no time spoil the show.

The shaking stopped when Jebi stopped drumming. Mr. Rai helped me to my feet. "She can be a shaman," he said as I slipped on my shoes. "I can guarantee you, she can be a shaman. Only she doesn't speak. But that is all right. It takes time. It takes time."

I returned to my seat. My legs had stopped trembling but inside, my stomach still shook. Someone asked how it felt. "Strange," I answered, surprised that my voice shook too. "Okay."

Aaron stared, not knowing how to take it. "My stomach's going up and down," I laughed.

Keri slid onto my lap, and I hugged her warm little body, feeling happy. Something was happening, something important.

GURU JEBI

We heard them shouting through the bedroom door. Keri lifted her head from the pillow. "What's wrong? Why are they fighting?"

"You keep me shaking every night past midnight," Jebi was saying in a loud, injured tone. "This is hard, hard work."

"You should pay him what you promised." That was Peter.

"Yes, but we have no idea expenses are so much," Mr. Rai said forcefully. "I will make nothing. Why you say to Jebi all these nonsense things. I am not cheater."

"Jebi is not the one who took on the risk," Peter admonished. "I am sorry we didn't make more money, but if we had, it would be you getting the extra profits, not Jebi. So you are the one who must bear the loss."

"Why I am coming here, bringing my shaman for your class, if cannot even make expenses," Mr. Rai demanded. "But I am not cheater, you will see. I am never cheater. I am agree, I will pay him. Now no more discuss of it." He had to give in. He needed Peter to bring more students to his school, needed Jebi to be his shaman.

"Jebi *should* get all the money, Mom. He's the star," Keri whispered, defending her friend.

The front door closed, and Peter's car drove off. I got up. Jebi lay curled up on the couch, his back to the room. Mr. Rai was sorting papers from his briefcase on the kitchen table. "Peter knows nothing about how we do things in Nepal," he said to relieve his feelings. "He should not butt himself in."

I went back to bed. When Jebi made me shake, it must have begun some process below awareness, for I came awake in the night, aware of seeing the inside of my mind, like a long dark mineshaft dug into the earth, studded with large rocks. Above was a high, narrow cavern, and from my vantage point, clinging to one steep side, the hollowed-out space stretched downward into darkness. It felt familiar, as though I'd been there many times without remembering, but always before, it had been still.

Now things moved and shifted by themselves. Rocks embedded in the shaft, once fixed and sure, now heaved and fell and rearranged. Those near the top moved lower, some fell, and others ground upward, the boundaries of my inner space, always so fixed and sure, now revealing they could move. Let them, I thought unfrightened. Let them heave and rend apart. Let everything change!

The odd sense of movement finally stopped. I tossed and turned, oppressed by the blankets, stimulated and restless. It was close to midnight. I got up and dressed, quietly pulled my jacket from the closet in the hall, slipped past Jebi, as he snored lightly on the couch, and went out into the cold night.

An unusual dense fog had settled over the neighborhood. I walked down the quiet street and turned at the corner toward the little white-steepled Swedenborg church. From there, the sidewalk angled downhill toward the railroad tracks. Tires hissed behind me as an occasional car passed on the main street. The side street was empty. It wasn't a bad neighborhood, but I felt uneasy, a woman alone at night passing the dark open space of the park.

Remembering Maile's protection mantra, I whispered it now, visualizing her smooth, light brown face with its high, scarred forehead. A man appeared from the fog, with a dog on a leash running out ahead. My heart pounded, but the man walked safely by, eyeing me like a co-conspirator in the strange foggy night.

I turned at the railroad tracks and walked the rails toward the stream. It was here I'd come last winter to watch the pale sun set, depressed, but gathering courage to end my marriage. At the bottom of the steep bank, under a layer of ice, the water whirled by. I'd come a long way since my last visit to this place. Energies long frozen were on the move. Free of my marriage, I could do what I wanted, feel my own life, magic and unique, as I did now in the foggy night alone. I could descend, at last, into the deep vibrations I sensed as Jebi drummed.

I'd come to shamanism hoping for miracles to convince me the spirit world—and God—were real. But I wasn't thinking of that now. Jebi's dark, magnetic force tugged at my soul, as though he'd put me in a spell. It began to snow; the flakes landed on my face like fresh little blessings, and I hurried home.

The next day was Saturday. The seminar was over, and Jebi and Mr. Rai had the day free. We took them to a thrift store to buy American-style clothing and presents to take home. Keri picked out a stuffed animal and presented it to Jebi. In return, he gave her a heavy green lion he'd bought in Thailand, cast in metal and decorated with real gold paint.

At home, I asked if Jebi could teach me his lower world journey.

He conferred with Mr. Rai in Nepali. "He says he can teach you," Mr. Rai reported. "He is very much willing to teach you because you are his ama, and he can tell anything to his ama. But it takes time. He had to study with own guru for years before he was a fully-cooked shaman."

"How long?"

They conferred again. "Six months. And you will need to come to Nepal."

I tried to breathe normally. "Would he accept me as his student?"

"Oh, yes, why not?"

Of course, Mr. Rai would say yes, for who but he would have the business of arranging my visit to Nepal. "Will you become my guru?" I asked Jebi directly in Nepali.

He gave me a look of intense scrutiny, and then said "Ho."

I would take Thorne and Keri with me to Nepal, I planned—next fall, when the house lease expired. Keri would be eight and Thorne eighteen. A great adventure. We would put the furniture in storage. If ever there was a right time to go, this was it.

"You must get up early in morning, wash, and prepare your *guru bette,*" Mr. Rai said. That meant money, an offering to Jebi when I took him for my guru.

"I know you are very much anxious to learn. May I?" He reached over my head, pulled my spiral-bound notebook from the top of the refrigerator, and opened to a blank page, where he drew a diagram shaped like an hourglass, and labeled the corners, center, and top and bottom with the numbers one through seven.

"This is the lower world." He named the deities to be encountered at each point, who had to be placated with offerings, or flattered or tricked to let the traveler pass on his descent. Coiled at the bottom was Sessnag, the primal snake with seven heads, great ruler of the lower world.

Jebi watched, nodding to confirm what Mr. Rai had said.

I studied the diagram. Clearly, I'd been given a road map with names and arrows and detailed instructions. But where did it begin?

As instructed, I got up early next morning, bathed, and dressed in clean clothes, choosing a red and white plaid jumper and white blouse, shaman's colors, hoping the ceremony would be finished before Peter arrived.

But the doorbell rang as Jebi set up his altar. A man and woman with an armload of expensive cut flowers had come for Jebi's help. They seemed shy, and to allow them privacy, I drove Keri to school. When I returned, Jebi was giving them final advice on how they might conceive a child.

At last they were gone, and Jebi called me to his altar. He lit charcoal in a metal pot and sprinkled dried leaf bits and dust on the glowing coals from a grubby, well-worn bag inside his pack. A pleasant, odd smell filled the room.

He placed a rudraksha seed necklace around my neck, a special one I'd seen him wear for ceremonies, interspersed with bells, red beads, and snake bones. He lit his oil lamp, and I placed my guru offering on his plate. He blew a mantra on me and blessed me with a shower of uncooked rice, then dictated a special mantra.

"Memorize it, light your oil lamp each morning and evening, and repeat it with an offering of flowers or incense," Mr. Rai instructed. "The oil lamp is called *deo,* symbol of Great God, Shiva, as a witness. Remember well, and do not reveal this mantra to others."

He translated the words of the mantra into English. They called certain gods and spirits, bad ones as well as good, to wake and come out and play. "From today, you has to give up garlic, beef, pork, and goat meat," he said.

At the airport, Mr. Rai spotted a man in a wheelchair on the floor below, stuck at the bottom of the escalator. His fine-grained face expressed concern as he took off running to help, his brown leather suitcase bouncing off his calves. "He has a good heart," I said, watching as he worked the wheels free.

"Ramro manchhe," good man, Jebi agreed.

Keri cried when they left, and Jebi cried too, tears streaming down the deep grooves in his face.

Later that day, Rebecca Brown, the woman who ran the Spiritual Emergence Network where they'd held the seminar, telephoned for Peter. I told her he'd already left for California, and asked if she'd enjoyed the class.

"It was great. Everyone liked it," she said, "but there was a Christian minister there who's been going around saying Jebi forgot to close the door to the lower world, and so my building is full of bad, heavy vibrations and thought forms."

"Oh, come on," I protested.

"People like that are dissociated," she said, "viewing the world in terms of good and evil and splitting themselves off from the parts they see as evil. I understand it, but that kind of talk doesn't do my Center any good. In spiritual emergence, we try to heal those splits."

"I see what you mean," I said, intrigued. "People like that think they're good, but they come across as smug and superior. Not loving at all."

"Lonely."

Knowing she'd understand, I confessed, "I feel like I need to just immerse myself in those energies of Jebi's—that I've lacked them, and need them to be whole."

"You should follow that feeling. And, by the way, tell Peter, if you talk to him, that when we cleaned up the backstage area, we found about twenty empty liquor bottles."

TRUST

How would you like to go to school in Nepal next year?" I asked Keri.

"But when would I see Daddy?"

"Well you wouldn't for a while. But we'd come back."

She looked away, eyes flat. This wouldn't be as easy as I'd hoped. As it was, with her dad only two blocks away, she could visit whenever she pleased.

That's what she'd been doing—running across the street to his house—when a car knocked her down.

I rushed to the hospital as soon as I got the call. She was in X-ray, but when they brought her out, she didn't seem badly hurt. "Maybe a broken elbow," the doctor said. "But she took a hard bump on the head. We'll keep her here and watch her a while."

They put her in a narrow bed and raised the rails. She was awake, but dazed.

The doctor leaned down. "Do you know your name, honey?"

"Keri."

"And how old are you, Keri?"

"Seven."

"Okay. What grade are you in?"

"Second."

I dropped into a chair beside the bed.

A little later, the doctor checked back. "The X-rays showed a minor crack in her elbow."

Keri sat passively and didn't complain as they casted her arm.

"What's your name?" the doctor asked again.

"Keri."

"How old are you, Keri?"

"Six."

"Okay." He gave me a significant look. "I'll be back."

I leaned on the bed rails and recited Maile's protection mantra.

The doctor came back half an hour later. "What's your name honey?"

"Keri." Her eyelids fluttered.

"How old are you, Keri?"

"Uh, five?"

He looked me in the eye. "I'll order a CAT scan. We need to check for internal bleeding in her brain."

Now I began to pray in earnest. "Please God, let her be all right," I pleaded as they rolled her away. Too scared to think, I recited Maile's protection mantra over and over, along with the Lord's Prayer, and the Hail Mary I'd learned from a classmate as a child. If only she could recover, nothing else would matter. "If there are such things as parallel lives," I prayed, "please, God, put us in one where she's not hurt."

As long as they didn't tell me her brain was damaged, it hadn't happened. I held fast to a here and now where she was whole. The world could pivot on this point, change as it would, so long as that one thing stayed true. I didn't stop praying, or let in a single outside thought, until they wheeled her back.

"We didn't see any bleeding," the doctor reported tiredly, not seeming to share in the surge of relief his words brought me. Keri's eyes opened as they lifted her into bed. The doctor bent down. "What's your name again?"

"Keri."

"How old are you?"

"Seven."

"Good girl. We'll let you go home now. Okay?"

She held out her arms, and I picked her up and helped her dress.

I had to wake her every hour to make sure she was conscious, but she was fine. A few weeks later when the cast came off, it was as though it had never happened.

"You're going *where?*" My old friend Mary reacted about the way I thought she would when I told her my plans for Nepal. "What are you thinking of? After what just happened!"

We'd been best friends since rooming together in college. She was the sister I never had, and though she lived in Portland, Oregon now, we'd remained stable constants in each other's lives, seeing each other through our two marriages and divorces, the births of her two boys, my three, and Keri. It was important to have her approval.

"She's okay, Mary. She wasn't hurt."

"You can't take a small child to a place like that. What will she do all day while you're...drumming and chanting?"

"They have schools."

"They have diseases. They have crazy drivers and kidnappers. What if she got run over again?"

"Lots of people take their kids abroad."

"Couldn't you have a more...conventional midlife crisis? Take a lover, go on a cruise, have a face lift, dye your hair? What does Evans think about it? Never mind, I can imagine. What does Thorne think?"

"He doesn't want to go. He's got a girlfriend. He wants to stay here and get a job."

"Good for him."

"Look, Mary, I want to do this. This is the right time."

"I don't approve, of course."

"You know you're just jealous."

"Think about having Keri stay with me instead."

"You're serious? You'd keep her while I'm gone?" Even under normal conditions, I knew Mary could provide a more stable environment than I.

"Yes, of course, if you must do this ridiculous thing. Is she there? Let me talk."

I handed the phone to Keri and listened as she told Mary about school and the older girlfriend who was teaching her to use makeup. "Yes," she said after a pause. "Yes. I'd rather stay with you."

I took back the phone. "Thank you, Aunt Mary. I can't tell you how grateful I am."

"It's a good thing that poor child has *someone* sensible in her life."

⌇

Narayan Shrestha was a young Nepali of the Newar merchant caste whom Peter had helped get started in the United States. Now he owned a successful import shop in downtown Boulder. I'd done legal work for him, and he invited me to an organizational meeting for a charity to benefit Nepal. That's where I met Vhim Rai, also from Nepal, who'd recently come to Boulder to work as a stockbroker.

"Are you related to Mohan Rai?" I asked.

"Yes. Not closely, but we come from the same branch of the Rai tribe, and I know him. He has his own trekking agency. There aren't that many important Rais."

Vhim lit up when I mentioned my plan to study shamanism in Nepal, charming me with his enthusiasm. Over coffee and croissants he told me that two of his aunts were shamans, as well as his mother's mother. "I can't believe an American would be interested in this," he said. "Most people my age think it's superstition."

"Do you?"

"I'm not so sure. When I go home to Nepal, I believe in it more."

We became good friends, meeting often for lunch, hikes and picnics. I called him *bhai*, younger brother, and he called me *didi*, elder sister.

❧

A few weeks later, Narayan asked me to meet him for breakfast, saying there was something he wanted to discuss.

"I hear you want to study shamanism in Nepal," he said when our orders arrived.

"Yes." Narayan was a businessman through and through, and I wouldn't even try to explain my reasons.

"I know many powerful shamans in my home village. I could arrange some good teachers for you."

"Well, thank you." I toyed with my scrambled eggs. "I've already arranged to study with teachers I met through Peter."

He spread a pat of butter on his waffle, drowned it in syrup, and took a big bite. "Has Peter set this up for you?"

"No, I'm doing it through Mohan Rai."

"I know Mohan." There was something odd about his tone, as though what he knew wasn't good. "In some ways, Nepal is just one big village."

"Well, what do you think of him?"

"Be careful," he said. "He'll milk you like a cow."

❧

Vhim and I met for a picnic lunch in Central Park by Boulder Creek. The water was high and spit up streamers of froth. "I suppose you were the one who told Narayan about me going to Nepal to study shamanism," I said.

"I did. I hope you don't mind."

"Of course not." I unwrapped my sandwich. "Narayan asked if he could arrange my trip. When I said I was doing it through Mr. Rai, he said, 'Watch out. He'll milk you like a cow.'"

Vhim thought a moment. "Did you ever notice how people tend to accuse others of their own faults?" he said finally.

"Yes, but what do you think of Mr. Rai? Is he honest?"

"I've never heard anything against him," he said. "And Rais are honest—too honest. They think everyone else is honest too. That's why they usually end up getting cheated."

"My friend Joe calls Mr. Rai his tricking agent," I said. Peter had recommended Mr. Rai's trekking agency to our friend Joe O'Laughlin, and Joe had nearly gone to jail when it was discovered that Mr. Rai had given him an unofficial visa extension with a rubber stamp from his own desk drawer. "But Joe likes him anyway," I added. "He says that's just how they do things in Nepal."

"I think Mr. Rai won't let you down on anything that matters," Vhim said. "He has a good heart."

"Do you think I'm a sucker—going off to Nepal to learn to be shaman?" I asked, pretending to be absorbed in picking clovers from the grass. "Is everyone laughing at me?"

He gave me an odd, compassionate look. "Of course not. Why would they?"

"Well, I just wondered. That time I invited you to our drumming group, you refused. I thought maybe you thought it was silly."

He watched the water. "It's not that at all. I told you I come from a shamanic family. I was afraid that once I heard drumming, I might start to shake. It could happen to me, and I definitely don't want to be a shaman."

"You mean, if you started to shake, you'd have be a shaman? You'd have no choice?" I searched his face.

"We believe if you're chosen by a deity or spirit of an ancestor who comes on your body and makes you shake, you'll never live a normal life."

"Why not?"

"If you refuse to become a shaman, the spirit will make you sick and give you bad luck." His eyes bored into mine.

"I wasn't exactly chosen," I said, looking away. "I chose myself."

Vhim was too diplomatic to speak his mind. He smoothed out the ball of sandwich paper in his lap and folded it neatly. "We all have our own paths."

BOOK FOUR

RAI DEAD

On the way to Oregon to drop Keri off at Mary's, we stopped at a diner in Wyoming with a yard full of chainsaw carvings made from tree trunks. "Look, Mom, look. That looks like Dad." Keri was grappling a large wooden head with a long, thin face and pointed beard across the grass. I bought it for her, knowing how she'd miss her dad.

Mary was glad to see us. She showed us the bedroom she'd fixed up for Keri, led us on a tour of Chief Joseph Elementary School, where Keri would attend third grade, and introduced her to the neighbor girl. We said goodbye at the Seattle Airport.

In Kathmandu, Mr. Rai's two senior wives greeted me with warm namastes and cups of sweet, spicy chia. Bindu, the first wife, was plump, soft-spoken, and shy; Thuli Kumari was outgoing and cheerful. They got along like sisters. *Thuli* means "big" in Nepali, and because there was a third wife also named Kumari, they called the second wife Thuli, and the third wife *Sani,* which means little.

A long hallway, with bedrooms to either side for the two Kumaris, led from Mr. Rai's front door to the living room. There was a kitchen at the far end, and a small office by the front door at the other. The living room was clean and airy; the windows, barred with white wrought iron curlicues, looked out across a garden to a smaller house behind. Several worn Tibetan rugs lay on the blue linoleum floor of the living room, and the far end of the room was screened off for Bindu's double bed and dresser. I speculated that Mr. Rai must rotate among his three wives. Several of his twelve children were away at school; the others slept with their mothers or laid out mats in the living room at night.

A glass-fronted bookcase in the living room held rows of books in English and Nepali, framed photographs of Mr. Rai's wives, children and two sisters, and Mr. Rai, himself, as a young man in his Gurkha uniform. A large silver stereo rested beside a stuffed mongoose on the top shelf of a second bookcase.

After we drank chia, Mr. Rai led me outside, along a dirt road lined with marigolds and red flowers. On the right were houses; on the left, beyond a narrow strip of weeds and grass, the land dropped off steeply into a treed ravine. He'd rented me a room in Mr. Bharat's house two doors down. We walked in without knocking and climbed a wide concrete staircase. Our footsteps rang, for the house was new and built solidly of concrete.

My room was on the third floor, next to a western-style bathroom, which lacked nothing but toilet paper. I said I didn't want to be a bother and could learn to use water as people did here, but Mr. Rai drew himself up and said, "You are American lady. You must be civilized," and went off to fetch an armload of separately-wrapped rolls.

A narrow bed with a colorful homemade quilt took up one side of my tiny room. Someone had fastened a Jimmy Hendrix poster to the wall above it, no doubt, to make an American feel at home. The room smelled stuffy. I opened the single window and leaned out. A four-acre field of growing rice stretched bright yellow-green in the slanting sunlight toward an area of scattered houses. Beyond them, on the horizon, a blue hill rose above a layer of cumulus clouds with sunlit tops. The air was soft and fragrant. Neighborhood sounds—children's calls, clangs and traffic noise, barking dogs, a bull's lustful bellowing, bird cries, and a rhythmic pounding—blended into a single harmonious chord. A dark, bald Hindu man passed slowly on a path beside the field, adding depth like a silent bass note.

The stairway rang with hollow footsteps, and two young men appeared with my luggage. I thanked them, unpacked, and walked back to Mr. Rai's. He took me through his garden, and showed me the outdoor toilet and the old house beyond where his youngest sister and her husband lived. I recognized them as the good-looking couple who had served as Jebi's helpers. Another, unmarried, sister and several old people lived there too. Mr. Rai introduced me to a bewildering array of family and neighbors, all smiling in welcome, and I bowed namaste to each, trying to memorize the unfamiliar names.

"Two houses," I marveled. "I had no idea your family was so big."

Mr. Rai beamed with pride. "All together, I am supporting twenty-seven people. Now Jebi coming will be twenty-eight."

He took me into his little office next to the bedroom occupied by Sani Kumari, the third wife, and sat behind his desk. He opened a drawer and pulled out a ledger he said he would use to keep track of my expenses. "I never ask clients for money in advance," he said. "I'll keep account. Later we settle up."

I told him the amount I'd set aside for my stay. "Will it be enough?"

"Of course," he said.

A letter lay on the desk, looking as if it had been crumpled and partially smoothed out. Mr. Rai frowned when he saw me looking at it, and shoved it into a drawer. "*Allen*," he explained, "I am in a little trouble here. Big German travel agency has gone bankrupt, owing me fifty thousand dollars."

"How awful. Have you talked to a lawyer?"

"Yes, of course. There is no help. Is not such a big amount for them maybe, but for me, a very bad loss. I am trying to think, how to come to side agreement some way..."

I didn't know about German bankruptcy laws, but special arrangements to defraud other creditors didn't seem likely.

Mr. Rai took a deep breath, deliberately filling his chest. "But this is not of worry to you. I am taking care. Now you are here, is good for my business. Everyone can see an American student has come to study at my shaman school."

Thuli Kumari cooked dhalbhat and curried chicken and served me in solitary splendor at the coffee table in the living room. The rest of the family ate in the kitchen, and then filtered in to watch me. I didn't think I was wolfing my food, but everyone kept saying, *"Bistari bistari,"* slowly, slowly. In a country where food was scarce, it must be polite to try and make it last, I thought. There was plenty on my plate, but I ate as slowly as I could.

Jebi arrived as I finished. We embraced, kissed each other on the cheek, and carried on a halting, well-intentioned conversation in mixed Nepali and English until Mr. Rai released me to go home to bed.

I'd barely dozed off when he was at my door, pounding and shouting, "*Allen, Allen,* come on, a Rai person has been killed."

Jebi was with him. I pulled on my jeans, grabbed up my sweater and camera, and rushed out after them. We caught a taxi at the main road, and I learned on the way that what Mr. Rai had meant to say, but had been too excited to find the right English words, was that a Rai lady had died of old age and was about to be buried.

In the taxi he apologized, "I am sorry to get you out so late, but I just got call. You see, I am one of few Rais with telephone. We Rais from the mountains live like tourists here in Kathmandu. Is difficult to keep up our village culture, so always I have to go to these things, keeping Rai society together. Even last night, at two in the morning, I had to go to help sick Rai person needing blood." He tapped the driver on the shoulder and told him where to turn. "You will see now traditional Rai ceremony," he announced like a tour guide.

We got out near Pashupatinath, a Shiva temple on the Bhagmati River where Hindus burn their dead. A Rai burial ground had been established on a nearby hillside. "Burial is best than cremation," Mr. Rai asserted, "because family has place to come and make offerings after."

A group of young men carried a rough plank coffin uphill to the gravesite. Men with shovels were still digging. We got in line behind a long procession of mourners, and Jebi kept repeating, *"Ram, Ram, Ram,"* calling on the Hindu god Rama and rolling his eyes like a frightened horse, showing the whites.

The men with the coffin began to argue about what direction the dead woman's head should face, and looked to Mr. Rai, as an elder, for guidance. When they opened the coffin lid a crack to locate the head, I caught a glimpse of shiny, wrinkled skin and snapped a photo. With many shouts and gestures, the men turned the coffin so the head faced east, and began to lower it into the grave.

A Buddhist priest, shaved bald, had gone down into the hole ahead of the coffin, and scratched at the earth with a small, leafy tree branch. "He is cutting steps so spirit can come out," Mr. Rai said. Clinging precariously to the dirt, the priest steadied the long, narrow box and guided it into place. Everyone shouted "Bistari, bistari!" rushing about all the while in a great hurry. "We bury on same day person dies," Mr. Rai explained.

A middle-aged man held a thick, short piece of burning rope above the open grave, and then the priest, still wedged against the steep side of the hole, waved his leafy stick over the coffin. "He is telling her spirit it is free to go up and out; it is not really being buried," Mr. Rai said. A relative of the dead woman knocked dirt on the coffin with a stick; other relatives scooped up handfuls of soil and threw them into the grave, as shovelers rapidly filled the hole.

Forty-five days later, in accordance with the Rai mudhum, a shaman would have to perform a ceremony to find out where the dead woman's soul had gone, or where it wanted to go. It could go away with the wind to the desert if it wished, Mr. Rai explained, or become a household deity—an ancestral god. But if it was a bad spirit, the shaman would have to kill it. Someone came around with pencil and paper to take down our names and addresses to let us know where the ceremony would be held.

Mr. Rai hailed a taxi.

"How does the shaman find out where the soul wants to go?" I asked.

He lit a cigarette, puffed, and leaned back in his seat. "We take a small basket full of ashes to the room where dead person has slept. Only shaman and family elders is allowed to go in. They pour ashes on the ground and level it, then put big basket upside down over the ashes so no one can touch. Shaman does mantra, spits ginger, and says, 'Come tonight and show in ashes what you are going to be, if bird, or cow, or lion or man.' Next morning, footprints will be there in the ash. We look at feet marks, whether bird or lion or what.

"If dead soul leaves footprint of bird feet, is very dangerous. Soul could be all over everywhere, could make nest in house. Shaman has to work for seven days to make it change mind. If footprint of lion, spirit will go away to hilly place, or if man footprint is there, spirit will go away somewhere else. Then, shaman only has to work one day. Maybe is dog footprint.

"Whatever footprint, family has to find out what dead spirit needs. They ask, 'What you need? What you want? We have offered good food and been friendly for so long, and we are all going to die one day too. Please don't take our souls.'

"Shaman and elders talk about dead person and how he died. Then family comes in and shaman starts his performance. Shaman says to elders, 'Stay beside me, listen what soul demands when it speaks through my mouth. If kukhuri knife, go get it, or if special clothes, or food, get it; if you don't have what the spirit wants, note it down and get it later.'

"Then the shaman speaks to dead soul: 'Dear soul, you are requested to come here and tell us what you need, what you want, and where you want to stay. Of the four directions, one in air, one in mountainous area, one in river, one in flowers, which direction?' Then dead person's soul comes on shaman's body. Shaman is shaking, speaking for dead soul. Maybe it says, 'I would like to be bear and stay in mountains.'

"If he wants to stay in flowers, he will be *dewa*. That is family god that withers and paralyzes others who pluck flowers or fruit from family garden. If he wants to be dewa, shaman gets angry and says, 'Choose something else, you can't do that.' But might be soul is determined still, and says, 'I want to stay in flowers and orchards.' Then shaman performs for seven days, and soul will be dewa.

"Then soul asks for its things, clothes, kukhuri knife, rings, whatever belongings it had in life. Family must tell everyone, all neighbors and friends, that soul has become dewa. All entire family will be affected, and neighbors. If they don't fulfill dewa's demands, garden won't do well, or maybe they get sick themselves."

Mr. Rai smoked like a European, holding his cigarette with the thumb and fingers of his left hand. "We all has to die," he said, repeating his words in Nepali for Jebi's benefit.

"Ho," Jebi nodded with respect.

"Next day, shaman makes pole for dead person's soul and ties up threads to pole. Everyone in family is holding glass or cup. Shaman puts a thread from pole into every person's glass. Only for eldest and second eldest of family, thread is tied around their neck. He pours rakshi from gourd into glasses. Then all peoples chant in Rai way, *'Solololololo,'* and each person breaks thread from own glass, or neck, connecting to pole. They drink, and then threads and pole is buried, so deads can't run away with others' souls."

They let me out in front of Mr. Bharat's big house, and I climbed the stairs to bed, wondering how I'd cope with all the excitement.

SCHOOLWORK

But life in Kathmandu settled quickly into a calm, if not boring, routine. I would get up, take a cold shower—there was no hot water in the western-style bathroom—recite my morning mantra, and walk over to Mr. Rai's for a breakfast of egg, toast, and coffee. Mr. Rai usually ate with me, and then left for his office. "Jebi will be here soon," he said that first morning, "and Mr. Ganesh to translate."

Mr. Ganesh arrived, limping slightly, and the women made a fuss over him, seating him in a comfortable chair and serving him coffee. He said his leg had been run over and broken by a motorcycle several months earlier. He was recovering well, but could no longer guide tourists around the city on foot. He was lucky Mr. Rai had hired him for this job he could do sitting down.

Jebi showed up an hour later. "We can start now," Mr. Ganesh announced as Jebi settled himself on a rug on the floor. "I'm just going to speak to him. *Jebi—?* I'm just asking our shaman, what does he want to teach you."

"*Bokshi, graha, massan, bhut, pret, mudkutta, shikarees, moch, sharma, deodeota.*" Jebi's large, dark eyes were glazed, his voice deep, resonant, and impersonal.

"Yes, well. I will tell you about Lord Shiva, you know." Mr. Ganesh crossed his legs with difficulty, pursed his lips, and stared toward the ceiling. I opened my notebook. "The principal god of the shamans, you know—."

"*Shiva ji,*" Jebi interrupted.

"Lord Shiva," Mr. Ganesh continued. "At the first, you see, Lord Shiva had no father and mother. He was created by himself." The little translator's voice took on the high, pedantic tone I remembered from my last visit. "In a Himalayan kingdom, King Dacha had a hundred and eight beautiful daughters. All of them except Sati, the eldest, got married to gods. Then Sati married Shiva. Dacha had never liked Shiva because he used to smear ash on his body for talcum, and used poisonous snakes for jewelry. He didn't have good clothes; instead he used a tiger skin.

"One day Dacha was going to perform a big ceremony. He invited all hundred and eight of his daughters and sons-in-law, except for Sati and Shiva.

"Sati wanted to attend the ceremony, even without the consent of her father and mother, so she went, but her father insulted her in front of her brothers and sisters. She was so upset, she threw her body into the fire. You know, *sati* is the custom of wife-burning. Moslem invaders brought the custom to India in the eleventh century."

"*Kiratiswaramahadeo,*" Jebi said.

"Yes, Jebi is saying Lord Shiva was god of Kirati, you know, Rai and Limbu, tribes first. Hindus adopted him from them. He is a mountain god, you know."

I'd forgotten how frustrating it was to try and get a straight story here. Jebi subsided into silence, quietly thinking his own thoughts. I knew he hadn't asked the translator to teach me Hindu stories, but Mr. Ganesh had hit his stride, chin uptilted, mouth open, eyebrows raised. He wouldn't be stopped.

"The fire refused to burn Sati because of its fear of Shiva, but Sati died anyway. When Shiva understood her death, he was overcome with grief. He put her body on his shoulders and started wandering the mountains without food or drink. The gods and goddesses said, 'If Shiva is mad, who is going to protect the world?' So they put insects into Sati's corpse to make it decompose and fall to pieces. They thought Shiva would come back to himself when Sati's body was gone. As Shiva carried her body, one by one, the parts fell off. A temple was built wherever a body part landed.

"Finally, there was nothing left of Sati's body, but Shiva kept going like a madman, walking naked. On the bank of a river, the wives of seven holy men caught sight of his nude body and fell in love with him. They followed him, forgetting they were married. When their husbands saw this, they were so mad, they cursed Shiva, 'May your phallic symbol be perished!'"

I looked up, startled, but Mr. Ganesh hadn't even changed expression. He must have told the story so many times to tourists that by now it was rote. I bent my head and compressed my lips to stifle a laugh.

"Since that day they worship the symbol instead of Shiva."

Mr. Ganesh had taken us to many temples last time I was here, pointing out stones he called "Shiva lingams." Women poured milk on them for offerings, but the stones were mostly so short and stubby, I would never have guessed what they stood for.

The translator stopped and glanced around. "Jebi...*Jebi*," But Jebi was in the kitchen, laughing with Thuli Kumari. The smell of cooking food wafted in. "I see our shaman has left us," Mr. Ganesh said. "Now I will tell you about Ganesh, the elephant god..."

Mr. Rai arrived for lunch. "How is everything? Okay?"

"Mr. Ganesh is telling me stories about the Hindu gods—which is interesting," I said, "but I was hoping Jebi would teach me about shamanism."

"Yes, yes, of course, he must teach you about shamanism. After all, that is what you have come here for." Mr. Rai shot out orders in Nepali, and Jebi and the translator responded with the peculiar sideways head wobble that signifies agreement in Nepal.

As we ate our lunch of rice, lentils and greens, Mr. Rai talked of his father, the powerful shaman of Dorokha. "In Bhutan, as a child, I was tail of my father, following everywhere when he does his work," he said. "I can tell you very many stories of true Rai shamans and mudhum way. But now, Jebi will teach you while I go to business."

Mr. Ganesh sat stiffly upright sipping tea, and Jebi fell asleep on a small Tibetan carpet on the floor. Bindu disappeared behind her screen for a nap.

"I forgot to tell you," Mr. Rai said, as he left for his office, "Dr. William, an American psychiatrist, is coming to study with you." He woke Jebi with a joke, and the shaman sat up at once, alert and laughing.

Jebi had no system for teaching. Traditionally, an apprentice shaman learned as things came up, by helping. Being a "civilized lady," of course, I couldn't do that. Nor did I have the months or years I'd need to learn this way. Taking matters into my own hands, I sat on the floor with Jebi and asked about the carvings and painted designs on his drum.

Mr. Ganesh, stranded on his chair above us, translated as Jebi explained the three faces of Brahma, Vishnu and Shiva carved near the top of the drum handle, and the wavy line representing Nag, the sacred snake, at the tip.

"Can you teach me how you journey to the lower world?" I asked next.

Jebi opened his pack and pulled out a small bag of vermilion, the red powder worshipers smeared on god statues all over the city to look like blood. He trickled lines of it onto a sheet of clean paper to form a diagram of seven squares, arranged as two horizontal rows of three, with the extra square off the end of the bottom right. Above this diagram, he drew a sun, Shiva's trident, and a crescent moon. "Witnesses from the upper world," he said.

I asked Mr. Ganesh to translate the word for witnesses, and he took the opportunity to launch into a long-winded explanation, but Jebi cut him off. "Lower world," he pointed to the diagram. He drew two wavy lines to its left with red powder, and said, "*Nag.*"

"Uh, you see, they have nag, means snakes, in the lower world," Mr. Ganesh explained.

Pointing to each square in turn, Jebi recited, "Nag, Nagini, Sime, Bhume, Subbha, Subbhini," and then, indicating the empty space at the top right where no square had been drawn, "Sessnag."

"Yes, you know, Sessnag, ruler of the underworld," Mr. Ganesh began.

"*Ke ho?*" what is this, I interrupted, speaking to Jebi, and pointing to the extra square at the lower right of the two-by-three grid.

Jebi explained that this square was the main entrance to the lower world, guarded by a doorkeeper. When he journeyed, he said, he came upon it through a watery tunnel. He spoke rapidly in Nepali, and again I had to rely on Mr. Ganesh for translation.

"All these people, Sessnag, Nag, Nagini, Sime, Bhume, Subbha, Subbhini, are called gurus," Mr. Ganesh said. "Jebi goes to the underworld in his astral body, first calling all the deities from the upper and lower world to put them on his body. He calls the *bayus*, the ghosts, as well. He asks, 'Give me protection so I can be successful on my mission.'

"He sees a tunnel with water everywhere, sees a doorman who refuses to let him in. He says, 'I have to meet Sessnag,' and the doorman lets him in. Then he meets Nag, the snake, and has to ask permission and promise offerings. Nag lets him pass, but Nagini, the snake wife at the next gate, is mean. He has to promise more offerings. Then he comes to Sime, local goddess of waters, and asks to come through. Again, she tries to stop him, but he persuades her. He comes to Bhume, a local earth god. He has to say, 'I'm going to Sessnag to get power to heal my patient.' He goes on until he comes to Subbhini, an old Rai woman, and says, 'Please let me in.' If she's mean, he offers to feed her with milk. She says okay, so next he goes to Subbha, her husband, and says, 'Sir, you are my guru, let me pass.'"

Jebi broke in to explain that Subbhini could cause inflammation and swelling in a patient's body, that Subbha could turn the patient skinny, and Nagini, the snake wife, could make a big, watery blister. "The patient will be thirsty, and drink gallons of water, but won't be able to urinate. His body will feel dead, with a very low pulse," Mr. Ganesh translated.

"Sessnag, the final destination, is a great seven-headed snake, the protector. When you reach him, you can ask for any kind of help and he will give it."

Then, Jebi showed me the offerings and where to place them on the diagram to placate these gatekeepers of the lower world and cure the illnesses they cause. I was pleased. This was the explanation for the diagram Mr. Rai had drawn in my notebook in America.

"Good. Jebi is teaching." Mr. Rai was home. Cordial but peremptory, he sent me away to rest. "Come back at seven for food," he said.

I felt rejected by his abrupt manner, but thought that after all, this was his home; he'd worked all day and might want time to relax with his family.

The afternoon dragged. With nothing to do, I studied my notes and arranged my things.

At last it was time to return to Mr. Rai's, and I cheered up when Maile arrived with little Dorje, now a toddler. She bowed, exposing her large front teeth in a welcoming smile, and I felt as though we'd never been apart.

LOVE SPELLS

Maile didn't come to teach the next day, or the next. The days wore on. Mr. Ganesh filled the time with his tales of Hindu gods and goddesses until I couldn't stand it, and would sit on the floor to question Jebi directly.

I asked about the upper world, and he drew a diagram of nine squares and taught me the names of the *grahas,* planets, who live in each square. He sifted lines of white flour through his fingers to form a rectangle divided into two rows of eight, with one square left over at the lower right, and then added vermilion powder over the flour lines to make them stand out red against the white paper. "Put offerings in the squares," he said.

Mr. Ganesh stepped in to translate. "His spirit will journey to the upper world, through the domains of the grahas, Rahu the terrible, Ketu, his wife, Chanchal the fickle, Bayu the wind, bloody Rakta, Chief Bir, Dhan the rich, Sharma, an ancient Brahmin, and Atma the soul.

"Rahu is a great black *mudkutta,* a headless spirit whose very touch can cause death. Rahu will say, 'You can't come in,' but Jebi will answer that he is on a mission to find Lord Shiva and learn what happened to his patient. He might have to promise an offering to Rahu during his yearly guru puja ceremony—a sacrifice of two chickens. Ketu, Rahu's wife, is light yellow in color. She will also demand an offering to let him pass.

"The upper world is bright, and at the top of the upper world, Jebi will call Lord Shiva, and the sun and the moon to be witnesses. Shiva will name the spirit that caused the problem for the patient, and tell Jebi what offering to give. The spirit might want blood, but if the patient is too poor to afford an animal for sacrifice, Jebi will promise an egg or some flowers instead, to be given during guru puja. If the outcome is going to be favorable, he will feel light. If not, he will feel heavy, and the teachers and spirits of the upper world will send him back quickly."

I was about to ask how the shaman causes his spirit to travel in the first place, when Mr. Rai arrived. After lunch, he told us a young woman in the neighborhood was the victim of some shaman's mohini. "If shaman puts mohini, that is love spell, on someone, and doesn't remove it after three months, the person will go crazy. This woman is completely mad. She gives wrong answers to questions, washes clean dishes, and every month gets angry and hits her husband."

I asked if Jebi would teach me mohinis.

He frowned. "This is very dangerous for you now. Maybe later. Now you could get sick, or do a lot of harm." He began to tell a story, but his stern expression lightened as he went on, and finally, he laughed.

"He is telling a bad thing that happened to a beginning shaman in Jappa when he tried to put mohini on a girl," Mr. Ganesh explained.

The girl, named Tulsi, was of the Brahmin caste, daughter of a rich landowner. She'd gone crazy because the young shaman didn't know to remove the love spell he had put on her. She would come home late from school, avoid her friends and family, and put a married woman's red tika on her forehead. That was what upset her father most, for girls only wear such tikas after their husbands have applied them. Tulsi wrapped her sari like a married woman, and every half hour, changed her clothes. She slept no more than two or three minutes at a time.

The father told his problems to a clerk from Jebi's village. "My daughter is not obeying me," he said. "I've slapped her a lot, but she's still wearing that tika."

The clerk knew Jebi, and fetched him to the Brahmin's house. As soon as Jebi stepped inside the door, the daughter cried, "You are not my husband. Who will marry with you? I've got my husband. You can't do anything for me."

Jebi said, "I only want to help you," but the girl kept on insulting him. In fact, Jebi didn't know how to cure her, but he thought, I have to do something. "Who is your husband?" he asked.

"Bakhta Bahadur Gurung," she said. "*He* is a shaman. I'll not stay with you."

Jebi knew of the young man, a student shaman in his early twenties from a nearby village. Tulsi's father was upset because the boy was a Gurung, from a mountain tribe that Brahmins consider lower caste. Jebi set to work to make an altar.

Suddenly excited, Tulsi faced him, shouting, "You are not my husband. I'll not go with you. You are going to put a mohini on me." She advanced on him, threw her skirt over his head, and sat on him. Her father grabbed her and threw her back. "I'll not stay with you," she shouted. Her father held her hands behind her back. "You can stop me now, but after dark I'll be going to sleep with Bakhta. You'll get sleepy and won't be able to hold me."

Because she had thrown her skirt over him, Jebi felt his shaman's power was gone, and told the girl's father he could do no more.

Before long Jebi's wife heard what had happened, and got angry. "Why did you go there?" she demanded. "You don't know the mantra to cure that girl. What did you think you could do? She must like you. Brahmins don't even allow others to touch their clothes, but she threw her skirt over your head. You must like her too. That's it, isn't it?"

Jebi told her it wasn't so, that he'd only wanted to help the girl.

The Brahmin girl continued with her crazy behavior, and her father didn't know what to do. When he heard that Jebi's wife was angry, he came to Jebi's house to explain what had happened and appealed to her, "My daughter will go to a lower caste. She may become a prostitute. If she goes to that Gurung, she will shame me. Where can I go? What can I do?"

Jebi's wife answered sharply, "Your daughter has no decency. She covered my husband with a sari. Is she a human or what? Let her die!"

"She has done a sin against you," the father admitted. "But let Jebi help her and I'll give you what I can. I have a good deal of property." So Jebi's wife agreed to let him help the girl.

Jebi said, "I may be able to do something." He told the father to go to the Gurung's house and take some soil from under a place where the boy had stood, a little from under each foot, not letting him know this had been done, and to tie his daughter so she couldn't run away.

The Brahmin promised to send a man with the soil. "My daughter is in class ten," he said. "I'll be giving her a good education. She should not marry this Gurung. Please try hard to cure her."

After he got the soil, Jebi told Tulsi's father to get some vermilion powder from her head or her pot. He mixed the red powder with the soil from under the Gurung's right foot, wrote the Gurung's name on a piece of paper he placed on the floor, and with the soil and powder, dabbed sixteen tika spots on the paper. He recited a mantra for removing mohinis and burned the paper, but he kept back the soil from beneath the Gurung's left foot. "The girl's sickness will go to the young man now," Jebi said.

The father went upstairs to check on his daughter. She had fallen into a deep sleep. After that, she stopped acting crazy, but still spent most of her time alone in her room refusing to speak to anyone.

Now the Gurung got sick and began to behave oddly, putting soil on his forehead for a tika. His father took him to shamans and doctors, but the boy said, "I don't want their medicine. This soil will cure me." Eventually, the boy's father heard of Jebi, but only as another shaman in the area who might be able to help. He knew nothing of the Brahmin girl. He brought his son to see if Jebi could heal him.

"You're my last hope," the father said. "Please cure my son so his life will be happy." While he was there, the Brahmin girl's father happened to come. The two fathers had never heard of each other. To avoid a confrontation, Jebi told the Gurung's father to come back the next day with soil from a place where the boy had stood with both feet.

"The doctor said my son has water on the brain," the boy's father said when he brought the soil. He pushed his thumb into his son's temple, and it made a white spot. "He said there was nothing he could do."

Jebi wrote Tulsi's name and made sixteen tikas on a piece of paper with the new soil from under the young man's feet, mixed with what he'd kept back from healing her. He said a mantra over the paper, and on sixteen grains of rice. Then he burned the paper and told the young Gurung to eat the rice.

"Why should I?" the boy protested.

"You shut up or I'll slap you," the father said.

"But why?"

The father slapped him. Sullenly, the boy ate the rice.

"Now you should get some relief," Jebi said. "Come back in two days and tell me how you're feeling."

In two days, the young man and his father came back. "I'm feeling better," the young man said. "Thanks to you."

Jebi excused himself to go to the toilet, but instead ran to the Brahmin's house and asked, "How is your daughter?"

"She is better," the father said.

Tulsi came forward with her sari wrapped properly for a maiden, and offered tea.

"I have guests," Jebi said, declining. "I must hurry home."

Ha! he thought. I can cure them both.

He questioned the young Gurung. "So you're a shaman? Tell me, what can you do?"

"I'm learning mohinis."

"Only mohinis? How many do you know?"

"Just eight so far," the young man said.

"Eight, not all sixteen? Surely you know you must master all sixteen mohinis before daring to use them—don't you?"

The young man hung his head.

"I see. Have you tried them on any girls yet? You can tell me. We're friendly," Jebi said. "Tell me the truth so I can help."

The father raised his hand as though to strike his son.

"Yes, I put mohini on a girl," the boy admitted.

"Who was it? A girl of your own caste?"

"You tell," the father threatened. "Tell or you'll die. I won't take care of you. Tell Jebi. He's given you so much relief."

"She is a Brahmin," Jebi said, as the boy remained silent. "Tell me about it. I may help you get that girl back."

The father was getting angrier and angrier, so Jebi took the young man into another room, and got him to admit he'd seen the girl on her way home from school and liked her white face. She was talkative and beautiful. The boy had waited in the path, and one day spoke to her and learned her name, then used it to place a love spell. But since he didn't know how to remove it, she went crazy.

"Why didn't you put your spell on a Gurungi girl? Did you like that Brahmin girl so much?" Jebi badgered. "If she agrees, will you marry her?" The boy was getting angry. "If you like her so much, your father is here, I'll call her father too."

"Please don't. I don't like her that much, to disgrace my family. How did you know about her?"

"I am the man who cured that girl," Jebi said. "I am a very big shaman, and I'm the man to hamper you."

The boy bowed low. "I will make you my guru. Please cure me. I was just testing to see if the love spell would work." Jebi raised his hand to slap him. "Please, guru, please forgive me for my mistake."

Jebi called the boy's father from the other room. "Now your son has told me everything. He put a love spell on that Brahmin girl, but now he's waiting for forgiveness and wants to make me his guru. He may if he wishes. He must bring a big basket of rice, and some money."

"Let the girl not be harmed," the father said. "It would be a sin."

"I'm your guru," Jebi sternly told the boy. "Now will you go on using mohinis—even on girls of your own caste?"

"No, guru." The boy bowed again, and Jebi did a ritual to remove the effects of the love spell from him.

"Now he's Jebi's student," Mr. Ganesh finished.

"Mohinis, no," Jebi said, and wagged his finger in my face. But he was smiling.

After dinner, as usual, Mr. Rai's house filled with neighbors to watch Maile remove the mohini from the young woman Mr. Rai had mentioned at lunch, the one who went crazy once a month and hit her husband. Maile's cousin, Nima Dawa, and the old lama set up her altar, with tall, cone-shaped tormas made of sticky rice, and flowers, and a water *callas,* and oil lamp.

The crazy woman's husband, a boy of nineteen or twenty, gently led his wife to Maile's altar. She was young and pretty, but much too thin, and slightly stooped, and she refused to meet anyone's eyes.

Maile drummed and chanted her long Tamang chants, and after ritual songs and offerings, divined that indeed, the girl suffered from a mohini. As Maile questioned her, a faint smile flickered over her face. Maile called on the Queen of the Forest, whose name in Nepali was Junglee, to cure her patient, and afterward, the girl's husband drew her to her feet and led her home.

"She will get better," Mr. Rai said. "That is for sure."

I wondered if I would ever find out whether she did or not.

Maile had not invited me to sit beside her at the altar, nor had I asked. I'd brought my video camera and kept busy taping. There would be plenty of time later to sit with the shaman and shake.

WHY HAVE YOU COME?

I learned the names of dangerous spirits —*pichas,* spirits of Newaris who have killed themselves, of which there are seven types; *chouda,* spirits of babies who die before their milk teeth come in; and *ched* who live in dirty places. "All of them can make you sick if you accidentally stray into their places or touch their dirty things," Mr. Ganesh explained, pursing his mouth as he said "dirty things."

I devised a blank form for taking notes, with spaces to fill in the meaning of each spirit's name, what it looked like, where it lived, how it acted, what other spirits it liked to be with, whether it could possess the shaman's body, what illnesses it caused, and how to heal them, the ritual steps and offerings it required, whether grains, rakshi, flowers, milk, eggs, uncooked rice, blood, or vermilion powder, its diagram, to be drawn on the ground with rice flour, its number for purposes of divination, and the mantras to make it go away. I collected the filled-in sheets in a folder of soft grey paper with large, black *devnagari* letters phonetically spelling the English word "file." The spaces for mantras stayed blank. I asked for them, but Jebi put me off.

The day was softly warm, the skies clear blue. Jebi was lecturing on the sixteen kinds of *moch,* spirits who attack pregnant women and babies. Through the window, Mr. Rai's first sister, working in the garden, lifted her face to the sun. "I have a lot of information here," I said, leafing through my file, aware of sounding disgruntled, "but I haven't learned to actually *do* anything."

Mr. Ganesh and Jebi conferred. I thought I heard Jebi say the word for husband, but Mr. Ganesh said only, "It will come."

I closed my "file," lacking the will to begin on a new class of spirit—sixteen more sheets to be filled in with arcane details I'd never use anyway back home, especially if animals had to be sacrificed.

But Mr. Ganesh was speaking. "As Jebi has already told you, it is not legal to use love spells unless people are married, but he can give you a love spell to make your husband love you."

I managed a laugh. So, he thought he knew what I needed. "How about a spell to make him get a job?"

"Oh yes," Jebi said. "I can give you a spell so a boss will like him."

"Fine, but will it make him want to work?"

"Certainly."

I didn't believe him. They never said anything you didn't want to hear. It was always, "Yes, sa'b, yes, sa'b," as long as you were right there in front of them. Maybe you were supposed to understand that their promises were only politeness. No one here would be dumb enough to take them seriously, for who can keep their word when, as everyone knows, the whims of the gods may intervene at any point.

I walked back to my room. The red and yellow flowers by the road were filmed with dust. I shut my door and wept.

❧

That evening, Jebi performed a ceremony for a girl of about eighteen. Her mother and father had brought her a long way down from the mountains to see him. She wore a bright pink pantsuit, doubtless her best, but very much at odds with her air of hopeless passivity. She'd been vomiting, refusing to eat, wasting away to unhealthy thinness. Mr. Rai told me her parents had refused to let her marry the boy she loved.

Jebi placed her beside him at the altar, and his compassion filled the space between them, palpable as a moisture-laden breath of coming rain. Surely she must feel it and respond—but she answered his gentle questions in monosyllables, refusing to meet his eyes. He divined her problem was mohini, and performed a ritual to remove it. She endured through it all with a sad, yet stubborn, air.

Next morning, Jebi did a backward mantra on her breakfast, passing a knife over the top of her food, pretending to cut it, then scraping the point on the carpet to remove a curse he said someone had put on her food.

I thought she might be anorexic, and asked her in Nepali, "Did you think you were too fat before you got sick?" She didn't understand. "Did you want to get married?"

She turned her head away, showing the conventional embarrassment expected of an unmarried girl.

Maybe the question was improper. I changed the subject. "What do you like to study?"

"History," she said, after a long hesitation, adding that she hoped to be a teacher.

She still looked sick, with dark circles under her eyes and no spark about her. Was she truly dying of a broken heart—or tuberculosis, or leukemia, or some other wasting disease? Or hiding a pregnancy that hadn't yet begun to show. Her parents would take her back home to the mountains, and I'd never know. Discouraged, I sorted through my growing file of notes.

❧

"After lunch, you will go to market with Jebi," Mr. Ganesh announced. "You have to buy one chicken, seven grains, and all the things for a moch ceremony."

But it wasn't to be. "Please tell Jebi I am sorry," I said later, heat rising to my face, "My menstruation has started."

"I will tell Jebi about your personal problem." The translator pursed his lips and nodded gravely, and for once I was grateful for his prim demeanor. He spoke to Jebi in Nepali, and I recognized the word *juttho*, which means contaminated.

"She cannot touch the things for the ceremony, or the altar," Jebi agreed.

❧

I walked with Jebi as far as Maile's new home, a large room on the ground floor of a nearby house where they had the use of a garden. A double bed took up most of one end; their clothes and household tools hung on large nails pounded into the walls. On the floor in one corner, they kept a kerosene stove, a stack of pots and pans, and a full pot of water. Maile wore a yellow T-shirt and a long, striped lungi wrapping her lower body. She namasted and accepted the gifts I'd brought—a watch for her, a shirt for the old lama, and for little Dorje, a sweater—holding each to her forehead as she praised it.

Jebi spoke in rapid Nepali, telling her about my contaminated condition. It was embarrassing, but she was a woman too. She offered us whiskey, tea, noodles, eggs, and beer. I chose beer, which she poured from a large brown bottle.

There were no chairs. I perched on the edge of the bed next to Jebi, trying to make my juttho self as small as possible. They chatted with jokes and laughter, and when Jebi left for market, he tapped me lightly on one knee, as though forgetting my contaminated condition. Maybe it wasn't as contagious as they'd said. I began to feel better.

Maile owned a tape recorder, a gift from a former student, and played a tape of an Indian singer, wailing in a high male voice. Little Dorje danced, bending his body from side to side as sinuously as a chunky two-year-old could manage, his arms swaying gracefully. Then Maile's sister arrived with two little cousins about Dorje's age, and losing center stage, he cried to be held.

But something interesting was happening on the floor. He squirmed down. The little cousins had found the shirt I'd given his father, still in its cardboard and cellophane package.

We all watched them play. It was easier than trying to converse without a common language. One of the children stuck her arm inside the plastic of the packaged shirt, clear to the top where the cardboard showed like a crown, and Dorje smoothed his chubby little hand across it. I knew intuitively how it was for them. This new thing on the floor held a message from God, letting us know that He presided over all, like the cardboard crest of the packaged shirt. To them, the whole world spoke of God. Why else did they explore it with such wonderment? They felt His presence everywhere, disguised, but almost ready to reveal itself.

I could remember how that was. And how it how it had been to lose it—when I'd gouged the blank face of my pink plastic doll so long ago, and thrown it under Grandma's porch, angry at God for abandoning me to a world of meaningless objects.

And after all these years, here I was, still trying to force Him back into the material world, straining to make this dead stuff live, trying to people it with ghosts and spirits and act "as if" it lived.

Maile bent above me with the large beer bottle, offering more.

"*Pugcha*," I said, covering my cup with my hand. Enough.

Mr. Rai had invited a Norwegian nurse from a health mission in Eastern Nepal to dinner, and to watch Jebi's moch ceremony afterward. She was thin and pale, with a long, serious face, wispy light brown hair, and the martyred air of one given over to good works. But she spoke English. Thuli Kumari handed us plates of chicken, rice and dhal, and a napkin and tablespoon each, and then stepped back and said, "Bistari, bistari."

"Bistari, bistari," Mr. Rai echoed.

"Bistari, bistari," Bindu agreed.

"Isn't it funny how they're always telling us to eat slowly?" I commented, pleased to have another Westerner to talk to. "Why do you think that is?"

"It is healthier to eat slowly." She lifted her fork at glacial speed.

"Maybe it's to keep us from asking for seconds," I joked. "Mr. Rai, why do you always say bistari, bistari when we eat? Do you think we eat too fast?"

"No, no, of course not." He chuckled. "We say it only as being polite. Means take your time, enjoy your food. This is time nothing else has to be done, just eat and enjoy."

"Oh." I tried to catch the nurse's eye, to laugh with her at how we'd misunderstood, taking it so literally, but she nodded with grave deliberation and kept on slowly chewing.

"This is very interesting," she said, when the lengthy process of eating was finished. She waved a hand toward Jebi's altar. "I would like to know more about it. We are learning in health care that we must work with these people's beliefs when we can. But why have *you* come? What is your interest in it?"

"I'm learning the healing techniques—so I can do them in America."

She stared at me oddly. "Oh, really? Why would you want to do that?"

"I—."

"You have not studied medicine in America, only law? You wish to heal...but using these shamanic ceremonies alone?"

I didn't know what to say.

☙

Jebi got into his costume, called his deities and spirits, and danced the traditional Rai shaman's dance. Aware I was videotaping, he took care with each gesture, acting out planting, transplanting, harvesting, threshing of the rice, and carrying home the bags of grain to be stored and eaten.

The moch ceremony took place outside, with the sick woman seated on the front steps facing outward, onlookers crowding the hallway behind her. The drumbeat rose and fell in a monotonous middle world rhythm, like the swelling and subsiding of deep waters, and Jebi's movements were slow and dreamlike. The chicken lay quiet on the ground, completely hypnotized. Jebi dripped water on its head to make it shake, twisted its head from its body, and poured out thick, dark blood on a dog skull set into a shallow hole he'd dug earlier.

Afterward, inside, he did my jokhanna. "You used to be mentally sick," Mr. Rai translated. "You had family problems eighteen months or two years ago. But you're all right now."

I didn't like what he said. He didn't need the spirits to tell him I'd had family problems—and I hadn't been mentally ill. Or if I had, how had it changed? I still didn't have a clue what was real. Only now, instead of pretending to believe in Evans' worldview, I'd switched to that of the shamans.

The Norwegian nurse watched everything with staring, pale blue eyes.

❧

Later, as I lay in bed, the ticking of my little clock, the night sounds—of crickets, occasional human calls, and distant barking dogs—arranged themselves into the dreamy pattern of Jebi's drumbeat. In times past, when people were ill from losing their connection with the growing rice, the traditional shaman would drum this rhythm to restore it. Everything people did in those simpler times was matched to the rhythm of the growing rice. They knew it; and the rice plants knew it too, each aware of their current places in the circle of life, and how they moved around it, now looking out on the world through human eyes; later, their bodies gone to earth, feeling themselves as rice plants, swaying among their green brothers in the fields, destined, as ever, to be eaten. When the shaman danced and made people remember the times when they were rice plants, they knew they were safe, embraced in an ever-renewing cycle.

But the traditional rhythms of that world were vanishing, overpowered by the clash and clatter of motors, jets, motion picture strobes, foreign images and tongues, digital pulses of computers, cell phones, pagers—a turmoil no shaman could hope to drum into balance. For now we live on oil, on foods grown with chemicals from oil, aware on a deep level that what we feed on doesn't renew itself like rice, but gradually disappears. Of course, we're frightened, for we know this leads to death. Whenever our minds happen to touch this deep level, we feel our fear and shoot back to the surface, for we dare not let our knowing embrace what sustains us. And so we feel cut off. What kind of shaman would it take to heal us now?

I couldn't get comfortable, turning on my narrow bed, kicking the sheet that wadded around my knees, resisting the conclusion that mankind was doomed. Human societies were changing fast, growing blindly. It was tempting to think of cities like cancers—rot and mold on the skin of a dying earth. But embryos, too, grow fast and furious, sweeping forward in a grand, foreordained pattern, reaching in joy toward a glorious destiny, dimly sensed. A vision of a growing seedling burgeoned in the darkness above me, each cell a separate human consciousness, white root tendrils probing moist dark soil as brave new leaves spread out to catch the sun and live upon its rays.

DR. WILLIAM

Dr. William arrived the next day, a large, friendly man in his sixties with happy, innocent blue eyes and a ruddy face surrounded by a ruff of shaggy, soft white hair and beard. He was taking a month's vacation from his psychiatric practice in Washington, D.C. to study Nepali shamanism. "But I don't have the talent to become a shaman," he pointed out, managing to imply not only that I did, but also that it was a fine and worthy endeavor.

I liked him right away, and able to be generous, said, "You already *are* a shaman, in our culture."

Mr. Rai had rented him a room on the ground floor of Mr. Bharat's house. I lived upstairs near the Western-style bathroom, but since he was having stomach problems, we traded rooms. The ground-floor toilet had a shower and sink, but no stool—only a hole with ridged metal shoe prints on either side to keep your feet from sliding as you squatted.

We started over with the lessons, reviewing the sixteen moches, sixteen sharmas, shikarees, jhagitras, massans, bhuts, and prets, but I didn't mind. It was good to have a friend.

On a day when Maile was our teacher, Dr. William asked her, "How do people tell the difference between a witch and a woman shaman?"

Mr. Ganesh launched into a long-winded explanation of how witches could be seen at crossroads, blue flames coming from their hands.

"So witches do harm, and shamans heal?"

"Sometimes witches heal," Maile said, "and sometimes shamans make their patients sick, just so they can heal them."

"Do people ever think a woman shaman is a witch."

"No, no," she answered. "Because I was taken by the Banjhankri."

"Is the Banjhankri a god?"

"He is Lord Shiva in the middle world," she said. "He is a little man with a long white beard and bushy white eyebrows, and his feet turn in." She held out her hands, palms down, turned inward.

"What happened after you were kidnapped?"

"She got a better imagination and insight to see whether a ghost or some bad spirit was working against her patient," the translator answered. "She started shaking every Sunday—you know Sunday is called *Gurubar*, the day of the guru. She heard voices."

I glanced at the psychiatrist, benignly leaning back on the couch. He wasn't making any judgments.

"She felt the sensation of a hand on her head when she started to shake. Then her father would have to get some incense and light it. After an hour of shaking, she would collapse."

"Does she still see the Banjhankri?"

"Yes, of course," the translator answered after consulting Maile. "Every evening the Wild Shaman goes around the world, East to West, North to South, and the four directions in between. He has to go around the world in eight directions each twenty-four hours to see the people and what they are doing. He can do it in one second."

And once in his travels, Maile had said, his shadow fell on me. Or had he come even earlier, while I was forming in my mother's womb, and made my feet turn in like his? But I knew I was grasping at straws, trying to make myself feel special because I wasn't yet shaking.

"What does Maile feel like when she goes into trance?" Dr. William asked.

"She imitates a tiger and moves around the patient. She goes unconscious when its spirit is on her. Her helper has to beat her to bring her out of it."

I tried to imagine myself being willing to lose consciousness to that extent, and knew it would never happen.

"Does she enjoy it?" Dr. William asked.

"She says it doesn't matter. With the patient in front of her, she has to do it."

"When she goes into trance, many astral bodies gather around, and she has to be able to tell which is one of her patient's souls. She can see them clearly with her eyes closed. They have faces. She feels light, as if her body is huge—tremendous, and she doesn't get tired when she dances. To make bad spirits go away, she sneezes, *Hashio!*"

Maile performed that night. But not wanting to make Dr. William feel left out, I didn't try to sit beside her at the altar and shake, but stayed on the couch with Dr. William and watched.

Dassein arrived, a festival equivalent in importance to our Christmas, when family members gather to touch their heads to their elders' feet and receive, in return, large, messy tikas on their foreheads, globs of a sticky red mixture of rice, yoghurt, and vermilion. The cows in the road were decorated with flower chains and sticky blotches of red and yellow on their flanks and heads. On the ninth day of Dassein, one hundred and eight uncastrated water buffaloes, and one hundred and eight uncastrated goats and roosters were to be killed in the public square of Kathmandu, a city whose very name means "cut mandate"—sacrifice worship.

Over breakfast, Mr. Ganesh explained that to save humanity from terrible monsters loose in the middle world, Shiva's wife, Parvati, took the form of the vengeful goddess Durga, carrying in one of her many hands the disc of Vishnu's power, in another a *vajra*, the ceremonial dagger from India, and in another, Shiva's trident. Riding a tiger, she slew the monsters, which is why, even to this day, animals must lose their lives to slake her blood lust.

Mr. Rai carried his sewing machine outside to the driveway next to his motorcycle, and Bindu brought a tray of red rice and yoghurt and smeared both machines in blessing, and then Jebi killed a chicken and poured blood on the machines straight from its neck.

"We even bless jets at airport at Dassein," Mr. Rai explained. "We make offering to Shiva's eldest son, Kartik, god of tools and machines, so no accident will happen."

He set up three fat squashes from the garden on bamboo legs in front of the house. A sheep, decorated with flowers, and smeared with red rice and yoghurt, was led up beside them. "Four sheep should be cut," Mr. Rai said, "but too expensive. I can afford only one, so these squashes are my other sheep." The gods didn't seem to mind. Jebi said mantras and hacked each squash in half with a swish of his kukhuri knife. Then he said a longer mantra, poured a handful of water on the sheep's head to make it shake, and whacked off its head. The sheep dropped heavily.

I wanted to ask if they would eat it, but Mr. Rai had disappeared.

"Up there, praying." Bindu pointed toward the flat roof. A pair of pigeons flew off the edge. She pulled me out into the street, from where we could see Mr. Rai untying the legs of another pair of birds. He held them aloft, let them go, and scattered grain so they could eat.

"I am Buddhist," he explained, coming down the outside stairs. "We don't believe on killing. I do sacrifice only for my wives, but to make up for sin of cutting sheep, I bought eight pair of pigeons to release."

After lunch, he took me aside and whispered, "Do not tell to others." He opened the door to his small, sacred shrine room. "We sprout grain here," he said.

It was dark inside. In the light from the doorway, I made out several flat enamel pans, each with a tiny forest of white sprouts curling upward.

"On first day of Dassein, we plant. After nine days they have sprouted, and we pick and put on our heads. I am showing this only to you, in private, because you are learning to be shaman in real Rai way. Since one year, I have been keeping sacred mangchhamma room."

Jebi's sister, Didi, a tall, frail woman in her eighties, came to visit for Dassein. Jebi was drinking, and the more he drank, the more he cared for her comfort, running to the kitchen to fetch her tea and a piece of doughy holiday bread she barely nibbled, and wrapping a pink baby blanket over her knobby shoulders. The pretty, quiet woman next to Didi on the couch turned out to be Jebi's wife, which surprised me because her smooth, brown skin, unlined face, and slender, upright figure made her look much younger than he. Jebi largely ignored her, and she him, but I saw her note the level of liquid in his glass each time he visited the kitchen.

Jebi's wife had photos of their three grown children, and I fetched pictures of Tom, Aaron, Thorne and Keri from my room to show her and Didi. "Good sons, good daughter," they said, as was polite.

I ran my fingers over the smiling faces of my children, feeling their presence for a moment. Keri's picture had been taken when she was only two or three, and Evans was in it too, his hair and beard still dark. "Husband," I said in Nepali, pointing, and then hesitantly added, "We are getting a divorce." They didn't react, but I knew they thought I had failed in my duty, though they would make allowances because I was an American woman, and therefore spoiled and drunk on freedom. Jebi's wife settled into herself, taking comfort in her own married role.

That night, Jebi performed, claiming he could cure a middle-aged woman of alcoholism. She was thin, with delicate, symmetrical features, bent shoulders and prematurely wrinkled skin.

"You have had a miscarriage. Yes, or No?" Jebi questioned her.

"Ho. It is true."

"You have three children."

"Ho."

"Your husband is mixed up with another woman. He is mean to you."

"Ho. *Ho.*" Tears filled her eyes.

"You are thinking of divorce."

She stared at her hands, clasped tightly in her lap, white along the tendon ridges.

"Because of this, you drink too much?"

"He is going to give her mohini," Mr. Rai explained, "to get her back her husband's love. And he will spell a mantra on cup of rakshi. After that she will never want to drink again."

I sat beside Jebi at the altar, and several times as he worked, he glanced at me, whispered mantras, and threw rice around my head and shoulders. I wanted badly to shake, but my body stayed calm and stolid. Finally, I moved to the couch beside his wife and sister.

A young man from the neighborhood took the place I'd left and spontaneously began to shake. Jebi handed him a bunch of half-dried kauli leaves that rattled as he shook.

"Jebi is testing to see, can he be shaman," Mr. Rai explained. Jebi shouted, demanding that the spirit that was in the young man speak and name itself. But the spirit kept silent.

"He can be shaman," Mr. Rai said. "That is for sure. Only he must speak and tell *who* he is."

❧

Jebi taught next morning, but got drunk and didn't come back after lunch. Mr. Rai was angry.

Dr. William and I spent the afternoon walking, exploring the surrounding network of dirt roads, passing free-roaming cows, half-naked children playing in the dust, stalls offering fruits and vegetables, Coke, Fanta, liquor, toys, toilet paper, electronic gadgets, and videotapes for rent.

On the way back, Dr. William told me he had lost his faith in God as a young man, but that as he grew older it had come back. I admired the peace he had achieved, but couldn't think how to get it for myself.

From the balcony on the roof of Mr. Bharat's house, we looked down on Mr. Rai's garden where his family dug and weeded. Mr. Rai's pretty younger sister spotted us and shouted up in English, "Nepali culture." The others grinned and waved, enjoying being objects of our study. Jebi hailed us from Mr. Rai's doorway, and ran across.

"Is Mr. Rai still mad at you?" I asked in my rudimentary Nepali.

"Ho." He acted out how Mr. Rai had shouted and shown his fists.

Mr. Rai shook his finger from below and scolded, and Jebi called back in a conciliatory tone, "*Namaskar*," the politest form of namaste.

Jebi had promised to heal Dr. William of his stomach troubles, and next day bought a black rooster in the market. As evening fell, he set up a freshly-cut banana stem by the house door and performed a khadco kattne ceremony to rearrange Dr. William's planets. I could see Dr. William would have loved to say he was cured, but as it was, he thanked Jebi and said it was too soon to tell.

Then Jebi performed a *kama kim* ceremony for Mr. Lok, a big, harmless-looking man without much ambition who lived in the old house at the back of Mr. Rai's property. Mr. Rai said that Mr. Lok was possessed by a ghost.

My notes said the symptoms of this kind of possession included high fever, lethargy, lack of appetite, and a sad expression. Mr. Lok did seem lethargic, but not the least bit ill. They must be running out of patients, I sourly concluded.

The ritual itself was from the Rai mudhum. Jebi readied a fire in a tripod of stones under a teepee of three bamboo rods. He placed a pot of oil on the stones, drew a rough sketch of the ghost, and wrote its name on a piece of paper, which he tied to the top of the bamboo rods where they came together. A helper built a little house of sticks and straw nearby, and Jebi began to drum and chant, inviting the ghost to come and live there. When the oil was boiling, Jebi recited the mantra for kama kim in archaic Rai with its characteristic, drawn-out *ah-ah-ahs* at the end of each phrase. Thuli Kumari handed him a cup of rakshi.

"He is telling the spirit, 'There is nothing here in this world for you,'" Mr. Rai explained. To prove it, Jebi threw the rakshi into the boiling oil. Flames exploded upward and burned the paper with the ghost's name and likeness, as the helper set the little house on fire.

"He has burned the ghost house. Now, nowhere to live, and the spirit must leave," Mr. Rai explained.

Dr. William's stay was coming to an end. Before he left, Mr. Ganesh and Jebi took us to Buddhanilakhantha, Old Blue Throat, a great Shiva statue lying prone on the ground, its neck painted blue to commemorate how Shiva drank the poison of the world to save mankind, which made his throat turn blue. As we walked up toward the shrine, Jebi drew our attention to a large nettle bush beside the path.

"Don't touch," he warned. "It will sting and give you blisters." Its dull green leaves were hairy and wrinkled. "I have a mantra that protects me," Jebi bragged. He whispered, blew on his hands, and picked off a large bunch of leaves. "The mantra kills the plant's power."

The plant looked harmless. I laughed and copied him, pretending to blow a mantra on my hands, and grabbing at the leaves. The moment I touched them, I felt my thumb pierced, as by a giant stinger. The pain was intense, like a scorpion's bite. I turned cold, and tiny blisters sprang up along the sides of my fingers. Jebi blew a mantra on my hand, and the pain slowly faded.

"This is *shishnu*," he warned. "Do not eat it."

I was fairly sure I wouldn't.

❦

For some unknown reason, Mr. Rai had been scheduling four or five sessions with Jebi for every one with Maile. When she finally came, Dr. William asked her a question he'd been storing up. "You said you see *one* of your patient's souls, and *one* of your astral bodies travels to the lower world. How many souls do people have?"

"Three principal souls," she said. "They rest in the body above the waist, in the heart, shoulders, or head. Altogether there are seven *satos*, but three are most important. You can tell when a patient has lost one of his satos because his eyes will be dull, and he'll look sick. If a child hears a dog bark and shrinks up with fright, or if he's scolded, he may lose his *atma sato*. He'll be afraid and develop bad-smelling diarrhea. *Bir sato* is the one old people lose. They become weary and tired, with little energy. A bad spirit, like a massan, may have taken the bir sato. The old person shrivels into himself and jumps with fright at every little thing. *Hangsa sato* is the third main soul. It stays with bir sato or atma sato, and never goes away until the person dies. When it leaves it makes him go unconscious."

"What do they look like?" I asked.

"A small, white, floating string." She held her thumb and finger two inches apart. "I catch it and put it in a jar for safekeeping during the ceremony, then blow it back into the patient."

Then she told us of a dream she'd had, of taking Dr. William and me to a place of clear, pure water to teach us. Afterward, she gave us tubs of butter, and we flew away.

"The butter may be your wisdom," Dr. William said. He was used to interpreting dreams.

I was astonished when she agreed. Somehow I'd been assuming her thoughts were too exalted, too foreign, to communicate in such homely symbols.

❧

On Dr. William's final evening, neither shaman performed. Instead, we had a rakshi party. Jebi retold the story of my encounter with shishnu, first to Mr. Rai, then Mr. Rai's wives and sisters, and then to everyone who came. Every time he told it, they all laughed harder.

"We have big bush of shishnu in the garden," Mr. Rai said. "We boil the leaves and eat them for greens. After boiling it is harmless. But shaman must not eat. Shishnu is shaman's friend."

"They threaten witches with it, don't they?"

"That's right."

Mr. Rai's secretary, a young Brahmin man whose name was also Mohan, explained in labored English that snot was a sure cure for shishnu burns. Someone translated what he'd said into Nepali, and everyone roared with laughter.

Jebi got quite drunk on Mr. Rai's good liquor. His wife didn't drink at all.

"Jebi." Dr. William took him by the shoulders and looked deep into his swimming eyes. "Do you know what will happen to your health if you keep on drinking?"

Mr. Rai translated, and added in English, "Yes, he drinks too much. At the airport in Seattle on night we are coming back from seeing *Allen* in America, I bought him a great big bottle of scotch. By morning it was gone."

"You should tell him what will happen to his liver," Dr. William persisted. "Ask him how long he thinks he's going to live if he keeps this up."

"I have already had children," Jebi said. "I have lived a long time. I don't care."

"Tell him he is young still. He is my guru," I said. "He has to teach me. He *must* care whether he lives or dies."

"I think I still have fifteen or twenty years left to teach my students," Jebi said. "That's enough."

His wife stared straight ahead, as though she hadn't heard.

We left, but the party went on. I said goodnight to Dr. William at the top of the stairs, and went out on the balcony overlooking Mr.

Rai's front porch. A crowd of men had gathered, some standing and smoking, others squatting and playing a gambling game with dice. Jebi's elderly sister, Didi, tall and frail in her long skirt, tottered slowly into the garden, then turned and went back to the house. She might have come out to urinate, and been so skilled she didn't need to squat—or maybe she just couldn't make it to the privy. She was very old. It was the last time I saw her alive.

HOW JEBI BECAME A SHAMAN

A good man has gone," Jebi said when Dr. William left. He wept openly, rubbing his blue bandana over his face.

I, too, felt sad. Mr. Rai shared our mood. On the front porch, waiting for lunch, we watched a boy in the road throw a pitted, red rubber ball high into the air. As it began to come down, the boy ran toward the cliff edge to catch it, stopping short as it arced out over the drop-off into the trees below. Mr. Rai's eyes followed the ball's descent. "Life is like that," he said. He spoke several slow sentences to Jebi in Nepali, and then said, "I am telling him, when my father was fifty-five, already he is getting old. And I am now, as well."

Maile appeared in the doorway, holding the edges of her yellow sweater with both hands, and gave Mr. Rai a long, kind look. "Elder brother, you are sad, remembering your father," she said. "Maybe it is time for a puja to honor your ancestors in the old Rai way."

"I have set up a mangchhamma room," Mr. Rai said. "Still, you are right. I have neglected Udhauli this year." He translated what he'd said into English for my benefit, his voice regaining its usual briskness. He lit a cigarette, tipped back his head, and blew smoke to dispel the sense of a disapproving presence.

"Hajur." Maile bowed and moved past him down the steps.

Jebi brought a whiskey bottle and three glasses from inside. "You should have a drink to make you happy."

Mr. Rai drank, and announced with dispatch, "*Allen*, we have arranged for Jebi to take you to his home in Jappa and show you massan."

I had been hoping we could get down to business now that Dr. William was gone, but my stomach tightened.

Jebi blew his nose into his blue bandana and said, "Ho."

"You must prepare by learning all the mantras Jebi gives. You has to learn by heart," Mr. Rai said.

"So far he's only taught me two—the protection mantra and the one for morning and evening."

"From today," Mr. Rai decreed, "he will teach you all mantras."

"Ama," Jebi said seriously, "I will teach you everything."

"You will learn many things for you only, unknown to others." Mr. Rai leaned toward me. "You must always keep secret. Then initiation — like Jebi's guru gave to him."

"How did he—?"

"Let us ask Jebi, how did he become shaman," Mr. Rai said, looking at his watch to make sure there was time.

✒

Jebi's parents came from the tiny mountain village of Sinduli, where his father owned a piece of land. They married when his mother was thirteen. But the rains came late that year, and the crops failed, so they left for the plains to find work. When his mother was nineteen, her first child, Didi, was born. Didi wasn't her real name; it was just the word for elder sister, but no one ever called her anything else. The next year Jebi's mother had a boy, two years later, another girl, and over the next few years, two more daughters, a son, and then twin boys. Jebi was the last of nine children.

Before his birth, the two eldest sons died of pox. The youngest of the four sisters died at age seven of tuberculosis. Though at first the family did well, by the time Jebi was born, his father had no work. He knew how to weave the conical *dhoka* baskets carried by porters, which he did for six days a week. On Saturday, he took the baskets to market to support his wife and six living children. When Jebi was a year and a half old, his father died.

Didi got married that year to a man whose father was a shaman. He owned an orange orchard, four bullocks to plow his land, and six cows, whose milk he carried to customers all over the surrounding hills. The father took care of his own four sons and their wives, and looked after Jebi and his mother and brothers and sisters as though they were his own, supplying them with milk, eggs and fish, and buying them clothing. Jebi remembered how this kind man paid for everything with money from a big wallet he kept in his breast pocket.

One day, for no reason Jebi ever knew, their benefactor sold his orange orchard for four hundred rupees and put the money in his wallet. Soon afterward, two strangers came from Sansing, eight kilometers distant, to fetch him for a healing. Usually, he took care of his patients and came straight home, but this time he didn't return. After three days and nights, his sons went looking for him. They searched all day. Finally, they found his body crumpled against a large rock several meters downhill from a trail. The money was gone from his wallet. The brothers cut their hair and mourned. They fasted for thirteen days, wore white mourning clothes for a year, and gave up meat, yoghurt, and milk. One after the other, the cattle died, until none were left.

When they saw that the land was dying, the four brothers gave the property to the farmer who'd been working it, and moved with Didi to Rowse Bazaar. Jebi was nine years old, with three sisters and one brother left. Then his youngest sister and his brother died of tuberculosis, and the other sister left home to marry among strangers, at age fourteen without a dowry. Jebi's mother became a midwife, and when Jebi was ten, he took a job carrying dirt from building excavations.

That year, his mother got sick. It was then that Jebi began to shake when he heard a shaman's drum from a distant field or hillside. His mother would put her arms around him and hold him tight to stop the shaking. She called shamans from all the castes and tribes—Kami, Damai, Gurung, Tamang, Tibetan, Mughur, but no one could make Jebi speak to tell the name of the spirit shaking him. Soon his mother grew so sick she could no longer work, and Didi and her husband came and took her to the hospital.

Every other day for three months, Jebi watched the doctor insert a long needle into his mother's swollen stomach and pull out a pint of light yellow water. At night he returned to his empty house alone, too frightened to work or even think. He had no money for food, but his landlady fed him and gave him a few coins when she could.

On a full moon night, as the first silver rays slanted in through the doorway, he began to shake. The moonlight crept closer and touched his legs. His teeth chattered; he was helpless to stop the trembling. There was no one there to hold him close and warm and tell him he was safe. The shaking kept on until the moonlight came over him and reached to the high shelf, touching a row of peppers his mother had left there, dried up now to hard, shriveled pods. The light spread out within the room. He could smell its cold, metallic scent. He kept on shaking until it narrowed to a small patch on the floor, and only when it was gone could he rest.

He would shake again when the moon was new. After those nights of shaking, he would curl up, exhausted, into a tight ball on his mat, relaxing only when the rooster crowed and sunlight came, bringing the good, normal scents and sounds of morning, when the warm air rising from the dusty ground would soothe him finally to sleep.

One morning, he arrived at the hospital to find his mother's bed, number eleven, had been screened off. He could hear her groaning with each breath. The nurse shouted, "Get out!" when he tried to enter, but he squeezed past the screen. His mother's open mouth, caked with white, worked silently as she gasped for breath. Her eyes were wide and dull, and she failed to recognize her son. Two large hospital attendants grabbed him and pulled him away.

He ran home and asked his neighbors for help. Five strong young men were with him when he came back to the hospital. The nurse protested, and the doctor said he could no longer be responsible, but in the end, they let him take a stretcher and bring his mother home.

It was seven in the evening by the time they had her settled in bed, still groaning and writhing, but weaker now. At eleven-thirty that night, the night of Asar Ekadassi when offerings are given to Vishnu and Shiva, Jebi's mother twisted her body one last time and died.

He sat by her bed, unmoving as a stone, and would let no one near to tend the body, until finally, when he got sleepy, Didi and her husband put him to bed on his mat.

Afterward, when the relatives had gone home, neighbors who'd lent his mother money came and told Jebi his debts amounted to more than a thousand rupees. To honor his mother, Jebi decided to pay off her debts by himself, and at eleven years of age, got a job on the railroad, staying with a cousin and working first as porter, then a cook, and finally a railway guard.

As a guard, he had a mean foreman, who came by several times a night to see if he was asleep and shouted at him if he was. He got in the habit of tying a wire to his toe so anyone coming would bump it and wake him up. At that time, there was a thief in the neighborhood, breaking into the storehouse and helping himself to whatever he wanted, and the foreman told Jebi if he caught the thief, he should beat him with his stick.

That night, when Jebi heard the clatter of the foreman's wooden shoes as he came to check on him, he put his head under his shawl and pretended to snore. As soon as he felt the tug of the wire on his toe, he jumped up and brought his baton down hard on the foreman's back. "Ow, ow ow!" The foreman ran off cursing.

Jebi thought for sure he'd be fired, but the big boss didn't like the mean foreman either, and promoted Jebi to be his own personal assistant. Jebi got to pump the long lever on a little trolley, just big enough to hold himself and the boss's chair, and make it run along the tracks, sporting a flag on a flagpole. When a train came, other workers would run and lift the trolley out of the way.

When Jebi had earned enough money to pay his debts, he asked for time off to go home. Didi welcomed him like a mother, and he wept when he left her to return to work.

He still shook when he heard the sound of drumming, and finally, when he was fourteen, his cousin found a Rai shaman who could help him. This shaman was old—at least forty-five—with many wrinkles in his face and eyes that joked. But he was deadly serious about his work. The altar had to be set up just right. When he needed to wake his sacred objects with mantras, he never piled them together in a bunch to save time by saying a single mantra on them all, but treated each object separately with careful reverence, reciting its own mantra and blowing it into life; and when everything was arranged in order, Jebi felt the power and would be shaking even before the drumming started.

It was the Rai shaman who made the spirit in Jebi speak, with offerings and many entreaties: "If you are a god, please tell us what you want—offerings of incense, food, drink, or flowers. We will bring them, or if you are bad, please also let us know who you are and what you want. You are here bothering this boy. Please let us make you happy."

At last the spirit spoke and said that it was a Rai deity who had been in Jebi's body for the last few years. Jebi took the Rai shaman as his guru. It was not unusual for guru and student to be of different castes or tribes in a land with thirty-two different ethnic groups. His guru was kind, and Jebi spent his free time following him to patients, helping and learning the way of each ritual. He was forbidden to eat goat meat or the stinging nettles called shishnu, for, the shaman said, "Shishnu is your ally against the witches."

When he had apprenticed three months, Jebi's guru gave him his own sacred oil lamp and in return, Jebi paid him a guru offering of a shirt and coat, a bottle of rakshi, and one big rooster.

The shaman taught Jebi and his other students mantras, reciting them line by line, for none of them could read or write. The students learned by heart, and if they didn't repeat the mantras correctly, their guru warned, they would go crazy.

When the students were ready, the shaman took them to a graveyard for a *gupha*, cave, initiation, a test to see if they could withstand the terrible massans.

It was evening. The twelve students had fasted all day and were prepared to stay for seven nights. Since there was no actual cave, the shaman set up four bamboo poles in a square in a part of the cemetery where lower castes were buried. He circled the square seven times, winding a thread around the poles to fence off a small piece of ground, and directed the students to cover the square with a thatched roof. Inside, he lit an oil lamp and told his students to stay there.

At midnight, the shaman put out the light, warning, "Do not leave the protection of this place or forget the words of your mantras, or you may die." He ducked outside the thread barrier, threw handfuls of popcorn and fried soybeans outward on all sides, and circled the small enclosure three times, calling the massans with moaning blasts of his hollow bone, played like a trumpet into the darkness in all four directions.

The harsh, ragged sound sent splinters of dread up Jebi's spine. All was quiet. The students scarcely breathed. Then a murmuring began, swelling gradually to the sound of many people wailing and crying. A great shadow loomed above the students in their little shelter. Their teacher was gone. All but three of them leapt over the thread and ran away.

Jebi felt someone punching at his chest and back and pulling him by his upper arms. The spirit let go, but Jebi refused to run. The sensations went on for half an hour. The two remaining students twisted and jerked beside him, grunting and crying out as though under attack. Jebi trembled, but kept on saying his protection mantra.

Finally, the huge shadow went away and their teacher came back. Jebi shook all night. In the morning, the other two students left and didn't come back, but Jebi stayed. For seven nights the same thing happened, yet somehow he survived.

His next task was to find his own massan bone. His teacher sent him to the graveyard alone on a night three days after a low-caste Damai man was buried. Jebi left his clothes outside the cemetery walls, and keeping to the shadows, made his way naked to the newly-filled grave, trembling at the raw earth smell.

He dug down, gabbling mantras for protection, loosening the soil with his kukhuri knife, scooping it out with both hands and throwing it aside. It took hours to dig the five feet down to where the dead man's head should be. He dug sideways and felt the hard, round shape of a skull, then ran his arm in along the length of the body, feeling for bones. He had no fear of being caught by other people, for no one dared come to the burial ground at night. But he was close to panic, fearing the dead man's ghost would harm him.

His fear gave him strength to break the corpse's joints. His fist closed on a lower right arm bone, and he twisted it free and hacked off a four-inch piece. He scuttled backward and threw the rest of the arm bone on the disturbed earth of the grave. Breathing in short gasps, and reciting mantras to quell his dread, he pushed dirt into the hole with both hands and feet.

He took the bone to the river and cleaned off all the flesh, then bathed himself as instructed. His guru had told him not to take the bone inside his house, so he hid it under a bush beside a wall.

Three days later, with his guru as a witness, Jebi opened a gash in his own arm with a razor blade, and sacrificed a black rooster, twisting off its head and anointing the bone with chicken blood mixed with his own. "I have your bone," he addressed the massan spirit. "Don't hurt anyone, especially not me or my family." After that the bone was his.

"At least once each year," his guru said, "you must feed your bone with your own blood. Keep it happy or it will turn against you."

Now Jebi was his guru's favorite student. He learned to set up the altar and perform with no mistakes. His guru told him, "Never sin. If an entity throws a bad spell, you have to defend yourself, but never try to kill it or do any harm. If you do, your children may not be born healthy." He made Jebi put a burning wick inside his mouth and promise to do no harm. "Only in an emergency, if you are under a spell, in intolerable pain," his guru said, "you can say your mantra forward seven times and backward seven times, and throw it on your enemy using a porcupine quill."

After six months, Jebi's guru made a ceremony, separating his own oil lamp from Jebi's. He gave his student a red and white costume and said, "Now you are a fully-cooked shaman. Go and heal the people."

When Mr. Rai had finished translating Jebi's story, I asked him how Jebi had met his wife. "Was it an arranged marriage?"

"Of course." Mr. Rai poured out more whiskey and continued.

Jebi had been staying with one of his aunts outside of town, working as a house painter by day, and a shaman by night. He never had time to sleep. "You have to get married and move closer to work," his aunt told him. "You are old enough, and it just so happens I know of a good-natured girl who knows how to keep house."

"If you want me to, I will," Jebi said, though he didn't know the girl. She turned out to be pretty and quiet, a girl of his own Chetri caste.

Soon after the wedding, Jebi's wife's elder sister, for whom no suitable husband had yet been found, married a Rai man for love. At first the family was upset, but he was a good man and they soon came to like him, especially Jebi, who felt affection for all Rai people because of his Rai guru. The brothers-in-law decided together to take their wives to Jappa, where they'd heard good jobs could be had.

Jebi found work as a carpenter. His children came one after

another, two sons and a daughter, but his brother-in-law bought land before having children. For some reason, no matter how hard Jebi worked, he couldn't get ahead. He was called as a shaman several times a week, and then, because he drank the rakshi his patients gave him, he was tired and made mistakes at work, and then was let go from his jobs. His brother-in-law let Jebi build a little house on his land, and saw that his family had food. His wife never scolded or asked for more. She was a good wife, and Jebi wanted only to make her happy.

"He says, maybe some day he will go and try to find his father's land. But his planets are not good." Mr. Rai stopped and grinned. "But now he has come to work in my shaman school, might be his luck has changed."

MASSANS

Jebi was especially powerful that night, and I felt my stomach and legs begin to tremble as he drummed, but not so much that anyone else could tell. The patient, a middle-aged woman, too ill to sit up by herself, lay curled on the floor. Jebi said she'd been affected by a ghost, and made a diagram with white flour on a piece of cloth, drawing sixteen squares he called rooms. "He is making rekhi," Mr. Rai explained. "Rekhi means, I am the universe."

Jebi placed offerings of rice made black with charcoal, betel nut, and betel leaves in each "room" of the diagram for the sixteen massans, and with his massan bone, transferred the patient's sickness to a rooster. Three times the rooster lay down as though dead—proof, Jebi said, that someone had put an evil spell on the woman. Each time the rooster lay still, he revived it with a mantra and continued. Then he sucked on the patient's stomach and spat out blood and a small bit of matter resembling decayed flesh. He ran out to the front porch, leaned over the edge, and spat and made loud gagging sounds the audience could hear inside.

Afterward, Mr. Rai helped the patient to the couch and covered her with a blanket from the foot of Bindu's bed. The next day she was gone. Mr. Rai said she'd gotten better, and relatives had come to take her home.

I dreamed of Jebi that night, buried up to his eyes in earth, with only his fierce, broad forehead sticking out.

Next morning Jebi's mood was light. He was full of jokes, proud of last night's performance, and basking in Mr. Rai's approval. "Now he will teach you mantras," Mr. Rai said.

"You write," Jebi said. I fetched my notebook and he assumed a serious manner. "Shishnu mantra." He waited until I was ready, and then one by one, dictated four words, making sure I'd written each before saying the next. He made me repeat them, and then pointed through the window at the large, stinging nettle at the end of the garden. "Now you try. Don't try to pick leaves without the mantra."

Bindu and Thuli Kumari laughed.

"Go." He shooed me out with a wave of his hand. I walked through the garden. A man I didn't remember, naked to the waist, was giving himself a cold bath at the outdoor tap, and several children gathered to see what the strange, white-skinned woman would do.

The bush stood before me, taller than my head, with a massed array of pointed daggers furring its stems and leaves. I reached a single finger to touch one thorny branch, noticing that the stickers all pointed one way, and discovering I could stroke them in the direction they grew without being pricked. The same was true of the sharp thorns on the leaves. I whispered the mantra three times, blew on my hand, and grasped a bunch of stems and leaves to twist them off. The pain came at once, cruel and hard.

I licked my fingers, hoping saliva would be as good as snot to ease the pain, and tried again. "Shishnu, you are my friend," I directed a loud thought toward the bush, ignoring the pain and trying to project good will into the very fibers of the fully-armed plant. "Don't hurt me."

"*Ouch!*" I jerked back my hand. Blisters popped out along the sides and bottoms of my fingers. The children giggled and ran inside ahead of me to shout a report of my failure.

"Licking won't help," Mr. Rai said. "Jebi's mantra takes time."

"What mantra did you say?" Jebi asked.

I whispered the words he'd given me.

"No, no." He shook his head and corrected the last word. I knew I'd written exactly what he told me, and that's the way I'd said it, but I crossed out the last word and wrote the new one in its place. "Again," he commanded, waving me outside.

He'd picked a huge bouquet of the shishnu leaves the day he showed us the power of his mantra at Buddhanilakantha, but I decided to start small, and chose a single stem with three leaves. I said the new mantra, steeled myself, and picked the leaves. Again I was stung. I brought the leaves to Jebi.

"Does it burn?" he asked.

"It burns."

"Keep trying. Tomorrow, next day, the day after."

I made namaste, wishing I could run to the bathroom by my room, blow on my hands and hold them under cold water, but Mr. Ganesh had arrived.

Mr. Rai said that beginning today, Jebi would teach me mantras.

"Sometimes, every once in a while, you may get a new mantra in a dream from your spirit guru," Jebi said. "It will be on a full moon night, when you have washed, cleaned your bed, and asked for it. You might only get one word in your dream, but then you can ask your human guru to give you the rest."

"But I don't have a spirit guru...yet."

That day Jebi dictated many mantras, including the one for Bir Massan. I was so thrilled he was willing to give it to me, I didn't even notice it failed to start with "Om."

"Massan mantra is very powerful," Mr. Rai said that night, pouring himself, Jebi, and me a drink from a large bottle of Star beer. "My father knew very well how to play massans. When he was drunk enough, he was a big joker. One day we were camping out with two uncles and couple other people near by a river. 'Elder brother, we are bored,' they said. 'Show us some magic.'

"We had built up big bamboo fire, but still we are cold and hungry. 'Oh, you forgot to bring flattened rice,' my father said. Flattened rice was special party food we all liked very much. My father picked up sand from the river, said the mantra for Bir Massan and river snake, and poured sand, one hand to the other. Suddenly fifty, sixty, hundred kilos of flattened rice are there to eat." Mr. Rai paused, tipped back his head, and drank. "But when you are shitting, you are shitting only sand." He laughed, and repeated it all in Nepali for Jebi.

Jebi chortled and slapped his thigh. "I once knew a really powerful massan player," he said. Bindu and Kumari came in to listen, Kumari helping herself to a glass of beer. "It happened when I was a child in Kalingpoke."

A cable car full of rice packed in plastic was being transported to the hill region, and stopped at five o'clock just under the massan man's roof. Police were set as guards, but in the morning four bags of rice were missing.

The police hadn't seen a thing. The massan player had stolen the bags with his mantra. He was a very old man by that time, but they decided to search his house, and found them in his room. "Did you take these bags of rice?" they demanded.

"G-no, I did-th not-th t-thake them," the old fellow said. He had a tongue-tied way of talking. "I'm just-th an old-th man. D-thu I look-th like-th Sthuperman to pick-th them up-th?" Jebi put on a dopey expression, stuck his tongue between his teeth, and thrust his head forward as he forced out the words, imitating how the old man talked.

"We see them here," the police pointed out. "Who brought them?"

"'I will hav-th t-thu ask-th my guru-th," the old man said. 'Sthit down, young boysth." The old man made an altar with an oil lamp and a plate, and took it outside to ask his spirit guru. Bir Massan can make things invisible, and while the policemen were blinking, the four bags disappeared. They found them back inside the cable car.

They stormed back to the old man's room. He faced them bravely. "I'll t-thurn you into bird-th. You'll be flying-th. Your guns-th will be your tailsth," he yelled in his tongue-tied way. "I was-th just-th t-thesting how d-thutiful you were. Shall I st-thart the cable car?" He moved his hands up and down, and said, "Dthing, dthing" to insult them.

The police were angry and summoned him to the police station for questioning.

"Oh, no, that-th's t-thoo far," the old man said. They could hardly understand him, the funny way he talked. "It-th's all uphill. It-th t-thakes me a half a d-thay to get-th t-there." Besides being tongue-tied, he was crippled.

But they insisted, and when he arrived at the police station, they said, "Old man, if you have such power, can you bring four boxes of money from the bank in Darjeeling?"

"I d-thon't-th know," the old man said, nearly swallowing his tongue. "I have-th t-t-thu ask-th my guru." That's what he always said.

"Just bring us four of the hundred steel boxes they have there," the policemen said.

The old man went outside with his plate and oil lamp, and then said, "Okay, my guru s-thaid he will bring-th them." The four boxes of money were already there.

The police phoned the bank manager long distance in Darjeeling. "Did you lock the bank properly?" they asked.

"'Yes, when we left an hour ago," the manager said.

"Better go and check."

The bank manager called his cashiers and they rushed to the bank, crowding into the cash room. Four boxes were gone. "Who came here?" they questioned the guards.

'No one came," the guards insisted. "We've been here the whole time." Their guns were on their hips.

The bank manager called the Kalingpoke policemen and told them what they'd found.

"We've got your thief," the policemen said.

"How could he have gotten there in only one hour?" the manager demanded. "It's six hours by jeep."

"We're testing our shaman," the policemen said. They made the old man return the boxes, and before they hung up the phone, the boxes of money were back inside the cash room in the bank.

The police said, "You are a naughty old man. Don't joke like this—and don't call your guru any more. You don't need to. We'll feed you instead." They collected food for the old man for the rest of his life.

"What finally happened to that old guy?" Mr. Rai asked.

"You have to be a very good friend of Bir Massan," Jebi concluded, draining his glass. "If not, he'll suck your blood and throw you away, *puk puk, puk, puk, puk.* Bir Massan finally killed that old man, thirty-six years ago. I don't know why."

Jebi continued to give me mantras, which I transferred afterward to separate sheets of letterhead that Mr. Rai had had printed for his shaman school, decorated with red outlines of the sun, moon, a Shiva trident, and "Om" in devnagari letters. I wrote the mantras with a red pen in careful capitals, and began committing them to memory.

Almost at once, I got sick, throwing up and squatting with my feet on the metal footprints by the hole in my bathroom floor, racked with waves of cramping diarrhea. After these spasms, I scuttled, shivering, to bed and pulled the covers to my chin.

Bindu brought me coffee with cream, smiled and sat on the edge of the bed to talk, chattering on in Nepali in a friendly way, as if I could understand. At lunch time she brought a thick soup of chicken and rice, and stayed to confide her secrets. "Don't tell the others," she cautioned, her eyes sparkling with rare *joie de vivre.* I began to appreciate her unique personality that only flowered when she got away from Mr. Rai and the rest of her family, and was free to drop her role of wife and mother.

"*Chup!*" she giggled, finger on her lips.

"Chup," I repeated.

The soup was good, but all I wanted was a plain piece of bread. Just one little bit of something made of wheat. I'd had enough of rice. It might be food to them; but I still didn't have the enzymes to digest it well. I was used to wheat. Wheat was my food. It was wheat I craved.

Jebi came in the middle of the afternoon, asked for the rudraksha mala he'd given me, gathered it into his hands and swept it over my body with a mantra. It felt good to know he cared, that he wanted to do something to help, whether it worked or not.

Later I felt better, got up, and walked to Mr. Rai's. Maile was there, visiting Bindu and Kumari. She took my wrist and held it, calm and mother-like, and did a divination, feeling my pulses and concentrating.

"Sometimes when you are alone in your room, you are afraid," she said. "You hear noises and think something's coming."

"That used to be true, but now I use my protection mantra," I said. I hadn't actually had such fears since childhood—with one or two exceptions. What she sensed could only be the faintest echo of those times. But maybe my pulses still jumped.

Then she divined, with pinches of rice laid out in small piles, counting grains, and said I was affected by *choke nas*. "Some greedy person has watched you eating and looked at your food with a bad eye." She dropped three grains of hard rice into a glass of water, and spelled a mantra over it, holding it near her breast and turning the glass as she whispered and blew. "Drink this." She supported her right hand at the wrist with her left as she held the glass out. "You'll feel better now."

"If I could just have something made of wheat," I said.

I went home to sleep, and woke in the morning lightheaded, with a stomach still shaky but no longer sick. I dressed and visited the shishnu plant, wet with glittering drops of dew that enhanced its poison, and after using Jebi's mantra, picked a few leaves. The children were watching, so I tried not to show how badly I'd been stung.

"Did it burn?" Jebi asked.

"It burned." The question and answer had become our morning ritual.

Afterward, Jebi seemed abstracted, sitting cross-legged on the rug and letting his gaze stay fixed where it fell. He answered Mr. Ganesh's questions briefly and without interest.

"I will tell you about the four ages of man," Mr. Ganesh began, when Jebi failed to suggest a subject for teaching. "You may know, the first age long ago was the *Satya Yuga*, the age of truth. The people then were carefree, unselfish, dedicated to God. Next was *Dwapar Yuga*, the second age, when Rama was born. It was very similar to the *Satya Yuga*. But sin appeared. Then came the *Tret Yuga*, the third age. This was the time of Krishna, of the *Bhagavad Gita*.

"Now we are in the final age, the *Kali Yuga*. *Kali* means black, but this doesn't have anything to do with black, or with the goddess Kali. The end of the world will be after this. When the world is full of sinners, it will be destroyed. Each *yuga*, each age, has four stages. We are now in the fourth stage of the Kali Yuga," he said, with no emotion but the pride he took in his scholarly knowledge.

"There was a man named Biruspacha, an ordinary man, also known as Kali," he went on. "He could communicate directly with Shiva. Shiva told him he was destined to someday have physical relations with his mother. Biruspacha did not want this terrible sin to happen. He went away, leaving his mother alone. He forgot all about her. One day it grew dark and rained hard. No one could see. A strange lady came to his door and asked for shelter. She was beautiful, and he slept with her. The next morning he found out she was his mother. He wanted to bury himself underground for shame, but before he did, he told the people, 'The day my body will rise from the ground will be when I am sinless—but on that day the world will end.'" Mr. Ganesh paused to sip his coffee through pursed lips.

"At the temple of Biruspacha there is a stone figure coming out of the ground," he said. "First the top of its head came out, then its forehead. In the sixties I saw it had come out up to its chest. Now it's out to its waist."

I shivered, reminded of my dream of Jebi, buried in the ground to his forehead, and realized the dream had connected me with the symbolism of a myth I'd never heard before, touching the collective consciousness of this land. How strong and meaningful Jebi's forehead had looked, emerging from the ground—all that power imprisoned, struggling to be free. Did he believe that, like Biruspacha, he had committed some grievous sin?

That evening, Mr. Rai invited two German doctors to Jebi and Maile's guru puja performance. Someone brought a black hen and rooster from the market, and Jebi used them to work on a patient from the neighborhood, a woman suffering flu-like symptoms. He hypnotized the birds, and possessed by his deity, sucked bloody matter from the patient and spit and gagged. On the floor beside him, I felt myself begin to shake inside, as he cut ginger over my head—but nothing showed.

When it was Maile's turn to perform, I sat on the couch with Mr. Lama. "She is a better shaman than Jebi," he whispered. "She calls all the gods, but Jebi only calls a few."

Then Mr. Rai had me sit by the altar, and both shamans tried to make me shake. But something stubborn and heavy held me still. The German doctors were impressed with the shamans' performances, and I hoped they hadn't understood my failure.

ILLNESS

Jebi, the mantra isn't working. Please tell me if it's right." I came in from outside with three shishnu leaves and as many blisters, and repeated the mantra I'd used.

"It will work," he assured me. "Try again. I'll come with you."

The morning dew was mostly gone. As the children watched, Jebi whispered his mantra, blew on the plant, and picked a large bunch of leaves. "Easy," he said with a grin.

I'd paid close attention, and copied his movements exactly, as I whispered the words, but I still got burned. It would probably take years to become desensitized to the shishnu allergens.

"You must say it forward, blow three times, then backward and blow three times—six times all together."

"But why didn't you tell me—?" I broke off, not wanting to sound disrespectful.

He stroked the bunch of leaves he'd picked. "Touch it. My mantra has removed the poison."

I grazed my fingertips along the stem and leaves. Nothing happened—no pain, no blisters. His mantra had made them harmless as a bunch of spinach.

"Try again," he directed.

"Tomorrow," I laughed, digging my thumbnail into the side of my index finger above the knuckle to ease the burning from the first try.

Mr. Ganesh was waiting inside. To make sure I'd understood, Jebi asked him to translate as he repeated his instruction to say the shishnu mantra three times forward and three times backward.

"Jebi says you must say the mantra three times," Mr. Ganesh reported.

"Must I say it backward too?" I asked to test him.

"No, not, that is..." He consulted Jebi. "Yes backward three times as well."

Jebi visited the kitchen and came back. We sat down to our lessons, Mr. Ganesh upright on his usual straight chair, me on the couch, notebook open on my lap, and Jebi cross-legged on the floor. Thuli Kumari had given Jebi a drink or two of rakshi. I could smell it on his breath.

"Today we talk about *bhuts* and *jhagitras*," Mr. Ganesh began, "dead spirits who die an accidental death. They are bad. After they die, they are forced to live out the length of their natural lives as spirits." He sipped his coffee, his eyes searching the ceiling. I had the distinct impression he was making things up.

"What happens to the spirits after that, when their time is up?" I asked. Mr. Ganesh drew a breath to speak. "No, please, I want to hear what Jebi says."

Jebi answered, and I recognized the word, *Nargalok*, lower world.

"They go on to other places." Mr. Ganesh translated, and then launched into one of his standard lectures. "There are thirty-two million species of living biologies," he recited. "Nirvana is the goal of all living things…"

I closed my notebook, moving carefully to hide my irritation, and made up my mind to tell Mr. Rai we needed a better translator. My stomach rolled with nausea at the smell of curried lentils cooking for lunch. I stood, slightly bent, letting my stomach hang suspended so as not to feel the sick sensations. "Please tell Mr. Rai I am ill," I said. "I'm sorry, but I have to lie down."

Bindu came later, after I'd thrown up, to see if she could help. I tried to smile. "My stomach is no good," I said. "I just need sleep."

She went away. I covered the bed with the extra blanket, and my sleeping bag, and huddled shivering, beneath.

At dark, Thuli Kumari brought rice pudding with butter and salt, smiling broadly when I took a few bites and pronounced it delicious. As soon as she left, I threw up.

I dreamed fever dreams of Mr. Rai's ancestors. Among the disordered, accusing images, one stood out sharply—the face of an ancient Rai man, his wrinkled skin stretched tight over delicate, symmetrical jaws and cheek bones, an older version of Mr. Rai. Triangular lids half covered a set of bright, knowing eyes that *saw* me. I started awake to the echo of his scratchy, angry voice.

Mr. Rai came later to check on me, and I said, "I think I dreamed of your *pitri*—that your ancestors are angry with me."

"No, no-o-o," he denied quickly.

"Maybe because you let me look inside your mangchhamma room," I persisted.

"Yes. Could be you are getting sick because of starting to learn mantras. Now spirits are taking an interest in you. It often happens this way."

"All I need is sleep." I pulled the covers to my throat, the nausea just bearable now, rising and falling in waves. I remembered how I'd learned to suffer on the plane, admiring the little old woman with her Buddhist secret. If I could let myself feel it completely, I thought—honor the nausea, give it its due—maybe then it would go away. But I couldn't. My body tensed against it.

"How is your trekking business going?" I asked to distract myself. "Did the German firm pay?"

"As a matter of fact, *Allen,* is not so good. I have many clients now wanting credit, but my partner doesn't want to give. Is bad decision. In this business, you have to trust." He pulled up a chair and lit a cigarette. "After all, they are trusting us with their lives in the mountains. I would like to get a different partner. Only thing is, money. Always money."

❧

I fell asleep and dreamed I was in a strange house with Jebi. Someone showed me letters spelling out the word, *"deodma,"* a word with no meaning I was aware of, and I knew it was for the shishnu mantra.

The dream shifted. I was back in bed, covered up, with two dark figures at the foot of the bed. The one to the right was a man, but the center of his face was invisible—an emptiness framed by hair and an edge of cheek and chin. "Why is his face like that?" I asked.

As I spoke, my own face began to shake, as though blinking in and out of existence, and I understood these half-invisible spirits were showing they could make me shake. I called out, "Why are we here?"

Mr. Ganesh answered from the next room, in his formal voice, "Ellen, do you want to eat?" I woke up ravenous, reached for my journal and wrote "DEODMA" in red ink.

❧

Later, Mr. Rai brought me a box of lightly-salted crackers. They smelled of wheat, of all the goodness of America, like home. I nibbled a few and began to feel better.

"You rest," he said. "Come later for dinner, then Jebi will do ceremonies for sick peoples. I will ask him to do for you also."

I soon felt so well, I decided to take a walk outside. It was always a strain, not knowing whether to meet peoples' eyes and smile or ignore them. So many people, giving me all sorts of looks—interested, puzzled, angry, or unreadable—but if I smiled, they often smiled back.

Maile was out in her garden picking greens when I passed her house. She invited me in and poured out tea from a thermos. Little Dorje lay sleeping on the bed, as her husband, the old lama, cooked rice on the kerosene stove in the corner. "He must cook everything for himself," she said. "Because he is a lama, he is not allowed to eat food cooked by others."

Mr. Lama beamed as I namasted. "What is Jebi teaching?" he asked.

"Now he is teaching mantras."

The lama spoke rapidly to Maile in Tamang, and she argued back, and then seemed to agree.

"Maile's mantras are more powerful," he said.

"I would like to learn Maile's mantras. Jebi always comes to teach, but Maile only comes sometimes." The conversation was straining the limits of my Nepali. "Jebi's mantras are short," I added. "Maile's are long, but I would like to learn them."

"Tamang mantras are very long," Maile agreed.

A small family appeared in the doorway, come for healing—an old man supported by a son or grandson, and a middle-aged woman. Maile asked them to wait until we finished our tea. They sat down on the floor.

"Many sick people come to you," I observed.

"They believe in me."

I was sure that the longer I stayed, the longer the sick man would have to wait. I stood and said I had to go.

"Have more tea," Maile said, as though she meant it. I sat back down.

"Mr. Rai has not paid Maile," Mr. Lama said.

"Why not?"

He shrugged.

I looked at Maile. "I don't know," she said.

"He should pay," the lama said.

"Yes, he should." I stood again, and now they let me go. I namasted to everyone and went out into the sunshine, queasy from tea and tension.

Back in my room, I curled up on the bed. Bindu brought some clean clothes Mr. Rai had sent out to be laundered, and a Nepali textbook for learning English. We sat together over the book and I taught her a few English words. "Do you feel better now?" she asked.

"I'm just a little sick. But Jebi will heal me tonight."

"No, Jebi has gone."

"Gone?"

"Gone. His old sister was taken to the hospital with pneumonia. He had to go to her."

CHOOSE

I toyed with the rice and lentils Kumari had heaped on my plate and sighed. My stomach still felt queasy.

"*Allen*," Mr. Rai said in that sharp way that forced my attention. "*Allen*, I think now, you should choose who is your teacher, Jebi or Maile."

I looked up, startled. "I don't—."

"I think maybe you are confusing, with Jebi teaching in Rai way, and Maile teaching Tamang way. Soon you start shaking, and maybe get crazy if try to follow two ways of shamanism."

"I never thought I'd have to choose." Butter congealed into dull little flakes on my lentils as I turned them over with my spoon.

"Jebi is good teacher," Mr. Rai said. "Teaching you shishnu mantra and all these things. I think his mantras are shorter, easier to learn."

He clearly wanted me to pick Jebi, and I could see it would make things easier for him. He'd only have to pay one shaman. It would be easier for me too, to learn only one set of mantras. But I couldn't give up Maile.

"I didn't want to say, but I have had dream about you," Mr. Rai said. "I think you are correct of your dream my Rai pitri are angry with you learning of Rai ways. But I have prayed to my family spirits. I have told them you are sincere student of shamanism who I am teaching mudhum ways—that you are a good person and they should not angry themselves. Instead they should give help."

"Thank you," I said, surprised. Up until now, Mr. Rai had taken no part in the spiritual side of teaching me.

"Only thing is, too confusing with learning both Rai and Tamang ways. I think better you choose now. In my dream, showed pitri are angry because is Jebi giving mantra in your ear, and Maile is pulling him away. Means two kinds of shamanism fighting. Is why you are sick now too."

"But Maile can teach me a lot—because she's a woman. In fact, I was hoping she could come more often," I said, politely as I could.

He pressed his lips together. "Okay, then I tell Jebi, go home."

"No," I said quickly. "I —."

"You think about it. Tomorrow, next day, make up your mind." He seemed annoyed. I decided to wait for a better time to bring up the subject of Maile's payment.

Jebi came in then, looking terrible, his cheeks drawn in, his dark skin dull and ashen.

"Jebi's elder sister Didi very bad in hospital," Mr. Rai said. "Doesn't sleep or eat. Very difficult breathing."

"I am sorry," I said in my awkward Nepali. "It is my hope she will become healthy."

Jebi rubbed his eyes. Thuli Kumari handed him a plate of food and he ate mechanically with his fingers. Finished, he pulled himself together and asked if I'd practiced with shishnu that morning.

"No, but I dreamed a new word for the mantra."

"Good." He mustered a smile.

"There was a man in my dream with part of his face erased. He made my face start shaking."

"Bir Massan," he said, speaking so rapidly that Mr. Rai had to translate. "He came because of mantra I gave you. I will give you all sixteen mantras, and while you are learning, massans will come in dreams. But after you learn all the mantras, they won't come any more unless you call. Add new word Bir has given you to the end of the shishnu mantra, and blow now four times instead of three, both forward and backward."

Next morning I tried it. The thorns looked heavy and substantial, and I wondered if the bush had learned to recognize me as that hated enemy who showed up each morning to tear off its leaves. I touched a small stem with four or five leaves, stroked it forward in the direction of the thorns, and repeated the four-word mantra forward and backward, blowing four times each. For a moment I thought it might be working; then I felt the sting. Jebi laughed.

"My guru gave me only one word of the shishnu mantra at first, and told me the rest would come in dreams," he said. "After four months of trying, I finally found out about saying it backward and forward, but I still got blisters. I tried every day. Even after I received all three words, I got stung. I wasn't able to control shishnu until my guru gave me my drum and shaman's costume."

That morning, Jebi gave me no new mantras, but said I should place offerings to the massans in a clean place because they were helping me now; though, in general, offerings to bad spirits that cause trouble, for example massans that a witch is using to curse someone, could simply be thrown down in the road.

Jebi took out his crumpled blue bandana and wiped it several times across his face and eyes. Mr. Ganesh asked him what was wrong, and explained, "He was up all night with his sister. She is very sick you know, in the hospital. I think we should let him go now so he can sleep." Despite his pompous ways, our translator could be kind.

CREATION

Jebi curled up on the couch, and because it was still early, Mr. Ganesh took me to the Tribuwan University library. Set on a pleasant, grassy hill, its size rivaling a library of a small American college, it housed English as well as devnagari volumes. Mr. Ganesh consulted the card catalog and retrieved a book called *History and Culture of the Kirat People* by I. S. Chemjong. It was dated 1966, and written partly in English and partly in Nepali. The little translator led me to a seat at a long, polished table.

I was excited to find that the English portion of the book told a creation story of the Kirati people, ancestors of the Rai and Limbu tribes. Jebi's Rai shamanism was strongly colored by Hindu influences, not only because of Mr. Ganesh and his interminable stories, but also because Jebi was Hindu. Now I would find out what true Rais believed.

In the beginning was nothingness, I read. Nothingness and a powerful force. The earth grew up out of the nothingness like a wooden bowl. God created a small burning light like the face of a small baby, then rays of burning light, and the blue color of hollow space.

To maintain the light everywhere, God made the small burning light move eastward and westward; the rays rose up in the shape of horns, and grew and mixed to form a great light covering all the directions. This gave the Creator pleasure in his heart.

With the light, heat increased and sweat accumulated, creating an eastern and western sea called "The Blue Seas of the Powerful Lamp." So much sweat accumulated, it filled the wooden bowl, and there was only water.

By the power of the heat and light, the seas shook, and a strong wind arose in the shape of two trees that covered the whole of space. They were called "The Powerful Trees of Wind Which Blow Around the Space." Then the bright, hot god created the shape of the universe, and Chotilungma, the Heart of Nature. For boundaries, he created two powers, Pakuru and Makuru, and by the mixture of these powers, nature brought forth new energy. He formed the states of waking and sleeping. By the power which is active, one can discern the innermost element of nature, and by this knowledge, can see and do anything and appear everywhere. This power of knowledge is called Ningwaphuma.

Ningwaphuma, whose name means "Mine of Knowledge and Wisdom, and God," came to earth with the other gods to help the people, and they regarded him as their grandmother and called him Yuma Sammang. But then these good beings created evil spirits: Epley, who causes evil deeds, Songdo, who makes one fail to keep promises, and Nahen who causes envy, jealousy, and anger.

Here it was again, I thought. Good permitting evil to exist—in fact creating it—as though the gods were bored and needed evil to make things happen so that stories could be lived and told—as when Parvati created the witches.

I read on. The Kiratis believed good men went to heaven when they died, to live in joy in the light of thousands of suns' rays. Mr. Rai had told me Rais didn't believe in reincarnation, yet I'd often heard contemporary Rais speak like Hindus of karma gained in past lives; and Jebi's mantras called on Hindu gods. Even Maile, who rarely mentioned Hindu deities, used Kali, a Hindu goddess. No doubt Maile's Tamang ancestors, living higher than the Rais, on the border of Tibet, had felt less influence of the Aryan Hindu invaders.

Through the afternoon, I scribbled notes. When a bad man dies violently, of suicide, accident or murder, he becomes an evil ghost, the book said. These must be like massans.

Among the people are oracles. Inspired by the good spirit of God, they fall down senseless and recite the mudhum of past days and instructions for good works. In the mudhum also, a practice is described in which a priestess recites the life of a flower, comparing it to a particular person's mentality. Then when the flower withers, the person weakens. When it freshens, he or she revives. This practice can also make a tree drop its leaves and resume them.

Here was true magic! Shamanic power—the same power Jesus must have used to blast the fig tree that refused to bear fruit. I turned the pages eagerly, looking for how those ancient shamans actually accomplished their magic. But whatever Mr. Chemjong may have discovered about that must have been hidden in the devnagari portion of his book.

I copied down the names of the gods for war, energy and ambition, health, and agriculture, all ending in *Sammang*, Spirit of God. Okwanama Sammang is the healer who makes sacrifices—the shaman. The healing priest uses no medicines, only prayer and sacrifice. He prepares an altar to attract the evil spirits, and if the prayer and sacrifices don't work, Mr. Chemjong said, he burns chili, rags and "dirty things" to drive them away.

It was the reference to "dirty things" that stopped my frantic scribbling. I just could picture Mr. Chemjong, lips pursed, eyebrows slightly raised, intoning "dirty things," exactly the way Mr. Ganesh so often did. This author was only a man, after all, full of petty prejudice, misconceptions, and pride of scholarship. And here I'd been all excited, thinking that somehow, because these words were written, they must be truer than the oral stories I'd been told.

Mr. Ganesh had been chatting with the librarian, and when I looked up, came over. "It is now 4:30," he said. "I think we must get you home." We made our way outside and down the hill, falling in with a scattering of students leaving campus on foot and bicycles. We found a three-wheeled taxi to drop Mr. Ganesh off in Tamil near his home, and take me on to Mr. Rai's in Baluwatar.

I asked Mr. Rai about the names of the gods I'd copied, and he said they were correct, but were Limbu rather than Rai. "Ningwaphuma is Shiva—Hemasang in Rai," he said, a name I knew from Jebi's chants. I consulted my notes. "Ningwaphuma, Mine of Knowledge and Wisdom—and God."

Jebi performed that night, a ceremony to extract a bad spirit from a woman with a rough, persistent cough. He had her lift the back of her T-shirt and unfasten her bra, and then pressed the underside of his brass plate against the bare skin of her back. The idea was to make it stick there as he beat the traditional middle world rhythm on it with his drumsticks, whistling mantras until it fell off and took the evil spirit with it. I'd seen him do this several times.

The woman's back was bent with the suffering of her illness, broad, and doubtless sticky with sweat; but though Jebi pushed the plate into place again and again with the end of his thumb and two fingers, he couldn't make it stay. At last he gave up and used his rudraksha mala and massan bone for the extraction.

Mr. Rai told me Jebi had spent the day at the hospital with his sister, and must be distracted by her illness.

The plan had been for Jebi to leave for Jappa in the morning to arrange the gupha initiation to show me the massans. Mr. Rai and I would follow four days later. In spite of Didi's serious condition, Jebi left.

After he was gone, Maile came to teach, greeting me with her usual toothy smile. She and Mr. Rai chatted with apparent cordiality.

Mr. Rai left for his office, and Mr. Ganesh immediately launched into a long Hindu story. I let him finish, and then said, "Please ask Maile, when she had the dream about teaching Dr. William and me, and giving us butter, what was the wisdom she wanted to give us?"

"About Banjhankri," she answered, and then began to talk about the things on her altar, indicating three short wooden stakes, elaborately carved like the handle of her drum. "These phurbas are Shiva," she said, calling him Mahadeo, Great God, in a loving tone. I remembered she had told me that Banjhankri is actually Shiva in the middle world. The things on her altar not only represented the gods, they *were* the gods.

"The phurbas are used for protection," Mr. Ganesh interpreted. "Her strings of beads are ornaments of Shiva. The bells she wears around her shoulders are for Bhagwati, a reincarnation of Parvati. She sings to the bells, telling how they were made by a blacksmith who gave them to the Lion. Then they were given to Bhagwati Raktakali, Blood Kali. *Udi* is the turban, with its end hanging down like Shiva's long lock of hair. In her chant, she asks these deities to be her guards. If she doesn't remember how everything must be done, and sing exactly right, the strings of beads and bells may break.

Maile dictated the words of the chant she used to begin her ceremonies, and I wrote them down. Mr. Ganesh explained, "She begins at the beginning of the universe, with Guru Pema Jungne who arose from a lotus flower by himself. The chant tells a story from the Tamang mudhum, of woodcutters who went into the jungle to cut a huge tree, so huge that even though they cut from both sides, the tree refused to fall. They went to a shaman to find out why. 'All around the tree are deities,' the shaman told them. 'Jeho Jiomo on the east, Jeho Singlekarbo on the south, Jeho Nanglekarbo on the north, Chamranglai Jeho on the west—and others. Beneath the tree is *kalo nag*, black snake.' The shaman told the woodcutters that God had instructed them to give offerings to these deities and get their consent to fell the tree. When the deities consented, the tree fell down.

"They burned the wood from the tree and turned it into charcoal. They took the skin of a dead bull, and the ironsmith made bellows from it. Then he tried to make a sacred water pitcher. At first he used clay, but that didn't work. Then the smith from the east brought gold ore, the smith from the west brought silver ore, the smith from the south brought copper ore, and the smith from the north brought iron ore. The smith from above brought bronze, and from these five metals, they made a sacred water pitcher.

"Out of the pitcher came a virgin deity, bright and beautiful to look at, the goddess, Jari Wari Dolmo. The pitcher had a little pipe down inside, and water came out and fell back into the pitcher. When this had gone on for a certain time, the pitcher came to life. Its spirit was awakened. Maile keeps it to the left of her altar and sings to it, 'You are pure as a virgin goddess.' The water is holy.

"If a patient begins to shake, Maile holds the pitcher to the top of the patient's head and pours a little water to make the patient break her speech. If the patient is going to become a shaman, she'll tell everything about the deity who is making her shake. If a witch is on her, the shaking will stop.

"The oil lamp on her altar, whose name is Nangsal Lamo li Mahadeo, is the Great God, Mahadeo."

Then Maile taught me to set up an altar, with tall cones of cooked rice called tormas to represent the gods, and other holy objects. "We must not take food or salt while the altar is in place," she said.

"Her deity is so strong it can hurt the other shamans at guru puja unless she controls it," Mr. Gurung translated. "When she starts to shake, all the deities merge into her body. When she stands and starts dancing, she thinks of her guru, and all her challengers become unconscious. The Banjhankri gave her a mantra for the rudraksha beads, to make them come to life. She can feel when they're alive."

"How?" I interrupted.

"They're a little heavier than usual."

As Maile explained these things, I fell under her spell, feeling the ritual objects as deities, alive and full of power. She spoke of her guru, Banjhankri, like a lover. "Banjhankri is like the earth," she said. "He is everywhere. If you need to remember him, think over the world. The mantra he gave me works to heal all diseases. It will cure any illness, no matter what kind."

I longed for her to give me this mantra, but feared she would not because I still wasn't shaking. Sucking in a shallow breath, I blurted, "Does she still think she can teach me to be a shaman?"

"Yes." Mr. Ganesh said impassively after consulting her, though I'd gone hot with shame. "In the time remaining, Maile can teach you to become a competent shaman." She smiled, watching my face as he translated.

"I will teach you Banjhankri's healing mantra," she said. "The name of Banjhankri in Tamang is Singbon. If he is angry, he can make you sick." She settled herself, with folded hands. "Ready?"

"Yes." My mouth went dry.

"Om...," she began.

In contrast to her long trance chants, the healing mantra was but a few lines long.

I thanked her, bowing namaste.

"We must say the mantras from the heart," she said. She taught me a mantra to open my heart, then other short mantras used for everyday healings, itching, joint pain, headaches, burns, and diarrhea.

Peter had said that among the Buddhist peoples of Nepal, shamans treated the living and lamas the dying. But though Maile's husband was a lama, she, herself, helped those who were dying, reciting the Tamang mudhum.

"When the person is ready to die, angels from heaven come to receive the departing spirit," Mr. Ganesh translated. I knew Maile had actually said "deities from Dharmalok," not "angels from heaven," but let it pass.

"She asks the dying person, 'Why did you take your food from the table? If you know the reason you ate your food from the table you may go to salvation. If not, you may not go. Speak.'

"If the spirit cannot answer, it cannot go with the angels. Maile has to recite the mudhum of her tribe so the dying person will know what answer to give. It tells the Tamang story of creation. In the prehistoric age, a god killed a demon, and from its backbone made a little table. From the thigh he made a blowpipe. From the knees he made little cups.

"The dying person must tell the angel, 'I had my food on a table made from the backbone of a demon. His knee was my cup, and I had my food there. I blew his marrow bone to call deities. In his skull I burned incense.'"

So, I thought, like a Christian, the dying person must acknowledge that his life on earth was full of sin, for by the very nature of things, even the act of eating to stay alive is a cannibal feast. If the dying person acknowledges this original sin, he is saved. But he must answer the question, as all questions are answered in this part of the world, with a story of how the gods once acted, for we humans can do nothing more than endlessly repeat their lives and stories.

"The remaining flesh and bone of the demon were cut into chunks and cooked in a large vessel," Mr. Ganesh continued. "Maile recites how the flesh that was not cooked turned into deadly insects like mosquitoes and flies. The meat that was not cooked, and even the raw blood, turned into insects. No insects came out of the properly cooked meat."

After lunch, full of confidence, I asked Maile to explain her ceremony step by step, feeling sure it wouldn't be long until I'd be ready to do it myself.

"Before we start drumming, we must concentrate," she said. "Clear the mind and heart. Don't think of appointments with friends or anything else. See Lord Shiva in front of you with his long locks and trident.

"We make seats for the deities we call. At the beginning of our chant, we invite them to sit to each side of us, and at our front and back, to protect us. 'I went to the east and got pine trees and made a beautiful bed for you,' we sing. 'I went to the west and cut down a pine and made a soft bed. I went to the north and cut down sandalwood and made a soft bed for you. I went to the south and got a special *surchan* pine to make a soft bed for you. I have everything for your comfort. Please, all deities, come and be comfortable.'"

Then she taught me mantras to awaken the rudraksha malas and the drum.

When she finished, we smiled at each other, and I understood she was truly giving me the butter of her wisdom. I felt gratitude and friendship. Kumari brought in tea, and I asked the translator if it would be all right to ask Maile how she had met her husband.

"Yes, of course." As usual, Mr. Ganesh answered without consulting Maile. "Why not?"

She smiled when she heard the question.

"When she first came to Kathmandu, she did not know many people," Mr. Ganesh translated. "One day Lama invited her to his house to eat, and she came. Then it was late, and he told her he had no way to take her home. They could not get a taxi so late at night. She had to stay over. After that, because of her relatives and his, they had to get married."

"But she is not sorry now?" I asked. "She has her son."

"No, she is happy with her life," he said.

"*Sukkha dukkha*," Maile added. Sweetness and pain.

After class, I set to work memorizing her mantras. It went quickly, for she loved them, and had communicated that love to me, perhaps with a special love-spell mantra. Their words were like poetry, in Tamang and Nepali, and their reach was as broad as the world. *Saat samundra tari,* seven oceans far...

Mr. Rai was late coming home. When he finally arrived, he sat down heavily and said, "I have just been to hospital. Jebi's sister has died."

A VILLAGE CALLED WEDNESDAY

I could sense what Mr. Rai must be going through. He took off his shirt, hung it on a chair back, sighed, and sat on the couch as though he didn't know what else to do. His eyes were clear and vulnerable.

The room felt different—bare—with Jebi's altar gone. The women had wasted no time cleaning up; not a grain of rice remained. Not even a lingering trace of incense. Mr. Rai's eyes were fixed on the wall where the altar had been. Every scratch and scar stood out stark in the bright light from the overhead bulb that turned the window, behind its curlicues of metal, to a dark mirror. The very air seemed different.

"I don't know why Jebi's didi had to die just now," Mr. Rai said. "The gods must be angry." He let himself sag forward. "When we are returned from Jappa, I will do offering to pitri as I have promise." He rubbed his face.

The phone rang, shockingly loud. He motioned Bindu to answer, chopping his hand downward, away from his face, to signal her to say he wasn't home.

"Hallow," she said in the small, shy voice she used with strangers. "He is not here." It must be a creditor. "Yes, yes, yes." No one could be angry with Bindu when she was like that, so quiet and compliant, nor expect her to be responsible.

Mr. Rai spoke to Bindu in Nepali, something about seeing people who owed him money in Biratnagar on the way to Jappa.

"Just go then," Bindu was saying. "You can tell Jebi about his sister when you see him, when you're there to comfort him."

"But what about her?" Mr. Rai indicated me with a slight eye movement, not realizing how much Nepali I'd learned. "She's expecting the gupha initiation, but if Jebi is in mourning, he cannot play the massans."

"What the gods have done, we must accept," Bindu said. "Ellen won't be angry. She is our friend." I wanted to agree, but thought it would be less embarrassing to pretend I had no idea what they'd said.

❦

That night I dreamed of a giant frozen ocean wave, somewhere north of the Arctic Circle, poised like a small mountain above a group of houses, ready to sweep them away. "It will melt harmlessly," people said, but I was frightened.

I greeted the shishnu bush as usual, still feeling sick. Bright morning sunlight scattered rainbows from the dew drops on its leaves. Three small children watched as I whispered my mantra, and giggled out loud when I jerked my hand away.

Mr. Rai had already left the house, and telephoned from his office as I sat down to breakfast. "Hurry up and pack," he said. "They are burning Jebi's sister at Pashupatinath. You come here to office and we will go together." I swallowed a bit of bread and coffee and hurried outside to meet the taxi he'd sent.

The fresh paint smell in his office triggered a wave of nausea, and I waited outside. We took another cab to the crematory ghats along the Bhagmati River at Pashupatinath, where Mr. Rai bought two flower malas and a bouquet of marigolds from a vendor's stall. We passed down a broad flight of steps to a series of widely-spaced platforms on the riverbank where corpses smoldered, sending up a smell of burning hair. I breathed through my mouth.

"Women are not supposed to be here because they cry too much and make everyone upset," Mr. Rai said, but pushed me forward anyway. "It is all right. You come. Don't worry."

Didi's body, covered with a bright yellow cloth, lay on the second platform from the stairs, overlaid with a neat stack of burning logs. She was so tall that the top of her head showed at one end, while her thin, stick-like legs protruded from the other. A tame fire slowly did its work, sending up clouds of white steam and smoke. Jebi's eldest son leaned against a wall and sobbed. Mr. Rai hugged him. The dead woman's niece, Jebi's cousin, stood by watching with bright, unreadable eyes. One of Didi's nephews stared out over the river. Mr. Rai handed Jebi's son the flowers he'd bought and gave him some money.

On the way to the airport afterward, he said, "I think maybe I should tell Jebi his didi has died and been burned. I am not sure what is best."

"Why would you *not* tell him?"

"Then he has to be in mourning time. For thirteen days, he cannot call massan or perform chinta. Most likely we will have to come right back from Jappa. You will not have gupha, I am very sorry to say."

"Why not stay here, then? Call Jebi to come back."

He rubbed his face. "No-o. Everything is set. We has to go. Maybe not tell Jebi till after gupha."

I shifted to face him, grabbing the back of the driver's seat as the taxi swerved to avoid a cyclist. "We can't do that."

"You are right of course. Don't say anything. Just let me handle."

We boarded a small propeller plane. Mr. Rai was good friends with the pilot, and he let me sit in the cockpit, and as we circled upward, pointed out Everest and Gauri Shankar, home of the goddess, Gauri Parvati, whom I knew from Maile's mantras. The engine roared. It was frightening so close to the machinery that kept us aloft, to think that, like a lawnmower motor, it could stop at any moment. We turned, leaving the mountains behind, and headed southeast toward Biratnagar on the Ganges River plain near the Indian border.

From the airport in Biratnagar, we took a three-wheeled cab through broad, dusty streets that shimmered in the midday heat, to a small hotel set back from the road like an oasis among a stand of trees. Inside, it was cool and dim. Mr. Rai left me in the dining room and went off on some business of his own.

I drank a Coke for nausea and retreated to my room, where a filmy fall of mosquito netting hung from a circular rod near the ceiling, enclosing a metal-frame bed in the center of the room. I untied the netting and lay down. With the window shade closed, it was almost dark.

Outside, beyond the city, the vast agricultural plains of India stretched southward, a land of endless small farms and villages that somehow reminded me of Anna Kennedy. Evans' mother had never set foot in India, but had studied its philosophies and learned Sanskrit to translate its holy texts. Her spirit fitted with this ancient land, and I felt her presence. "Am I going like a pirate, Anna Kennedy? I'm surely a long way from home."

Later, feeling better, I took the indoor staircase to the flat roof, surrounded by treetops and furnished with chairs and tables for guests. Crowds of hawks, crows, pigeons, sparrows, and countless other birds I couldn't identify flew restlessly from branch to branch, twittering, screaming, and calling in the heat and brightness. When Mr. Rai came back, we had dinner, and then he left again to meet a business associate.

I studied mantras in my room, and then reached out of the netting to pull the long string on the overhead light, and quickly drew in my arm and curled up. The room was dim. White curtains floated in the open window. A mosquito was trapped inside the net, and cruised, whining, past my ear.

It was still too hot, and my mind was churning. What would I do if Mr. Rai refused to tell Jebi his sister was dead? We'd come so far for the gupha. I was a rich American who wanted to be a shaman, and he was a can-do guide who lived by getting clients what they asked for. What if he and Jebi had cooked up some sort of phony initiation experience, and he insisted on going through with it because I was paying?

If I saw any black dwarves that turned into giants, as massans were supposed to do, I'd be sure to notice the direction of the light source, and remember that shadows grow and shrink. But I couldn't believe Mr. Rai would really try to fool me, or lie to Jebi about his sister's death — use him that way to make money.

I clapped my hands at random toward the whining. It paused, then resumed. Shamans must have many tricks. Jebi might well use trickery to test my courage. His teacher may have done the same to him. But he wouldn't find me lacking. I'd simply slip into my scientific, rational state of mind and tell myself there were no spirits. That should make them disappear!

In the morning, Mr. Rai and I took separate bicycle rickshaws to the bus station. Even at dawn it was hot, and Biratnagar was wide awake and bustling, shop fronts rolled up, street vendors out, handcarts of merchandise trundling through the broad, flat streets. People dressed less well here than in Kathmandu. More faded lungi skirts than beautiful saris, more men in dhotis than western suits, and many, like our drivers, in tattered shorts with no shirts at all.

My rickshaw man was young, with close-cropped hair. His well-defined muscles strained as his thin brown legs pumped the pedals. I felt conspicuous, riding at ease while he sweated — unfairly privileged and frightened of the strangeness. But mostly what I felt was sick. Silently, I recited Maile's healing mantra, gathering my attention to my belly button, and felt a shift inside, as the nausea lessened with each repetition.

At the station, we climbed aboard the bus at once, to claim front seats. It soon filled to capacity, and the driver started up with grinding gears. He drove fast on the paved one-lane road to Jappa, using his horn like a train whistle — as far as I could tell without effect — to warn off pedestrians, men, women and children, men with large bundles of raw cotton on their heads, cars, carts, bicycles, rickshaws, dogs, and herds of cows and sheep — swerving skillfully to avoid collision with oncoming trucks, bulls, and anything else too large, or deaf, or stubborn to get out of the way.

At every stop—and there were many in each of the closely-spaced towns along the way—he got out for a smoke. His assistant would jump into the driver's seat, gun the motor, add water, and check the fluid in a little container from which a hose ran down through a hole in the floor to somewhere underneath. Mr. Rai, tired and hung over, got out to smoke, and stayed away so long I feared we'd leave without him.

And at each stop, more people crammed aboard, crouching in the aisles, and perching atop a large hump in the floor beside the driver that housed the motor. Mr. Rai scooted toward me to make room for a little old woman on our narrow seat. The mood was friendly, those already aboard cooperating to help newcomers find places and arrange their baggage. Mine was the only white face in the crowd.

We sped along the straight, black road through flat, green countryside dotted with thatched-roof shelters. Children played right up to the edge of the pavement. Goats, driven by small boys with sticks, thronged the way, and lone cows and buffaloes ambled beside the road. Even so far from the city, an endless line of people walked the verges, carrying bundles and baskets. The driver chuckled and slowed as he steered around a pair of goats copulating in the middle of the highway.

Piles of white clouds massed to form a solid grey storm front, obscuring our view of the distant foothills. We passed through Jappa, a fair-sized town, and stopped on the outskirts. It was raining heavily by now, and Jebi, smiling hugely, ran to meet us with an open umbrella.

"Don't say anything about his didi," Mr. Rai whispered, as Jebi rushed us into a sort of restaurant open to the street. Brusquely, he ordered Jebi to fetch us food from a high counter in back. "You eat now," he said to me. "After we tell him his sister has died, everyone will be upset. Most likely, they will forget all about food."

Jebi came back with several bowls and glasses, and set them on the long table of rough boards that ran the entire length of the restaurant. Trying to make contact with him, I asked, "Are you happy to be home?"

But he was focused on Mr. Rai. "What is happening with my sister?"

"I haven't heard." Mr. Rai rearranged the food—two small bowls of garbanzo beans, a glass of milk for me, and a sort of crunchy fried dough snack. Behind the high counter, half hidden by a partially-drawn curtain, a woman at a dresser painted her toenails. I spooned a few beans into my mouth, disliking their dry, grainy taste, and inwardly cringed at Mr. Rai's lie. No doubt Jebi expected Mr. Rai to tell him what he wanted to hear instead of truth. That's how they did things here. But clearly he suspected there was something wrong.

The woman behind the curtain finished her toenails and began to brush her daughter's long black hair. Urged by his mother, a boy of about ten at the next table struck up a conversation, asking in careful school English, "What are you doing here?"

"We are visiting Jebi Bhandari," Mr. Rai told him.

The mother beamed with pride at her son's success with English, and remarked in Nepali, "I know Jebi's wife."

As I looked into her warm, brown face and took in her words, my perception shifted. I'd been aware of people around us, but now they took on solid reality—a square-built man in a coarse, faded shirt, with his heavy wife and three polite children, on the far side of the restaurant, a man with a long, worried face behind the counter, the woman and girl in back, three boys loitering outside—real and distinct, their separate identities coalescing like raindrops from a mist. The diffuse anxiousness of floating unanchored in a crowd of nameless strangers gave way abruptly to a physical sense of coming to ground among a large and peaceful family.

We settled into the back seat of the taxi Jebi found, an old Land Rover. It seemed the driver had lost his key. A small crowd gathered to help and advise. They unpacked our luggage from the back, put it back, and then pulled it out on the ground once more, to no avail. The key was nowhere to be found. The driver raised the hood, and amid a great deal of loud talk and pointing, managed to connect two wires. The motor coughed into life, and we set off under clearing skies, taking a dirt road north through a crowded green landscape toward a range of low hills in the distance. "Go slow," Jebi cautioned the driver. "The road is no good." The hills were still far ahead when we reached his home.

Jebi's sister-in-law, round-faced and smiling, shorter and stouter than his wife, showed me to an upstairs room in her substantial house where I could leave my bags, and then led me out back to Jebi's home, a thatched hut on stilts. We climbed an outdoor ladder to a large room floored with rough planks where Mr. Rai was talking to Jebi and his sons. Through the cracks in the floor we could see down fifteen or twenty feet to a lawn of green, fine-bladed grass.

Jebi's pretty wife, in a sari blouse and lungi, her fine, straight hair drawn back to reveal classic features, invited us to sit on the edge of a bed and brought chia. A pleasant, rain-washed breeze stirred the coconut palm fronds growing at eye level beyond the broad windows.

Beyond the main room of Jebi's aerial hut were two smaller rooms used for sleeping. A broad, shaded balcony surrounded the whole structure. I became aware of a steady pounding, like a distant heartbeat coming from the north, across a field and nearby stream.

"Jebi, sit down," Mr. Rai said. Jebi turned a chair sideways from the table to face us, and strained forward, his hands clasped between his knees. He fixed his eyes on Mr. Rai's face.

"I am sorry to tell you, Jebi, your sister has died in Kathmandu. We found out—."

"*Didi?* Didi died?" He rolled his eyes, sobbed out loud, and covered his face with his hands. He dropped his head, and half moaning, half howling, rubbed his eyes and forehead with obsessive violence on his arm. No one came to comfort him, not even his wife. She set a cup of chia on the table and retreated, and then after a few minutes, brought a towel for his tears. Mr. Rai followed her out to the balcony where the relatives had gathered.

I knew that public displays of physical affection between sexes were considered improper, but I felt so bad for Jebi, watching him sob and shake all by himself, I finally stood and hugged him. He grabbed my waist like a drowning child, pressed his head against my breast, and sobbed.

I patted his back and let him cry until Mr. Rai came back. Then he sat up and wiped his face. Suddenly, with a wild look, he struck his forehead with his fist and said in English, "No good man. Program no."

"It's okay," I reassured.

He struck himself again. "No good man." He put his hand on his heart, and said in Nepali, "My heart is broken. It hurts."

His brother-in-law shouted up from the lawn outside, and everyone but Jebi left. He began to cry again, holding onto my waist, groaning and repeating, "My didi, my didi." I didn't know what to do. Finally, Mr. Rai called us to join the others on the porch of the main house, where a group of fifteen or twenty people had gathered.

At the bottom of the ladder, I asked Jebi where the toilet was, and he showed me a wooden structure about a hundred yards north, built on boards across the narrow stream that flowed, shallow and straight, through an artificial ditch cut into the grass of the flat meadow. He rushed off to fill a grubby orange plastic bucket with fresh water to use in lieu of toilet paper.

꙳

Mr. Rai recruited me and my camera to take pictures of Jebi's stilt house while the light lasted. "Take from all four sides," he said. "I had no idea Jebi has to live in such a poor place. I will ask his students to give money to build him a proper house."

"How much would he need for a new house?"

"About twenty-five hundred dollars." Mr. Rai pulled his lips down over his teeth. "It can be done."

"They should start with a proper outhouse," I remarked. "This one is a terrible health hazard, with the waste going right into the stream."

As I walked around the hut taking pictures, I couldn't help wondering what Mr. Rai thought was wrong with it. Large and airy, surrounded by lovely green countryside, it was much more pleasant than Maile's single room in the dirty city.

Jebi climbed back up the ladder to his home, and stayed there for a long time, sobbing and calling for his didi.

Mr. Rai drank rakshi on the porch of the main house with a group of local men, talking about another Mohan Rai who lived nearby and was married to Jebi's wife's sister. Several of the men spoke English, including a schoolteacher who promised to translate any letters I wanted to send to Jebi. They were all drunk. "Remember us, and the name of our village, *Buddhabari*—means Wednesday," the schoolteacher said. "Because we are your brothers, and you are our sister, you must not forget."

Then Jebi appeared, and dragged me off to the room where I'd left my bags. Noticing my purse on the floor where I'd dropped it, he grabbed it and said "money" in English, stuffing it out of sight behind the bed. He tugged me down beside him, sobbing, and hugging me, and kissing my face like a child as he called me ama.

Mr. Rai followed with Jebi's wife, who sank down on the bed on my other side. She leaned into me and began to cry. I took her hand and held it, as Mr. Rai scolded Jebi, calling him "black," and saying, "Be a man." But Jebi only sobbed louder, refusing to look up as Mr. Rai berated him, "Don't you see you are making your wife cry?"

At that, Jebi's wife let out a cry, laid her head on my shoulder, and said that now that Didi was gone, I would be her elder sister. She fell across my lap and sobbed.

Suddenly, like a jealous child, Jebi pushed her off.

"No, no, no," I said. "My two good people." I put an arm around each, wishing I knew more Nepali words of comfort.

Mr. Rai yelled at Jebi, and suggested I take a walk outside so that

Jebi and his wife could get themselves together. I left, but Jebi followed, holding tightly to my hand.

"I am going to walk," I told him. "You must go back to your wife."

He refused to let go, and steered me north along the road toward the foothills. It was late afternoon, and the green of the fields was intense.

"How beautiful," I said.

As we walked, the steady heartbeat sound I'd noticed earlier grew louder, until I saw that it came from a large wooden building beside the road. "It is a mustard mill," Jebi said, and took me inside. On the right was a sort of large funnel for husking, and on the left, a long wooden arm with a great mallet-like end going up and down against a stone, making the loud, steady pounding noise as it crushed oil from mustard seed. The yellow-brown oil ran down through a square wooden trough, and was collected in plastic containers. Jebi dipped his finger in and wiped it on my hand. He was still a little drunk.

The fields were lit with magical green-gold light, and inside the dim interior of the mill, long rays of sunlight lit up dancing motes of dust, as the great wooden arm kept up its steady pounding. The moment glowed numinous—Jebi, my guru, showing me the heartbeat of the world.

We walked slowly back, but Mr. Rai, waiting by the roadside, waved us on. No doubt the family was upset by Jebi's behavior, and he wanted to save Jebi, in his fragile condition, from being scolded. But maybe it was my behavior that angered them. I felt I shouldn't have come.

It was nearly dark. We passed a large school building with a football field, and a series of houses set far back on beautiful green lawns. Jebi stopped and began to call for Saile, a word that means third daughter. It was what everyone called his wife's younger sister. He pulled me toward the house, balancing on stones across a small ditch of running water. His sister-in-law came out and led us upstairs into a main room in her house, and introduced me to her husband, the other Mohan Rai, and several teenage children. She lit a few candles as it rapidly grew dark, and offered us beans and rakshi.

I still felt ill and declined, but Jebi took the rakshi. "I cannot eat," he said. "My sister has died. I will have to be in mourning for thirteen days and eat only after sundown—boiled potatoes I cook by myself, and no salt, only a little ginger. One meal a day." He began to cry again in front of them all, hugging me and calling me ama. I didn't try to stop him; I couldn't be that cruel. Saile's husband said something sharp, but Jebi argued back, so belligerent the other man backed down.

Suddenly Jebi jumped up, dragged me to a door made of grey-green vertical boards at the top of the stairs, and loudly demanded the family open it. His brother-in-law put a hand on his arm and tried to reason with him, but Jebi shook him off and pulled at the door. More concerned with calming Jebi than anything else, the man swung the door open. I saw inside. It was a long, narrow room, in which I could make out a tripod of bricks about two-thirds of the way toward the back of a dusty board floor. "Rai mudhum," Jebi said.

Appalled, I realized that this was their chula, in their sacred mangchhamma room, home of their ancestral gods. A non-Rai like me shouldn't even be allowed to look. The family must be horribly offended. I placed my hands together and bowed toward the chula, at least to make a show of respect. "I honor your ancestors," I said.

"She is my shaman student," Jebi told them.

I hoped that made it seem all right. "We should go now," I said, and moved toward the stairway.

Jebi was drunker than before, and as we crossed the ditch, his feet slid off the stones and he splashed through the stream.

The air was thick with glowing fireflies, a matrix of tiny lights no more than a few feet apart, ten to twenty feet high, filling the fields as far as we could see, blinking slowly on and off. The road itself was relatively clear of the lights because of the many people walking there, but denser bands of fireflies flanked its sides.

"This is beautiful," I exclaimed.

Jebi concentrated on walking, and as we passed the school and football field, he pointed toward a group of houses on the left and said, "Bokshi." Apparently a witch lived there.

"No bokshi," I said, like a Western parent to a child.

"Bokshi," he insisted, spitting repeatedly.

I wondered what my friends back home would say if they could see me with this childish, drunk man, who spat on the road and wept—my guru. But nobody ever said shamans had to be wise or holy. They were just people who knew how to contact spirits. In fact, it was probably Jebi's hypersensitive emotions that gave him his talent. Maybe I, too, should be fostering my hysterical tendencies instead of trying to suppress them.

Two young men came up behind us, conversing as they walked. Jebi swung around, ready to fight. "Who are you?" he challenged. They said something soothing and sped up to pass. We walked on.

When we got home, Jebi's whole family, including his wife, were sitting calmly on the porch of the main house. No one seemed at all upset.

I was relieved. I knew I should have put a stop to Jebi's displays of affection right away. Compassion had caused me to violate a social taboo I'd never been programmed to observe, but that was no excuse. What if Jebi had been breaking one of my own taboos? If he'd been taking off his clothes or offering me boogers from his nose to eat, I would have pushed him away, no matter how sorry I felt for him, even if I knew he was only doing it to ease his pain.

Jebi spat again as we climbed the steps to the porch, and Mr. Rai scolded, "In civilized parts of the world, it is not proper to spit."

Jebi's wife and sister-in-law tried to feed me—chicken, rice and dhal, a cup of rakshi, and a small bowl of *kirbhat,* rice cooked in milk with a little sugar. I tried to eat. The kirbhat was good, but I couldn't get much down. "I am a little sick," I said, hoping they wouldn't feel rejected. "Please excuse me."

I went straight to bed, but once there, my eyes refused to close. Thousands of crickets shrilled, and little animals, squirrels, rats—I didn't know what—scampered across the metal roof no more than three feet above my bed. I'd told Jebi that witches didn't exist, but if I really believed that, then why was I here? I could be logical and scientific, and say that witches were only poor, sad women in search of revenge against those who spurned them, but I could have said that at home.

I curled up, skirting an edge of fear at my dawning understanding. We can't always be in a logical, scientific state. We have to sleep sometimes, or we're sick, or low on energy, and passive to forces around us. A mosquito whined; I covered my ears with my hands. Jebi and Maile didn't spend much time being logical. They fully believed in spirits, witches, capricious deities, and planetary influences. The only way they knew to feel safe was to "bind" these threatening forces with mantras and rituals.

The crickets ceased all at once, as though on cue. A moment passed; my thoughts stopped too, suspended in eerie silence as the world held its breath. Then the crickets started up again, a grainy, impersonal, high-pitched backdrop for the night. If spirits really existed—and how could I say they didn't when I'd personally experienced that little man all made of heat waves standing by my bed—then they had to be taken into account. Because they really can affect us. If I wanted to deal with spirits, I'd have to admit they were real, learn to be receptive, use mantras instead of denials for protection. I whispered Maile's mantra into the darkness and blew it on my chest.

Later in the night, I woke to total silence. It was dark, and the crickets had stopped. Then I heard Jebi's voice from the yard, sobbing and calling for his didi. His wife was with him, making soothing sounds, urging him to be quiet, and gently scolding as they circled the house. After a while, Mr. Rai's voice joined in, and finally all was still.

In the morning, Jebi's face was puffed and raw from crying and drinking all night. He brought a basin of hot water and set it on an outdoor table so I could wash my face. I carried the water upstairs to the room I'd slept in, looking for privacy to wash my body and change clothes, but it was full of people who showed no sign of leaving. I left the water by the door, closed my suitcase, and took it downstairs.

"Primitive conditions," Mr. Rai said. He hadn't been able to wash either.

Jebi, under control for the moment, shook hands goodbye. "Sorry, program no," he said. His wife extended both hands, and I squeezed them and thanked her.

On the bus back to Biratnagar, we passed two little girls, three or four years old, squatting by the roadside with their little weewees facing traffic, talking and laughing as their backsides squirted soft yellow mounds. I felt grubby; everything was dirty, sticky. No one cleaned up; they left all that to the lowly sweeper caste, and if no one from that caste was on hand, oh well.

Mr. Rai bribed the pilot for seats to Kathmandu. While we waited, he bought a Star beer for me and whiskey and water for himself. "I am sorry for you not seeing massan," he said. "Maybe can arrange near to home."

"It's okay," I said. "At least I got to see more of the country."

"I knew you would not mind," he said. "Only God can say when someone will die. We must accept." He held his cigarette close to his face and watched me shrewdly through the smoke. "You know," he said, "there are many kinds of healer. For example, *homay* doesn't shake himself. Just heals with mantras." People were massing up by one of the boarding gates, and Mr. Rai looked up. "We has to hurry. Flight leaving now."

I followed him up the steep metal steps to the plane, feeling sad. My time here was drawing to a close and he was already thinking up ways to let me save face if I failed to shake and couldn't become a shaman.

An American five dollar bill had to pass from Mr. Rai to the pilot before we could board. The flight had been sold out. Mr. Rai rode in a jump seat in the pilot's cabin, and I sat next to a middle-aged Welsh woman, a textile designer who worked with mountain Rais on a British-funded project making Harris Tweed from nettles. "We don't use dyes," she said, "because of the boiling."

"Boiling uses too much firewood," her companion explained from across the aisle.

The Welsh woman told me a third member of their group had been bumped from the flight to make room for a man who was supposed to be sick. "That is the man they said was sick," she loudly announced, indicating a dark-skinned man in the seat beside her companion. He was wearing a traditional Nepali cloth hat, printed with pink and black trapezoids, and creased to form a long ridge running front to back. He stared out the window as though he hadn't heard. "He's not sick!" she said. I felt proud of her for asserting her British sense of fairness, and hoped she wouldn't find out Mr. Rai had bought our seats.

We talked to more Britishers in the Kathmandu airport—a tall, elderly man, slightly stooped, who looked like an ambassador, and his cordial wife. His face was kind, but her tone clearly let us know our place—somewhere far below hers. I told her I was here to learn to be a shaman.

"How do shamans get their powers?" she asked with feigned interest. I could almost read the labels on the file drawers in her mind, "native superstitions," "primitive herbal remedies," "anthropologists," "dangerous cults," "pathetic hippies."

"From God," I said, and her eyes involuntarily widened, but only for an instant.

If I'd said Shiva or Kali, she could have sorted me quickly into "native superstitions," but this answer confused her—a white face speaking good English, invoking her own deity. She recovered at once, blinked and smiled. "I do wish you the best of luck." She pressed my hand and shunted me off to file drawer labeled "religious nut."

NOTHING EVER GOES AS PLANNED

Back in Kathmandu, Bindu said that Maile and her family had moved while we were gone—to a larger room in the same house. I decided to pay my guru a visit.

She showed me how she'd arranged their things in the spacious, freshly-painted room—bed in one corner, drum on the wall, Mr. Lama's cloth-wrapped books, and his *thankas*— intricate Buddhist paintings on cloth—rolled up on a shelf. As in her old room, one corner served as a kitchen, with the kerosene stove, several pots, a thermos, and a large enamel basin for washing greens and dishes. Most of the family's clothing had been laid out on a shelf, though there was also a small bureau.

"I can't give you tea because of my monthly," she said, inviting me to sit. "On my monthly, I cannot cook or touch sacred things, or perform healings or teach."

Jebi, still in mourning, couldn't teach either. Instead, over the next few days, he and I took many walks, visiting his relatives. At his cousin's house, a baby was screaming with colic. The mother said it was because she'd eaten hot peppers and they'd gotten into her milk. She handed the wailing child to Jebi and, evidently forgetting he wasn't supposed to do healings during the mourning period, he soothed it with a mantra. Then he proudly introduced me as his student.

"Does she shake?" the baby's mother asked.

"Yes," he said.

I didn't correct him.

Another day, Jebi took me to visit his nephews, Didi's sons. The walls of their tenement were hung with colorful god posters depicting Shiva, Vishnu, Parvati, Kali, and Laxmi. In a place of honor on a bureau, framed in brass, was a photograph of Sai Baba, a dark-skinned man in a long orange robe with Negroid features and a big globe of bushy black hair. They said he was an avatar of Vishnu, as Rama had been, and could perform miracles, materializing sacred ash, gold rings, and jewels, and appearing in several places at once.

Outside in the courtyard, Didi's sons were performing a ritual of mourning. A small mound of dirt had been heaped up in one corner, and the brothers were cooking a pot of rice on a triangle of bricks, using a fire of special wood. When the rice was soft and sticky, they rolled it into little balls, which they placed on a large leaf tray. Other leaves had been formed into bowls and filled with milk, water, mustard seeds, and white flour.

Didi's sons, dressed in white rags and shaved bald, took turns bending over an outdoor spigot, splashing water over their faces and smoothly-shaved, dark, shining heads, washing themselves nine times. A Brahmin priest droned mantras from a book, which was actually a thick stack of separate pages wrapped in a silken cover. He turned the pages one by one as the eldest son made offerings from the leaf saucers. The ritual dragged on and on, until even the gods must have been out of their minds with boredom. They'd been at it nine days already, with three more days to go. At the end of the ceremony, Jebi said, the eldest son would ram his head into the mound of dirt to break it up.

The next day, when we returned, the rituals were still going on. The hired Brahmin priest sat on a patch of bare ground surrounded by little bowls of foods, drinks, and flowers, reading aloud and mechanically making offerings from the bowls. In payment for his services, the family had to give him a mattress, pots and pans, blankets, foods, baskets, woven mats, and other household goods; but for their lunch, they cooked only rice, for they had no money left for dhal. Jebi told me Mr. Rai hadn't yet paid him for teaching.

"Has he paid Maile or Mr. Ganesh?"

"No," he said.

❧

Finally Jebi announced, "The thirteen days of mourning are over. I can teach again." He bragged to Mr. Rai, "I will make her shake, I guarantee." He was drunk, but I couldn't help feeling hopeful.

He said something else in rapid Nepali, and Mr. Rai answered sharply. I left them, crossed the garden as usual, shivering in the chill, and picked three shishnu leaves.

"Does it burn?" Jebi asked, as I laid them on the coffee table.

"A little."

He made no comment, neither joke nor reassurance. I couldn't help reading judgment in his silence.

Mr. Rai came out from one of the bedrooms in a brown leather jacket and Canadian lumberjack hat with sheepskin flaps. "I go to office now," he said. "Program tonight."

Jebi didn't look up.

Mr. Ganesh arrived then, crossed his legs and announced, "Now, Jebi will explain about the ceremonies they do in his village." But Jebi had followed Mr. Rai outside. "Uh, he is talking to Mr. Rai, of course. Yes. Uh, Ellen, did I ever tell you about the time I found the young American runaway named Gina for her parents?" He leaned back with an air of well-earned enjoyment, and sipped his sweetened tea.

"Yes, you did, Mr. Ganesh."

Jebi came back, and went straight to the kitchen.

"Her name was Gina. You see, she had come to Kathmandu and met the wrong kind of people. Drugs, you know, of course..."

"Yes, you told me that story, Mr. Ganesh. Here's Jebi now."

Jebi had fortified himself with rakshi and his eyes shone white like a blind man's.

"You see, in the village, they have many ceremonies. Jebi—."

Jebi answered Mr. Ganesh's questions in his deep, calm voice, looking up occasionally, but failing to connect with either of us. The friend with whom I'd walked all over the city, the grief-stricken, childlike man who'd needed my comfort, even the drunken shaman who'd recklessly promised to make me shake, had disappeared.

"There are yogis, *saddhus*, you know." Mr. Ganesh said pedantically. "Holy men. They go around the villages in the nighttime, circling the houses and blowing on the horn of an extinct animal, reciting the mantra for massan, to protect the people, you see. The next morning, they come back, and the people in the houses give them food. They have big black coats with pockets sewn on the inside to keep the food they're given. One pocket for millet, one for butter, one for rice..."

I began to fidget. Mr. Ganesh spoke with Jebi. "There is a devi, a goddess, you know," he resumed.

I know, I wanted to protest. I knew what a devi was before I came here, and you tell me every time you say the word. He droned on about the devi causing itches, and the offerings required to cure them.

When I could stand it no longer, I said, "Mister Ganesh, this is interesting, but I'm not an anthropologist. I want to learn about shamanism, not religion. Can Jebi teach me something shamans do?"

"Of course, about the shaman*isms*. Jebi—?" They had a lengthy conversation.

"This is about the shaking persons. The person starts to shake, maybe a bokshi is making him shake, a witch, you know of course, or a ghost, or the bad spirits. They call Jebi. Jebi tells the shaking person, 'I've given all the offering you wanted. What else do you need?' The person shaking will have to stop eating contaminated food—should bathe every morning properly, and twice a year give a she-goat offering. He also has to cook his own food and fetch his own water. This is called *swayampoke*, means own cooker."

"Jebi was working with a shaking man here a few weeks ago," I said, not caring if I sounded rude. "He didn't say anything about offering a goat or cooking his own food."

"Yes, of course, it depends on what is causing the person to shake."

"But is that what Jebi said just now?"

They had another long conversation.

"Jebi wants to tell you another story," Mr. Ganesh began afresh, ignoring the hanging question. "Dimal is a tribe that has a *Garampuja* ceremony. *Garam* means hot..." Jebi got up and went out.

I sighed. If the ceremonies Mr. Ganesh was describing were anything like the funeral rituals for Jebi's sister, I could imagine how boring they must be. I pulled my legs up under me, sighed again, and doodled faces with pointed chins and ears and long pointed tongues sticking out from between twisted lips.

Jebi came back. "He's ready to join us now again. I will ask about the shaman*isms*."

I smelled food cooking for our lunch. Maybe later, Jebi and I could go for a walk. But Thuli Kumari came in with only two plates, fried noodles with vegetables and bits of egg for me and the translator, and Jebi left. As we ate, Mr. Ganesh entertained me with the story of Gina and her grateful parents.

❦

That evening, Jebi set up a fresh altar. He didn't ask me to help. A well-dressed Newari couple arrived, the wife a short, broad-faced, small-featured woman with round dark eyes that shone like beads, the husband taller, with a heavy nose, soft, long-lashed eyes, and a reluctant, long-suffering air. Jebi dressed up in his costume and drummed until the woman shook. He watched her with a cool, assessing look. "Who are you?" he asked in a conversational tone. She shook more violently, head down, refusing to speak.

He called for Thuli Kumari to bring him a red-hot spoon, drumming lightly as he waited. After a few minutes, as the patient continued to shake, he roughly lifted the back of her shirt, handed me a bunch of shishnu leaves, and told me to say the shishnu mantra and pretend to beat her. I waved the leaves at her bare back as I'd seen him do, careful not to touch her skin—not failing to notice that, miraculously, my own hands weren't burned. Kumari came in with a large metal spoon, glowing red. Jebi brandished it at the shaking woman, threatening to burn the spirit within her.

She gasped and "broke her speech," calling for incense.

"A deity has come on her," Jebi said, "not a witch."

The woman said, "I am Hartimati, protector of children," and then began to shout angrily at her husband.

Mr. Rai explained that several years earlier, the woman had asked her husband to make an offering to Hartimati, and he had refused, joking that he would give the goddess old shoes instead, and incense of burning tires. Now, through his wife, the goddess screamed her righteous anger, demanding apology.

As she vented her rage, the woman's shaking died away, and when she was calm, she turned her face aside with a sneaky look. Jebi said something friendly and she raised her head and smiled, clear-eyed and fresh.

Perhaps I'd only imagined the sneaky look.

Jebi pulled off his headdress, finished for the evening. I was disappointed he hadn't called me to his altar to make me shake, but knew I hadn't even been close. He probably knew it too.

❦

Feeling reckless the next morning, I picked a large bunch of shishnu, ten leaves or more. Blisters came up quickly.

"Tomorrow, pick only three," Jebi said without much interest.

"What do you want to teach today?" Mr. Ganesh asked him, with an aside in English that he would ask about the "shamanisms."

"He will teach about Rajbangshe. Rajbangshe is a tribe of dark-skinned people..." I tuned him out. If I'd been shaking by now, I might be learning something real.

Mr. Rai arrived, and I closed my notebook with a bang, and gave him a meaningful look. He set his hat on a chair and raked his fingers upward, making the hair on the back of his head stick out like short feathers. Mr. Ganesh kept talking, waving his pointing finger. "I'll be with you in a moment," Mr. Rai said, and went to the kitchen to find Jebi.

I heard Jebi shouting—about money, I thought—and Mr. Rai answered, "You have not yet made your student shake."

Jebi emerged from the kitchen, stuffing a folded hundred rupee note toward his pocket, missing, and finally succeeding on the third try. "I am working for you all these months. It's not my fault. I deserve to be paid," he said.

"Don't shout," Mr. Rai shouted. "I will pay you when I get the money."

"You should be the one shaking," Jebi accused. "You are the one standing in the way. It is *you* who has broken your promises to the gods. Maile says so too."

Mr. Rai drew back. "Jebi is very drunk," he said to me.

Next morning, I picked three harmless-looking shishnu leaves and let them sting me. Afterwards, Jebi tried to teach me the different drumming rhythms for traveling in each world. I couldn't get them right, and tape-recorded his drumming to practice later.

Then he opened a battered canvas satchel and talked about herbal medicines, holding up odd-shaped pieces of roots and bark, seeds and ground leaves—remedies for diarrhea and vomiting, headache, moch, malaria, fever, dysentery, broken bones, and for removing curses. I tried to memorize the way these botanical materials looked, but knew I'd never be able to find them in the wild without help.

After lunch, Jebi left, and I went back to my room. I flipped to the beginning of my journal, where I'd recorded a description of the old Rai woman's burial. Our names had been taken for an invitation to the ceremony to be held forty-five days later to send the dead woman's soul to its next abode, but we'd never heard of it again. As usual, nothing ever went as planned. If I left it to Mr. Rai, I'd waste the little time I had left listening to Mr. Ganesh tell stories. I wanted to see Maile.

DO-SI-RE

It was the first day of Dipawali, the Hindu festival of lights. Mr. Rai's house had been decorated with alternating splotches of red and yellow, forming a trail from the front door to his mangchhamma room. This was a pathway for Laxmi, goddess of riches, he explained, when she came to bring good fortune. Houses all over the neighborhood were strung with lights, and when darkness fell, oil lamps flickered in each doorway.

A group of children and teenagers gathered in front of the house, caroling, "*Do-si-re, do-si-re.*" Someone sang a solo, made up on the spot, which poked fun at people who lived here, and everyone laughed. Thuli Kumari took a large tray of loops of sweetened party bread outside, and passed them around to the singers.

Learning it was the custom to give gifts, I hurried out to a roadside stall and bought a large bottle of Johnny Walker for Mr. Rai and his family. He thanked me and opened it right away, pouring drinks for everyone, including the group of men who had gathered to play cards and gamble. Bindu declined, but Thuli Kumari drank with the men and got jolly. She brought out bowls of crispy puffed rice and mixed crackers for snacks. Jebi gambled with the other men. I drank too, but soon developed a headache and went home.

Next day, Jebi failed to show up. I studied mantras and walked in the neighborhood alone. The wandering cows had been decorated again, as during Dassein, with smears of red and yellow yoghurt on their foreheads and flanks, and flower malas on their necks.

Dipawali was a time for visiting relatives. Arriving at Mr. Rai's house while he was gone, I found Bindu cooing over a tiny baby in a soft pink blanket. Someone shouted from the courtyard in a wounded tone, "I know very well this is not my house. That's no way to talk." It was Mr. Lok, who lived in Mr. Rai's old house by the shishnu bush, the man for

whom Jebi had done the kama kim ceremony because he was lethargic
and had no job. He was yelling at a young woman.

"He is shouting at my daughter," Bindu said.

Santa Dev Rai, a serious young man, husky like an American,
who'd recently rented a room across the hall from me in Mr. Bharat's
house, explained that Mr. Rai's eldest daughter had run off with a boy
her father didn't approve of. The baby was hers. Mr. Rai had banned
her from the house, but learning he was away from home, she'd come
for a holiday visit to her mother. Mr. Lok had made the mistake of
challenging her.

"Don't ask me any questions," she retorted. "You have no right
to ask me anything—ten years living in this house, giving nothing in
return."

Santa Dev took the role of peacemaker. "Just leave her alone," he
counseled Mr. Lok. "She's upset. You can understand that. It isn't your
fault." Mr. Lok pouted. "All Rais are hot-tempered," Santa explained to
me in English. "I have to calm Mr. Lok down so he won't tell Mr. Rai
his daughter was here. Please don't say anything, or there will be big
trouble."

Out front, more carolers appeared, raucous young men chorusing,
"*Do-si-re, do-si-re, do-si-re,*" and shouting out improvised verses with
a great deal of boisterous laughter. The longer they sang, the more
insulting the verses became, until someone finally went out and gave
them money to go away.

Mr. Rai's daughter took her baby and left, and Mr. Rai came home
soon after. Kumari handed him a plate of rice and dhal.

I waited until he'd finished eating, and then said, "Mr. Rai, Jebi
doesn't have anything left to teach me, and Mr. Ganesh is driving me
crazy. I don't think his translations are good. All he does is tell those
stories of Hindu gods that he uses to entertain tourists when he takes
them around the city. Over and over and over. I want to work with
Maile."

"All right," Mr. Rai said easily. "I will tell Jebi to go home."

"No, no. I want to work with Jebi too. But I want him to teach me
something useful."

"Yes," he agreed. "Of course he can teach something useful. I will
see about it." He sat on the floor with two cronies, his secretary, whose
name was also Mohan, and the big policeman, to play a gambling game.
They were throwing cowries shells, betting on whether the shells would
land slit side up or down.

I watched in silence, thinking sarcastically, "Sure you'll see about it."

"By the way, *Allen*," Mr. Rai said, glancing up in time to catch my sour expression. "I meant to tell you. I saw a dream about little sister Keri last night. She was all in dirty clothes and with a dirty face. She told me, 'It snowing, this is how we like to play in snow,' and I ask, 'Where's mom?' 'Out to market for vegetables for Jebi,' she says." He laughed.

"I guess that means she needs her mother."

"I think, means she's okay."

His friends agreed. "If dirty clothes shows in dream, means person won't get sick," Mohan, the secretary, said. "If clean clothes, means they are sure to get sick."

"Since I have told dream, if it is bad, means it won't come true," Mr. Rai assured me. "If a good dream shows, we never tell, or it may lose power."

"I see." Again, they were saying only what they thought I wanted to hear, but dirty clothes mean neglect in any culture. Playing in the *snow* in dirty clothes! I turned and left, unable to bear my own bad mood. It was early, but I went to bed.

I woke to the sound of do-si-re singers racketing their way around the neighborhood, now with a flute and drum accompaniment. They stopped outside my window by Mr. Bharat's front door. I pulled the curtain and looked out. A crowd of twenty-five people, including Bindu, Thuli Kumari, Sani Kumari, Santa Dev, Mr. Rai's handsome sister and brother-in-law, even the old lady who lived in the back house with Mr. Lok, and Mr. Rai himself, were out there singing and dancing in the street. I pulled on my T-shirt and jeans and joined them, bad mood forgotten.

SHISHNU

That night I dreamed Jebi was struggling to open a door. Someone wrote "EXIT" backwards in the dirt with a stick. I woke up, groped for my journal, and wrote it down, planning to ask Jebi what it meant in the morning.

But Jebi never came—nor did Maile. The day was cold and drear. Late in the afternoon, tired of memorizing mantras, I went for a walk. My mood was too heavy for greeting shopkeepers and smiling at children, and I thought if I walked through the Tunal Devi temple, I wouldn't have to pass the shops. But finding no coins in my pockets to offer at the shrine, I skirted the temple grounds, feeling paranoid, though no one laughed or pointed. The American lady had become an ordinary enough sight on these paths after all—the one who was trying to be a shaman, but couldn't.

The way slanted upward, past an open field, and joined a larger road beside a high brick wall and a market area, and then branched off sharply downhill to the left. Further on, to the right, it fed into a paved road. The sun appeared beneath the edge of a cloudbank, and I turned back at the top of the hill, wanting to be by the temple when it reached the horizon, the magic time when Maile said Banjhankri traveled the world to check on his people. I picked a blue flower from a hedge and waited on the bank of a little stream beside the temple grounds.

"Help me, Banjhankri," I prayed as the sun went down, throwing petals in the water and watching them float through a weed-choked turning and catch in soggy mounds of trash. A shawl-wrapped woman with a baby watched impassively from the end of a concrete platform a hundred yards away. She isn't judging me, I told myself. She's here because she's nowhere else. If she finds herself here, why should she blame me for finding myself here too?

The sun was gone. I headed home, relieved that for once my landlady, Mrs. Bharat, wasn't out on the front step with her spinning wheel, and I wouldn't have to greet her. The bathroom hadn't been cleaned. It stank of urine. I switched on the light and leaned toward the mirror, examining the fine lines on my face, the permanent sunburn damage on my neck, a red that never went away, my pale blue eyes under too-light lashes, their small pupils ringed with jagged lines of yellow, staring back with unwelcome consciousness.

My period had started. No more memorizing mantras and trying to shake. In a way, I was glad.

✧

Next day, Mr. Rai asked me to come to his office and help write a letter to the German bankruptcy court, though he said it was probably useless. He didn't think he'd ever get his money back. "It is very bad, *Allen*. But I am continue to work hard and keep going. After all, I have got these twenty-nine peoples depending on *me*."

He ordered an office assistant to make tea, and I set the sugary mixture beside an old manual typewriter and pounded away. The phone rang. Mr. Rai took it in his office.

"I have learned Vhim Rai is in Kathmandu," he announced as he signed my letter and folded it into a thin airmail envelope edged with blue and red stripes. "He has telephoned and asked permission for you going with him to Dengmaya. You doesn't need my permissions. Why not you go?"

"Vhim? In Kathmandu?" I couldn't help beaming.

Vhim met us at the Sun Kosi Café for lunch, gave me a big hug, and called me Didi. "She is my sister," he explained to Mr. Rai. "Just like a family member."

The two Rais ordered pork. I settled for a vegetable dish, and Mr. Rai made sure it wouldn't include garlic. Vhim was excited about the medical clinic he planned to bring to his home village of Dengmaya, and described it with enthusiasm, meanwhile sorting through his food, as though examining it for stones. Three doctors, his classmates from St. Xavier's High School, where they'd studied under Father Miller, had agreed to run the clinic, and Vhim was arranging flights to Tumlingtar, the mountain town from which the group would continue on foot to Dengmaya. "Please, *Dai*," he asked Mr. Rai, calling him Elder Brother out of respect, "could you spare one sleeping bag for our trip? I promise to return it in good condition."

"Of course," Mr. Rai said. "But it is very hard to get air flights. I can arrange for you. In fact, I can arrange all equipments, foods, porters, everything, and you will save money."

"Luckily, I have a pilot friend," Vhim told him. "And I am all set for food and equipment. I've bought the food, but I'd like to leave it in your storeroom a few days until we leave, if you don't mind."

Mr. Rai puffed away at his cigarette, an unaccustomed tension pulling at his mouth. "I don't mind. No problem," he said. "I hope everything works out. But if not, Younger Brother, remember, I am always here to help."

ॐ

The next day Mr. Rai came to my room in Mr. Bharat's house and led me upstairs to an office where Mr. Bharat had spread out several newly-printed catalogs of merchandise for his import business. "Why not you order Christmas presents for friends and family," Mr. Rai suggested.

I looked at the prices. "I don't know if I can afford them."

"These are very much bargains," Mr. Rai urged. "You can order now and pay when you are home in America."

I chose a number of metal idols and several woolen shawls, but in the end Mr. Bharat said there was no way he could ship them before Christmas.

"Never mind," Mr. Rai said. "We will find good things here in stores."

He seemed subdued. When I remarked that I hoped Maile would come back soon to teach, he assured me she would, then shook his head and said with unaccustomed candor, "I know I may be a bad person for ignore my family spirits. They will find a way to punish. I know this from long time."

ॐ

But when I was finished with my monthly "personal problem," Jebi was the one who came to teach. I finally told him about the dream I'd had of someone writing "EXIT" backward in the dirt, and he said to add it to the end of the shishnu mantra. Now that there were five words in the mantra, I should repeat it five times forward and backward.

I went outside to try. A band of low clouds lay against the mountains ringing the city, but the sun was well up, and the day would be warm. The vigorous shishnu bush stood at attention like a well-armed soldier guarding its corner of the garden. I decided on my own to add "OM" to the beginning of the mantra and repeat it and blow six times. I approached the bush in a workmanlike manner, ready to endure whatever stings it would mete out. I stroked the thorns forward, barely grazing them, repeated the mantra, and picked a bunch of five leaves—and didn't get stung! I carried the leaves inside and laid them on the table.

"Did it burn?" Jebi asked.

"No, it did not." I smiled with pride.

"Well done," he said, happily surprised.

I continued to handle the leaves, turning them over in my hands, enjoying my new insensitivity to their poison, and then set them on the rug.

Jebi left the room, and when he came back, asked, "Can you touch them now?"

"Why not?" I reached for the leaves, and then jerked my hand back as they stung.

Jebi laughed and laughed and said that while he was out of the room, he'd done a backward mantra on them to take away the effect of my mantra. I laughed with him, pinching my fingers against the pain, happy that my mantra had worked when I picked them, but even happier because his backward mantra, undoing my mantra, was proof it had been my mantra and nothing else that had taken away the sting in the first place. This was more like it. Things were starting to move. My trip here wouldn't be totally in vain.

A few days later was Bhaitika, the holiday when sisters bless their brothers in return for gifts and money. After the rest of the family finished their rituals, Mr. Rai called me to the center of the room where the sisters of the family had been applying tikas to their kneeling brothers' foreheads. Bindu handed me a tika plate furnished with red and yellow rice-yoghurt mixtures and heaps of marigold petals. "You must give me tika," Mr. Rai said. "You are now my little sister and I am your elder brother."

I placed a large spot of sticky red on his forehead, and called on Laxmi, goddess of riches, to bless him, as I'd heard the other women do, and then added a small yellow dot in the center of the red and sprinkled him with petals. He handed me a ten rupee note. "Thank you, Bhaihini."

I felt honored. He must have decided I wasn't totally hopeless.

The women placed walnuts on the threshold to represent the head of Yama Raj, King of the Dead, and crushed it with their heels to assure their brothers of long lives. Thuli Kumari poured me a glass of Iceberg beer, and I crowded onto the couch like one of the family, joining in the jokes and banter.

Jebi came in later, drunk and crying. He'd had a fight with his family. They wanted him to give them money, but he'd spent all he had on the Brahmin priest. He put his head down on his arms and wailed. "No sister to give me tika. Oh, Didi, why did you have to die and leave me?"

Mr. Rai lectured him like a child, saying we must be lion-hearted, not chicken-hearted in the face of death. "We all has to die. Cry only little bit. Worry about living, not deads."

Recovering himself, Jebi sat me down beside him at his altar, whistled mantras, and began to shake. He told me to drum along and recite all the mantras he'd taught me. After a while my insides shook, but nothing showed.

"Did you shake inside?" he asked.

I nodded, pleased he'd guessed.

Someone handed him a glass of whiskey, and another for me. I took it, joking in Nepali, "Like teacher, like student." Everyone laughed, especially me, with ill-controlled hysteria, and Mr. Rai grinned, his eyes strangely dark in the dim light of the oil lamp, his forehead crinkling like tissue.

That night I dreamed a mathematical formula:

$$\frac{D}{I} = M$$

I woke up, blinked to clear my eyes, and wrote it in my journal. As soon as I saw it written, I knew exactly what it meant: Deity D, divided by specific Intention I, equals Man M. The deity is power to do all things. An intention to do a specific single thing divides it, and forms a person for the doing.

It followed that:

$$\frac{D}{M} = I.$$

With Deity D, the power to do all things, above, and Man M petitioning from below, the result is Intention I, a portion of the deity's power. But whose intention was it, whose power? The man's or the god's? Or would there be a difference?

And further, I realized:

$$MI = D.$$

M times I, the person magnified by the intention, equals Deity D. A man pursuing an intention is, in fact, a deity.

I closed up my journal and lay back. The dream was a sign. I had the intention; it was a mathematical certainty that the deity must come.

"SOMETHING IS BLOCKING YOUR WAY"

Vhim showed up for our lunch date with a stylish-looking Frenchwoman named Thérèse. Tense and petite, she claimed to be a professional photographer. She was friendly enough—too friendly, I thought, watching her rub her bare arm over Vhim's. He was inviting her on the trek in return for taking pictures of his clinic.

"I am completely at loose ends here," she said. "I don't even have a place to stay." She shot him a meaningful look and riffled her short, blond hair. It fell back into perfect shape.

"You don't mind if she stays with you one night, do you, Ellen," Vhim asked, "since we'll be leaving in the morning." He moved his arm away.

She arrived in a taxi at dark. "No hot water, surely you are joking," she said, and didn't spend long in the bathroom. She spread her pad and sleeping bag beside my bed, and hefted a cast iron statue of Lord Shiva from the altar I'd arranged on my low bureau, announcing, "I too am on a spiritual path."

"I'm not sure if shamanism is a spiritual path, or just a set of techn—."

"I'm working off all my karma this lifetime. This will be my last time on earth." She set down the god, struck a match from the pack beside my little copper oil lamp, watched as it burned down to her fingers, and waved it out. "Unless, of course, I decide to come back as a bodhisattva to help others who are less evolved."

In the morning I packed my jeans, shirts, underwear, sleeping bag, foam pad, water bottle, filter, and the medicines Vhim had asked me to bring from America, mostly vitamins and aspirin. We piled our things on Mr. Rai's porch and I collected the sleeping bag Vhim was borrowing from Mr. Rai. "Let me show you the shishnu bush out back," I said, and led Thérèse through the garden.

The spikes stood out long and dangerous. As she watched, I whispered Jebi's mantra, blew, and gingerly picked off several leaves.

"You should first talk to the spirit of the plant," Thérèse advised, as

I bit the side of my finger to ease the blister forming there. "Tell it you are friendly and will try not to harm it." She extended a hand as though to touch the bush, but drew back.

"Just picking a few spare leaves," I pretended to address the plant. "No harm intended." I laughed, but she didn't get the joke.

We sat on our packs enjoying the sunshine, waiting for Vhim. I felt like a kid at the start of school vacation. Thuli Kumari was hanging out clothes on the clothesline, and I recognized three T-shirts of mine, and a pair of sweat pants. If Mr. Rai was making his wives do my laundry, his money problems must be more serious than I thought.

Vhim and his doctor friends, Prem and Ganesh, showed up in a taxi, and we loaded the gear and headed for the airport. There were five other members of Vhim's group, but he had sent them on ahead, on a roundabout route through the hills, to meet us in Dengmaya where the clinic would be held. Thérèse was outraged when she found her ticket to Tumlingtar was only standby and mine wasn't, but she needn't have worried. Vhim had old school friends among the pilots and we all got seats.

She and I shared a room at the hotel in Tumlingtar. I developed a tickle in my throat, and spent a long, restless night suppressing a cough, working my throat around to scratch it. Finally, I couldn't help coughing, and Thérèse heaved a great, long-suffering sigh and pulled the covers over her ears.

The next morning, two of Vhim's brothers and several cousins from Dengmaya arrived to carry our gear, and we got underway about midday, hiking up the broad, sandy beaches of the Arun River and crossing a long, hanging bridge, strung high between the rocky cliffs, and made of open ropework, with a walkway of widely-spaced planks. The river far below looked small and unreal—until I remembered that a fall would mean certain death.

On the other side, we stopped for tea, but not food, and then climbed steeply upward, away from the river.

Vhim walked with me, talking about his father, a former Gurkha captain, with drinking companions all over these hills. Thérèse, ahead of us, had been taking pictures, but now unscrewed her lens and snapped the case around her camera. "We should have started earlier," she said. We caught up and passed her, and Vhim pretended not to hear as she pointedly repeated herself, but his shoulders stiffened.

It was dark when we reached our stopping place for the night, the home of one of Vhim's aunties, an elderly Rai woman, thin and a little stooped, but smiling in genuine welcome. Her clothes were simple, but her large earrings and nostril ornament were real gold. She led us inside, inviting us to sit on the floor of the main room as she cooked.

This was true Himalayan life in a traditional Rai house without a chimney. The room soon filled with smoke, so that down near the floor was the best place to be. Vhim's auntie set a pot of water on the fire and began to chop up vegetables.

"I told her she must boil everything for a long time," Vhim said.

We hadn't eaten all day, but I knew if she used garlic, I'd have to go hungry. Jebi and Maile had both forbidden it. "Could you ask her to leave out the garlic—at least for my food?" I whispered to Vhim.

She peered through the smoke in my direction when he asked her, and began to laugh. Other family members came in from a side room, studied me with surprise, and laughed too. Vhim laughed with them. "They don't think a white-skinned person can be a shaman," he explained. "They think it can't be learned."

I smiled with stiff lips.

"But she will leave out the garlic." He put an arm around my shoulders.

Relatives and neighbors kept filtering in; and each new person had to be told about the crazy white lady who thought she could be a shaman. Then everyone laughed all over again. The joke was good for more than an hour. I kept smiling until the muscles of my mouth and cheeks were sore.

It took a long time to prepare the food. Finally, Vhim's auntie handed us tablespoons and plates heaped with more rice than any Westerner could eat, topped with potatoes, greens, and radishes.

When I passed Therèse her plate, the spoon fell on the floor, and she gave me a look that said that was no more than she'd expected.

"Take mine," I said. "I haven't used it."

The young men had mountain-sized portions of rice, as much as their plates could hold, piled high, and in no time at all, they had scooped every bit into their mouths with the fingers of their right hands.

The family kept on cracking jokes and laughing about the jhankri woman, so that it was actually a relief when Vhim and Therèse started fighting. Therèse had kept up a stream of critical remarks about Vhim's lack of organization, how we'd had to skip lunch, and hadn't eaten until after eight at night. "This trip was *very* poorly planned," she complained. "We are all hungry and tired. We should have had the porters carry food, or had real food for lunch at that tea stall."

"Why didn't you say you were hungry, then?" Vhim stood. "Come on, we'll discuss it outside."

She followed him out, and we could hear them arguing. It turned into a shouting match, and the two doctors got up to help. After a while, Thérèse came in with Ganesh, and they sat apart, quietly talking. Before long, she announced she was sorry. "I am hypoglycemic," she explained. "I get very...grouchy...when I don't eat." She accepted her plate of food from Ganesh and her hands shook as she ate.

Vhim came in with Prem, and Thérèse apologized, but I noticed Vhim didn't reciprocate.

After dinner, Vhim's brother, Desh, showed Thérèse and me to an outdoor wooden platform where we could lay out our sleeping bags. Thérèse hadn't said a word since dinner, and crawled into her bag at once.

I stayed up, talking to Prem on a knob of grass above the dusty pathway in front of the house. He was one of the few Rais to earn a scholarship to medical school in India. Now, he said, his dream was to study psychiatry in Britain, but he was newly married, and so much in love with his wife, Rita, that he couldn't bear to leave her.

Vhim wandered over, heard Rita's name, and began to tease. "He's always thinking of her. He comes up to me and says, 'Vhim...' I say 'What?' and he says, 'Ri-i-i ta.'" He drew the name out in a swoon, rolling his eyes like a lovelorn cow.

Prem laughed. "It's true."

Vhim ambled off, and Prem asked what had made me interested in shamanism. Under his gentle questioning, I heard myself saying things I'd never realized before. He was a natural psychiatrist.

"At one point in my life I thought I was the only sentient being in the world. I understood that nothing I saw or heard or felt could prove otherwise," I said.

Prem listened with total, non-threatening attention, his eyes fixed on my face.

"In fact, I never really got over it. I just decided to act like everybody else—"as if" I wasn't alone in the universe. Otherwise, I couldn't function. But you know, I still do think there's only one consciousness. I guess I just confused the big consciousness with my own little piece of it," I concluded, surprised at my own words.

Prem nodded, letting me talk.

"I still don't have a clue how it works. I guess shamanism is a way of trying to find out."

"The mystic intuition," he said. "Things we can't prove, but still believe."

"Believe! I wish I could. How *can* people believe without evidence?"

"Most do." He poked at the dust of the pathway with a stick, tracing patterns invisible in the darkness.

"Yes, but you've studied science. Don't you look down on people who don't think rationally?"

"I'm in two worlds." He turned his stick over and doodled with the other end. "As an educated Rai, I tend to think like a Westerner, but still I'm ready to believe in ghosts and spirits, because people in my own family have had such experiences."

"It's hard to escape what you learned as a child," I agreed.

"You were raised to think like a scientist. But the rational mind can only take us so far. Maybe you've reached the end of what it can do."

A goat bleated high up on the hillside. "You're probably right. We all have to be in two worlds. Our senses don't give us the whole story—and neither does logic," I conceded, realizing only as I spoke that it was true.

We said goodnight, and I climbed up to our sleeping platform. The sky was bright with stars, huge and glowing like little suns. I slipped into my bag and slept easily until one or two in the morning when we were suddenly wakened by a strange, trumpeting sound, like the call of a wild beast in the distance. It moved around, coming first from one direction, then another, closer and closer, and louder and louder, as it circled. Thérèse started upright, her light hair flaring in the moonlight. "What's that?"

We listened a while in strained silence, and then I knew. "A saddhu." Mr. Ganesh had talked about them. "They go around in the night blowing a horn and reciting mantras to protect the houses from ghosts called massans. In the morning, they come back to be paid with food." The trumpeting drew near as the saddhu circled the house, and then receded. In the morning, sure enough, a ragged stranger showed up at the door begging food.

We packed up our bags and took them to the house, waiting for someone to tell us what came next. "I'm hungry," Thérèse complained.

Vhim appeared and drew me aside to a sort of boardwalk beside the house. "It's beautiful this morning, isn't it?" He breathed deeply, raising his fists and pretending to pound his chest in a pantomime of health, and then grabbed my arm and propelled me down a short flight of steps. "I want you to meet my other relations."

I looked back at Thérèse, hunkered down beside our packs, hugging her own thin shoulders and looking miserable.

"Never mind," said Vhim, as I hung back. He was still annoyed with her. We walked a short distance to a nearby house. The land around sloped up gently toward a bank of rolling hills that mounted to distant, higher elevations. The lady of the house, a middle-aged Rai woman, welcomed us inside. One of her daughters, dressed for school, poured water into a tall black iron pot with a fat belly, part of an apparatus with three levels that took up a substantial portion of the main room. Vhim explained they were making rakshi. The lady dipped out large sample cups for us to taste. "It's almost done," she said. Another daughter worked on painting an outside wall with a brush and bucket of whitewash. We stayed for a long time chatting, forgetting breakfast in the glow of the rakshi. Thérèse would be wild.

Around the corner, in front of another house, Dr. Ganesh was pressing his stethoscope to an old woman's chest, listening intently. "She's in congestive heart failure," he said in English. The lady smiled. "She probably won't last more than a couple of days, but we can't help her. No medicines, no equipment."

Prem joined us. "There's another woman here with the same problem." He shook his head. "Also, a bad case of emphysema. We can do nothing."

Vhim's auntie fed us rice. The porters had already left with our gear. My daypack with my jacket and sleeping bag were gone. "They've taken them on to Dengmaya," Vhim said. It was only a few hours distant, and the day was warm. I wasn't worried.

Vhim hurried off ahead to make it to his home village in time to greet his other group. "Just follow the trail," he said. "If you get lost, my father is well-known around here. Just ask anyone the way to the Captain's house."

The land rose gently for a while, and we relaxed into a comfortable stride, crossing a set of low hills, and reaching a fork in the trail on the downhill side. "I think this is a shortcut," Prem said, veering off to the right. "If not, I'll come back and catch up." Ganesh took the other fork, and Thérèse and I followed. By noon, Prem was still gone, and Ganesh had begun to ask directions to the Captain's house from everyone we met.

"Oh yes, the Captain, that way, *utta*," was the invariable answer, accompanied by a raised arm pointing up and over the next range of hills. We had brought no food, and stopped at a house perched high above a canyon where Ganesh bought a lunch of oranges, fresh honey in the comb, and an unnamed fruit with hard, edible seeds. Big broad-leaved plants with red flowers like North American paintbrush grew under orange and banana trees on a hilly landscape, interspersed with scattered patches of tall bamboo.

Ganesh kept on asking directions as we hiked down one long hill and up the next. "He doesn't seem to have much confidence in what they say," Thérèse observed, "since he keeps on asking." She was sweating, her hair beginning to separate into strings.

In spots, the path plunged steeply downward, but gradually led higher, ever more narrow and rocky, until there was barely room to walk between high dirt cliffs to either side. I got a second wind, and then a third, taking strength from the small, smooth-barked tree trunks I grasped to pull myself along. The air was soft and warm; everywhere were large-leafed trees and huge white flowers like lilies.

We walked for hours, until the light began to fade and the air turned chill against our arms. We hiked a mile or so along a ridge, and then in full darkness, turned a corner and could see lights in the valley below. Ganesh went to a nearby house to ask directions.

"Dengmaya is just down there where you see those lights," he reported. "But it's a half day's walk. I think we should spend the night."

The house belonged to a family of Brahmins. They invited us onto their porch, wanting to be kind, but they couldn't let us inside because we were low-caste and unclean. The wife brought out plates of rice and vegetables, and the husband ate with us on the porch. Ganesh assured me there would be no garlic. "Good Brahmins eat neither garlic nor onions," he said.

An old neighbor man, small and bent, appeared from the darkness at the Brahmin's elbow. "He's probably Rai," Ganesh explained. "This Brahmin is the village headman. He is also a shaman." Indeed, a shaman's drum hung on a wall inside his door.

The Brahmin turned from his meal to perform a divination for the old man, perfunctorily laying grains of uncooked rice on a metal plate. He made a quick diagnosis, recited a mantra, blew on the old man's head, and turned back to his food, without sparing his patient another glance. I was shocked, but the sick old man went away in apparent satisfaction. Through it all, Thérèse maintained a brittle silence.

"They will allow you to sleep on that bench." Ganesh pointed out a narrow wooden ledge at the opposite side of the porch. His own bed would be the shelf we'd been using for a table. The Brahmins brought out a thin, dirty blanket for Therèse and me to share. Therèse began to protest, but Ganesh said it was probably the best they had.

"I've got to find a toilet," I said. Ganesh waved vaguely toward the road, and Therèse insisted on lending me her flashlight, though I said it would ruin my night vision. I wandered off in search of an isolated place. Even at night, there were people everywhere, walking the road in groups of two and three. My only chance for privacy was to climb a few feet over a steep cliff edge. The flashlight came in handy then, but I lost my footing and it slipped from my hands, fell open, and the batteries bounced out.

Recovering my balance, I did my business clinging to a tree root, then groped around and found the flashlight. The batteries couldn't be far. I inched down, peered into the darkness, and ran my hand across the crumbly earth, searching for a long time with no success.

"I'm sorry. I didn't mean to lose your batteries." I handed Therèse the empty flashlight shell. She set her lips and nodded.

We were both exhausted, and lay down gingerly on the bench beneath the skimpy blanket. Our bed was barely wide enough for one, much less two. The night was chill, but neither of us liked the other enough to cuddle together spoonwise, the only thing that would have made sleep possible.

I had just slipped into an uncomfortable doze when something cold and wet lapped my feet where they stuck out over the end of the bench. A calf tied on a short rope by the corner of the house was licking our toes for salt. Therèse groaned.

Just before dawn, the family began a puja on the table by our bench. The father held a two-sided *dameru* drum, rotating his wrist so that the stone beater, which was tied with a string to the drum's hourglass-shaped body, whirled out and struck each face in turn, making a loud rattling sound. The mother swept the air with the long, coarse hairs of a severed black and white yak's tail to banish evil spirits, as the rest of the family made offerings and recited prayers. When they finished, they honored us with tikas of sticky red rice and garlands of flowers. Meanwhile, Dr. Ganesh went off to visit a cancer patient.

He soon returned, and our spirits lifted as we started out, for now we could actually see our destination, a cluster of houses on the hillside across the valley, backed by the dramatic vista of snowy Makalu. Word of the doctor's presence had spread, and a young man bounded up the trail to ask him to treat a woman with a broken leg. He tended to her, and we walked on, down and up again, and finally arrived at a fine, large house, whose outside had been plastered red. The Captain himself wasn't home, but Vhim and one of his father's wives came out to greet us, bringing chia. The day was warm and sunny, with a sky full of white, puffy clouds.

"What took you so long?" Vhim asked.

"We kept on asking directions," Ganesh said, "and went where they pointed."

"Of course, they were pointing in the right direction," Vhim said, "if you could fly like Hanuman. You should have followed the river instead of going straight, up and down over the hills." I laughed at that until I coughed. Thérèse frowned.

Now that we were safe, the fever and nausea I'd been fighting overtook me. Vhim's brothers had set up our tent in front of the house. My daypack and sleeping bag and jacket were inside. I crept in and lay down.

Vhim stuck in his head, asked what was wrong, and crawled in. "I've engaged a shaman to do something for me and my brothers tonight," he said. "You see, my father has seven wives. I am the eldest son, from Ama, his first wife. My brothers are from other wives. Always in a situation like this, there are jealousies. Each wife wants her own son to be given preference, and the sons usually turn out to be enemies. But I want to change all that. You know, I have hired my half-brothers, Ek and Desh, as porters for the group, and I plan to bring Ek to America. There's no reason we can't get along and help each other. That's what the shaman's ceremony is for."

"You're quite the idealist," I said. "I hope it works."

"I know you'd hate to miss it. Try to feel better. This shaman is very old, very experienced. A real Rai shaman from the mountains—not a city shaman from a different caste."

At nightfall I staggered from my sickbed and hiked across the valley with the others, up a gentle hillside to a house with a broad front porch where two hundred or more people had gathered. We foreigners sat on a dirt bank near the house. Someone brought us cups of rakshi.

The shaman was thin and quite tall, in his seventies, Vhim said, but still flexible. His head was nearly bald. His altar was similar to Jebi's, but with more peacock feathers, and a black egg instead of a white one. The villagers treated him with respect. A group of old men, obviously long-standing friends, surrounded him, lending advice.

As soon as it was dark, he began to drum, using the familiar Rai beat Jebi had taught me. As his deity possessed him, he shook and grunted words of prophesy for Vhim and his brothers. Then he grasped for something in the air and trapped it in his water pitcher. When he stopped for a break, he called a woman to his altar, and Desh explained that in the shaman's trance he'd found a sato floating like a white string in the air and put it in the pitcher. Now he was returning the soul to its owner.

Then a banana stem was planted in the yard, and one end of a long string tied around it. Vhim and his brothers held the other end as the shaman danced, recited mantras, and swept a hypnotized rooster along the string from them to the banana stem. I recognized the khadco kattne ceremony to rearrange their planets, like the one Krishna had done that had so changed my life. It lasted a long time, but no one seemed bored. There were no TVs to go home to, and this was what was happening.

When the banana stem had been chopped, and the rooster killed, the shaman took a break to palaver with his friends, and Thérèse and the Americans from Vhim's other group left. "I'm staying," I said, ignoring signs of rising fever. "I want to see what happens."

Local people took turns at the shaman's altar, and for each, he drummed, shook, and made passes over their bodies with two bamboo brushes, shaking something from one of the brushes into his hand—usually a small brown stone.

Desh, a likeable young man with a reputation for wildness and drinking, stayed beside me and explained that the dark-colored stones were impurities extracted from the patients' bodies. When it was Desh's turn with the shaman, the old man told him to do a puja for his family gods.

Then Vhim said that I, too, could have a turn. "When he shakes something out of the brush, don't look at it," Vhim warned, "or the bad spirit will come back to you."

He led me to a seat by the shaman and lent me a ten rupee note for the altar. Up close, I couldn't help feeling awed by the shaman's aura of authority. As he drummed, he kept glancing down at my leg, which felt as though it were about to start shaking. He said something to the old man beside him, waved the brushes over me, and shook something out on his hand. "*Seto*," he said, the word for white. Others echoed, "Seto." I didn't want to look, but everyone was pointing to the shaman's open palm. There, instead of a dark stone or seed, were several white grains of rice.

He spoke to me in earnest Nepali. I couldn't understand, but later Vhim explained, "He said a deity is coming. You can be a shaman, but something is blocking your way."

My spirits lifted. Let them laugh. The shaman has spoken. This white woman *can* be a shaman. I accepted another cup of rakshi and settled down to watch the divinations from the porch of the house, where space had opened up as people went off through the hills to bed.

There was no lack of patients for the shaman. People had come from miles around to have their fortunes told and their illnesses cured. He spoke sternly to this one, kindly to that. Some he counseled at length, consulting his elder friends; others he dismissed with a few words. After midnight, Vhim and Desh said goodnight, but I was determined to stay to the end. This was my chance to see a real Rai shaman work.

Several cups of rakshi later, however, my resolution faltered. I thought I must be very ill, but it was nearly dawn. Surely the shaman would soon stop. Daylight came on, but still he drummed and shook as powerfully as ever. The sun rose high. The birds were awake, well into their morning routines, as were the villagers, passing on errands back and forth along the paths. At last I gave up, stumbled down the winding trail, and crawled into the tent. Thérèse was still asleep. I searched my pack for Tums, trying not to make a sound, and then collapsed.

But before I could sleep, an old Gurkha soldier, a veteran of the Second World War who had served in Italy, stuck his head in the tent and shouted in mixed Italian and Nepali for his "daughters" to wake up and come out for their Nepali language lessons. Thérèse sat up and told him sharply to go away.

I crawled out, gave the old man a weak smile, and hurried around the house toward the bamboo outhouse high on the hillside. In a clear spot, I paused to vomit, and then tried to push dirt over the shameful evidence of my weakness. A woodcutter with a broad, bony face like a Tibetan's, came over grinning, counted the pulses in my temples, and clicked his tongue in sympathy. "Poor sick person," he said, and went off smiling.

I trudged on, up the steep hill to the outhouse. The only way to get in was to climb a too-short ladder, then lever myself up to the door with both arms. It took all my strength. I stayed inside in the dim private space a long time, trying to enjoy my suffering.

All that day I shook with fever as I dozed in the tent and recited mantras, especially Maile's Banjhankri mantra for healing any illness, trying to aim it just right to make it work. I broke out in a drenching sweat, and slept.

I woke in full darkness as Thérèse slid into the tent. As she prepared for bed, I tried to separate her name into its two parts, "tear" and "erase," but they stuck together in the middle.

"You know you snore," she remarked as she pushed her legs into her sleeping bag with conscious grace.

The clinic had been set up outside the Captain's house, close to our tent. All the next day and into the night, sick people drained down from the nearby hills. The doctors never stopped to eat or rest. They were surprised at the number of asthma cases. Chronic bronchitis and gastritis accounted for another large portion of their patients. They had nowhere near enough theophyllin, bronchodilators or antibiotics.

I felt better, and got up to watch. Prem treated patient after patient, examining them quickly and asking questions about their symptoms and medical histories. He gave out advice and medicines, and even recommended shamanic treatment. "I have often seen it work," he explained. "The mind and body are one."

He spoke with an old woman with aching joints, then lifted her shirt and listened to her heart. "There is nothing I can do," he said in English, "but she believes the cold metal of my stethoscope against her back will heal her." He listened intently, moved the instrument here and there, and in Nepali said, "Very strong heart."

I soon tired, and crawled back into the tent. In the evening, Vhim and his brother Kumar prepared a spicy curry for the group, but Thérèse cooked her own meal in the tent, fishing a hair from her pot and holding it up so I could see that it was mine. She laid it aside and cooked noodles in a thin chicken broth. When it was ready, she offered me a bowl, which I accepted with gratitude.

"It is important for anyone on a spiritual pathway to perform acts of charity," she said. "I try to do several every day."

I ate every bit, feeling the nourishment soak in.

⟡

We left the next morning, hiking steadily downhill. Millet was ripe in the fields, with pods shaped like holy Buddhist vajras. The rice crop had turned golden, and tall stands of sorghum towered above the houses. That evening, we camped at a place called Chilqua, and next day followed the Arun River, stopping on a wide, rocky beach where, still weak, I rested in the sunshine. Thérèse had turned into a strong trekker and nearly stopped grumbling, but I overheard her complaining with Vhim's brothers of his autocratic ways.

At Tumlingtar, we found our flight to Kathmandu had been canceled, but a plane would be leaving that evening for Biratnagar with three empty seats. A bus ran from there to Kathmandu. Thérèse lifted her chin and announced, "I'm taking one seat." A man from Vhim's other group claimed the second. I needed to get back, but not if it meant another night with Thérèse. She was doing her karma too fast, *really* going like a pirate, and bad things were sure to happen, if not on the plane, on the eighteen-hour bus ride to Kathmandu—delays, flat tires, breakdowns, misunderstood directions, thefts, abandonments, betrayals.

"I'll wait," I said.

Ganesh spoke up, "I'll go."

The rest of us had dinner in the hotel, and afterward built a campfire and sang English and Nepali folk songs as Vhim played his guitar. Sharon Conlin and her friend Suzi, two women from Boulder in Vhim's other group, knew *Rickety, Tickety Tin*, a grim old Irish ballad about a girl who had killed her family one by one. We sang it with enjoyment.

> *And when at last the police came by,*
> *Sing rickety-tickety-tin,*
> *And when at last the police came by,*
> *Her little pranks she did not deny,*
> *For to do so, she would have had to lie,*
> *And lying, she knew, was a sin, a sin,*
> *And lying she knew was a sin.*

Vhim and Prem taught us *Pan ko Pat*, a funny song about betel leaf, and Prem finished with a hauntingly beautiful Nepali love song.

"That was for Ri-i-i-ta," Vhim teased.

Alone in my room at the hotel, I dumped my pack on the empty spare bed, hugged myself for joy, and turned around twice like a dog making a nest. I had always considered myself reasonably competent, but Thérèse had criticized so much—I combed my hair too near the food, made coffee too strong, snored, dropped clean utensils, lost her flashlight batteries—that I became clumsy, even ill. Next time I felt like criticizing or putting someone down, I'd remember that witchy, self-righteous face of hers, that scolding, tense French accent, and forebear. I *hoped* this was her last lifetime on earth. I never wanted to meet her again.

A BALL OF ASHES

Vhim managed to pull a few strings with friends among the Royal Nepal Airline pilots, and next morning, we broke into cheers beside the little runway as a special plane touched down to take us back to Kathmandu. The sky was clear, and the pilot pointed out the white, gleaming masses of Everest, Makalu and Ama Dablam from the plane.

For a moment, coming out of the sunlight into the relative darkness of Mr. Rai's office, I couldn't see at all. The room had no window; a single lamp cast a spot of light down on the desk. Mr. Rai sat behind it, small and shrunken, his skin and eyes as yellow as old parchment. I couldn't hide my shock. "What's wrong? Are you ill?"

"Just now I am having a few problems." He looked up without smiling, all his fire gone out. I peered through the smoky space at a stranger—a small oriental man crouched in a dim cubicle in this distant corner of the world. "I am getting better," he added.

"Have you seen a doctor?"

"I will go," he said. "Just cut down on drinks, is all. I know what he will say." He tried to laugh, but it came out a dry cackle.

He did cut down, and for a while quit altogether. His color improved, though he remained distant and preoccupied. One evening, as he and Jebi sat in his living room after dinner sipping tea from glass tumblers, he told us how his father had died. "He went to see his mom, because they had had a disagreement, and he wanted to fix up. She thought he was drunk and tried to send him home, but he said, 'Not yet. I want to stay and talk longer to you and my brothers and sisters, because nobody knows what will happen.'

"Then Dad pick up handful of ashes from chula and squeeze together. 'We are just like this ball of ash,' he said. 'Put out in the rain and it scatters.'"

Mr. Rai sighed. "After that, my dad returned to home and told mom, 'Give my shaman things to Mohan.' He went to bed, and later when my mom got in beside him, he was cold. And that is all, how he left us behind." He stared into his glass.

I'd wanted to tell Mr. Rai and Jebi what the old Dengmaya shaman had said, but it didn't seem appropriate to Mr. Rai's somber mood. Instead, with some embarrassment, I related how the mountain Rais had laughed at the idea of a white lady thinking she could learn to be a shaman.

"Why not you become shaman," Mr. Rai broke in, energized. "Look at Jebi. Neither is he of Rai tribe, yet he is good shaman, having Rai guru to teach him."

I decided to tell them everything. "Then I met an old Rai shaman in the hills. He did my jokhanna and said I *could* be a shaman—but something was blocking my way."

"I agree," Jebi said. He set his glass down hard. "I can do something to take care of it. I believe it is a goddess protecting you." Mr. Rai listened, nodding. "But if the protection goes away too soon," Jebi warned, "you could go crazy."

"You keep studying mantras as Jebi has taught you," Mr. Rai said, with more animation than I'd seen since I returned. "For ten days you study, and then we will see."

But Jebi said, "I will test her and do jokhanna now."

He dressed in his costume, drummed and had me dance the Rai shaman's steps, then told me to cut ginger with a feather as he stood behind me and guided my hands. He whistled mantras, and I sliced the feather downward, knocking off a bud that rolled across the floor and landed cut side up, a good omen.

"He is finding out what will give you power," Mr. Rai said. "He has tried mantras of hunter spirits and massans, but they were not right. Then he has tried mantras of Rai mudhum. This is what has worked for you."

Jebi nodded vigorously, as though following Mr. Rai's English. Then he tried to make me shake, but as usual, nothing happened.

"Keep practicing," Mr. Rai said. He held his right hand up, edge on, carefully centered with the thumb toward his chest, and raised it to his forehead, down to his heart, and up again. "Don't just think, 'I am *Allen* with my own history.' Think, 'I am shaman here. Tell me something. Let me do something.' You must be very much proud that you are shaman and you are sitting down at your altar to perform. I will ask for help and grace from my father," he added.

"STOP, GO BACK!"

Mr. Rai told me that later that night he'd had two vivid, frightening dreams. In the first, he and I were flying through the air, skimming over woods and meadows along a river valley in the foothills. He felt anxious. "Why are you taking her so fast?" someone asked, and he began to sweat. Down to the right, a group of tigers were tearing at a deer carcass. "Go the other way," the voice directed. We landed on a hillside, and I began to drum traditional Rai rhythms and shake. He shook too.

Then, all at once, we were flying again, and coming to rest at a shrine to Lord Shiva, where we drummed together and shook.

The dream had frightened him, sweeping him back into the old Rai shaman ways he thought he had escaped.

The next dream was even more telling. He was crossing a high suspension bridge above a clean, clear lake. Flowers beckoned on the other side, but the bridge was faulty, and I was following close behind— too close. "Go back," he shouted, waving his hands to shoo me off, but I refused. "I say, go back."

I smiled and kept on coming. He knew I would fall if he didn't tell me exactly where to put my feet, so he pointed out the places where the ropes were solid. So many flowers. He ran ahead into the field. I kept on following, and he whirled and shouted, "I told you not to follow me!"

He'd brought a packed lunch, and a monkey was trying to get into it. The monkey spoke and said, "Please save me a little food." Mr. Rai opened the sack and left half a sandwich among the flowers.

We started up the mountain. He noticed I was barefoot, and shouted again, "Go back!"

"No, I have shoes in my daypack." I kept on coming. We reached a high plateau. The sun was rising.

A bearer said, "Here's your coke, Memsa'b, and here's your whiskey, Mr. Rai."

"Mr. Rai! A half liter of whiskey at six in the morning? No!" I scolded.

I took photos of the sun coming up, motioning Mr. Rai to move aside, get out of the way.

We kept on going to the summit, and he woke, still angry that I'd followed. "But now I have come to know how determined you really are," he said.

MONEY

I too dreamed that night—that I was in someone else's personal elevator, going up. It was large and empty, with scarred green doors. I didn't know whose it was, or what floor we had reached. The doors opened, and I entered a deserted room furnished with a dusty red plush couch and chair. I felt I shouldn't be here.

In the morning, Mr. Ganesh was rushing out of Mr. Rai's front door as I approached, and stopped me to confide, "Mr. Rai still hasn't paid me. You are my last client for shamanism." He was trembling with anger, but trying hard to keep his dignity. "If he doesn't pay his translator or his shamans, he must not expect his student to learn."

"Why isn't he paying?" I asked, as Jebi followed him out.

"He has paid no one. Maile has not been paid. Has he paid you, Jebi? I know you need money for your family."

"A little," Jebi said, his loyalties divided.

Mr. Rai didn't comment on Mr. Ganesh's absence, and after breakfast, Jebi said Mr. Rai had instructed him to take me on an all-day hike. Thuli Kumari handed us a sack lunch, and we headed out to the edge of the city and climbed into the foothills to a place called Boombah, a Buddhist nunnery. On the way back we traveled through a forest of tall trees, all of whose lower limbs were missing, hacked off for firewood by the city's exploding population.

A few days later, Mr. Ganesh returned and conducted class as though nothing had happened, relating Hindu myths and describing village ceremonies. Mr. Rai came home at noon and dismissed him for the day.

"Will Maile come again?" I asked, for she'd not taught once since my return from Dengmaya.

"Oh yes," he said easily, and sure enough, the next day she appeared, though Mr. Ganesh made a point of telling me that Mr. Rai still hadn't paid her. I said I was sorry for the problem about payment, and that I'd speak to Mr. Rai.

Maile had obviously been thinking how to teach her difficult

American student. "You do not need to recite the mantras in my Tamang language or in Nepali," she said. "It is enough if you say them in English."

She taught me a ritual to cure joint pain. "The shaman begins outside the patient's house," she said. "As we speak the mantra, we move toward the west, into the yard, up to the house, and in the door. We chant that the door is guarded. We call three brother spirits to help, the souls of ancient shamans. We find nine large leaves and make them into offering cups, in each placing millet, herbs, ginger, rice and hot peppers.

"We circle a little rice and incense before the patient as we chant that a group of nine brothers dwells in the cups, and we ask them please to take away the pain. 'Take the pain to the place where the ginger grows. Take the pain to the place of the nine millet seed curls. I am proceeding to the west,' we chant. 'There are rocky roads all over. I have reached a country where they grow the tree with the big leaf, where they yoke the bullock to plow the land. I am about to reach this country. I come to the bank of a river too big to cross.'

"We leave the cups in a clean place, and chant, 'Stay at your abode, brothers, even if someone tries to make you come out. Even if bad people call you, stay at home. This is a promise.'" Maile hooked her index fingers, and in quick succession, clapped her right hand on her left, her left hand on her right, and again, right on left. Once more, she hooked her fingers, and exclaimed, "Truth!"

Then she gave me a mantra to extract the rest of the joint pain with an egg.

"Does the shaman have to be possessed and shaking for this?" I asked.

"Certainly," she said.

Mr. Rai had not yet asked me for money. He was keeping accounts, but whenever I brought it up, he put me off and said we'd settle later. That evening, I insisted on paying him to date. The total was more than I'd expected, but I would still have enough to get home. "I hope now you can pay Maile," I remarked when we were finished.

"Who tells you I don't pay Maile?" He turned on me so fiercely I took a step back.

"Mr. Ganesh mentioned it."

"Don't worry about anything. I am doing it," he said, taking pains to hide his anger. I gathered my things and hurried to my room.

"You should not have mentioned to Mr. Rai about payment for Maile," Mr. Ganesh complained when Maile arrived next morning.

"But you told me it was a problem."

"You overheard it."

No, I thought. You *told* me. But I dropped it.

Maile agreed I shouldn't have spoken, that it made Mr. Ganesh look bad.

At first I argued that it was terrible they hadn't been paid, but they were so serious, so sure I'd been wrong to mention it to Mr. Rai, that I finally promised to apologize. Evidently I'd broken some taboo.

As soon as Mr. Rai came home, I screwed up my courage and spoke. "I'm sorry I mentioned anything about your arrangements with Maile." I tried to smile. "It was not my business."

"Don't even think about it," he said, waving me off, but it was obvious he didn't forgive me.

Bindu came to my room before dinner, sidling toward the bed and smoothing the covers, something clearly troubling her.

"What's wrong?" I asked.

"Nothing." She put a hand on my arm, inviting me to read her mind.

It wasn't hard. Mr. Rai must still be in a bad mood, making life difficult for his family. I knew it was my fault. I'd threatened his authority with my meddling. After all, how else could he keep his people properly subservient except by withholding their pay? That was how it was done here, and I should know better than to interfere. Never mind what I thought of the way Nepali men treated their egos to the fun of being "big men." How could there be order in the universe if their proper authority was undermined?

"Your husband is not happy?" I asked in my simple Nepali.

"*Kushi chaina*," she said—literally, happiness is not.

I tried again, after Mr. Rai had eaten and was leaning back in his chair, smoking and sipping from a glass tumbler that held an inch of brown liquid. "I didn't mean to offend you," I recited my planned apology. "I don't understand how things are done in Nepal. Please forgive me for interfering in how you are managing. You have arranged everything to teach me. I could not have done this by myself, and I am very grateful."

"There is no problem," he said as before, but this time I felt he meant it.

Later, Bindu grabbed me around the waist and tried to pick me up to show her joy.

FIRE WALKING

Today, *tharo jokhanna*," Jebi announced next morning. He'd finally decided to teach me something useful. But it was a type of divination that could be done without the shaman going into a shaking trance.

"We start with a handful of uncooked rice the patient has handled. Take up a pinch of it, say the mantra, and lay the rice down in the plate." He dictated a mantra, whispering so Mr. Ganesh wouldn't hear. "Then count the grains. If there is an even number, a deity is bothering your patient. If there's an odd number, it's a bad spirit or a witch. You should get the same number of grains three times in a row."

I thought the odds against that must be astronomical, and said so.

"If it's double the number of grains, that counts the same," Jebi continued. "Or the shaman can ask for four out of seven tries, or six out of ten. Or just ask for an odd or even number in answer to your question. As I already taught you, each spirit and deity has its own number, but sometimes spirits make the rice grains lie. If a massan spirit lies and says he's not the one causing the problem when he is, give him less of an offering."

"I don't see how this could work."

"The shamans cannot teach this method well," Mr. Ganesh observed. "When Peter was here, everyone got confused and angry."

"I'm not angry," I said. "I just don't get it." Mr. Ganesh didn't answer, but looked at me a little too long. Maybe I *was* a tiny bit angry. Frustrated at least. I scanned back over my notes. "It seems to be an interaction between the shaman and the rice grains," I guessed, "asking questions and interpreting the answers on the spot—not cut and dried like a computer program."

"Yes," the translator agreed, conferring with Jebi in rapid Nepali, then adding, "No, that is, Jebi says, no." Mr. Ganesh obviously hadn't the slightest idea what I was talking about.

"Please tell Jebi I have noticed he has only been teaching me things a person can do without shaking," I said.

When Mr. Rai came home for lunch, I asked him straight out, "Does everyone think I should be shaking by now?" I pinned him with my gaze, willing him to tell the truth for once, not just say what I wanted to hear.

"Ye-e-s," he said thoughtfully, drawing out the word.

I let my hands fall in my lap.

"However, you should not worry yourself," he backtracked. "It takes time. Every things takes time."

"Yes, I know, but my visa's running out."

After lunch, we held class outside. The air was cold, and the sun's rays felt good on my bare arms. Jebi began to explain how he used the drum for guru divination while in a shaking trance.

He asked me to place a handful of rice grains in the center of the drum as he held it out horizontally and tapped a four-beat rhythm on the bottom, one hard stroke followed by a softer second echo, then a third, harder than the second, and finally a fourth, softest of all. As the drum skin vibrated, the rice grains jumped and formed patterns. He whistled a mantra asking the spirits to tell him what he had to know.

"I watch the patterns formed by the rice grains," he said. "If pairs form, it may be there's a quarrel between husband and wife." He held the drum out and showed me several pairs. "If in threes, there's a quarrel with neighbors. In fours, a family member may be sick. In fives, the patient's desires are never fulfilled. If the rice spins, the patient is fickle minded." A number of grains were dancing near the center of the drum. Jebi raised it vertically, still beating. "If all the grains fall off and none of them stick, it's not a serious problem. If rice stays stuck to the drum no matter how hard I beat, I tell the patient, 'You may have an enemy trying to hurt you.'"

It all sounded highly unlikely.

At dusk, Jebi built a bonfire in front of the house. Mr. Rai said, "He will teach you to walk on fire. Take off your shoes."

First, Jebi tried again to make me shake, throwing rice grains and whispering mantras, but as usual, he failed.

Then, he drummed, instructing me to copy whatever he did. By now the fire had formed a good bed of coals. He danced and I followed. I knew the steps, and paced and whirled beside him, dancing on and on until my feet dragged the ground like mud-caked boots.

Then he danced straight into the fire, his bare feet landing on the bed of glowing coals. I jumped in after him without a second thought, my feet thudding heavily among the coals. I felt no pain. Back and forth we danced, stamping and drumming, as the crowd of onlookers exclaimed in amazement.

Jebi grinned with pride and said, "Good student."

Jebi and Ellen Firewalking

The next day, Mr. Rai said that one of my friends from America had telephoned, and he'd invited him to dinner. It was my patent client, Igor Gamow, a professor in the Chemical Engineering Department at the University of Colorado and inventor of the hyperbaric mountain bag which had revolutionized the treatment of altitude sickness on peak climbs. He was here with a group of students on a "Semester in Nepal." I'd given him Mr. Rai's number before I left.

Thuli Kumari cooked chicken and curried vegetables and laid out bowls of party food—mixed nuts, flavored crackers, and fried noodles. Mr. Rai opened a large bottle of whiskey, set it on the table, and sent me off to meet Igor at the Blue Star Hotel, half a mile away on the winding paths, and guide him back.

As I waited on the sidewalk in front of the hotel, Igor zoomed up on a rented motorcycle. "Get on," he said, patting the seat behind him. We swept to a grand roaring stop in Mr. Rai's driveway.

Mr. Rai enthroned Igor on the couch and handed him a large drink, hesitating only a moment before pouring himself a like amount. I knew he hoped to persuade Igor to use his services for the student treks, but Igor was working with Narayan in Boulder, and there was no doubt in my mind it would be Narayan's friends and relatives in Nepal, not Mr. Rai, who got Igor's business.

After dinner, Mr. Rai asked Jebi to do a jokhanna for Igor. "He will tell your fortune," Mr. Rai explained.

As Jebi came out in his costume, I tried to imagine what it must be like for Igor to see this for the first time, but Igor sipped his whiskey as though nothing at all could surprise him.

"You have no wife or children. You are like a bird, going where you wish," Jebi said after he'd drummed and spoken for the god. Mr. Rai translated.

"No," said Igor. He tipped his head back, slightly smiling. I thought this answer a bit unfair, for though Igor did have a wife, they had no children, and he could and did go where he wished.

"Your wife is kind-hearted and so are you," Jebi said. "Your wife wants you to be more kind-hearted."

"No," said Igor.

"You start projects, remember something else, go off, talk and talk, come back and have to start the first thing over," Jebi tried again.

"No," said Igor, but his superior smile had begun to look a bit strained.

"Your wife's planets are stronger than yours. Your wife is very lucky. She protects you."

"Yes," said Igor, surprising us all.

"You plan a lot before you go to sleep at night, but sometimes you forget your plans and promises."

"No." Igor's lips twitched downward.

"Ask again," Jebi said to Mr. Rai. "He's hiding."

Mr. Rai asked again.

"Well, maybe." Igor laughed. "Sometimes I let the trivial things go."

"You see?" Jebi said in Nepali.

"Yes, you're a good shaman," Mr. Rai answered.

Jebi took off his costume and accepted a cup of rakshi from Kumari. Mr. Rai poured more whiskey for the rest of us.

"I like to drink with Sherpa families in the mountains," Igor said. "They are good people."

"You would like Rai families. They will drink with you too," Mr. Rai said.

"Do they let you sleep with their daughters?"

I was stunned. From what I knew of Rai men, if a traveler even looked at their daughters, they'd chop him with their kukhuri knives, but Mr. Rai was much too urbane to take offense, and answered, not missing a beat, "Maybe. It depends."

Igor asked about my studies, and I told him Jebi had taught me to walk on fire.

"That's easily explained." He drained his glass and Mr. Rai filled it from the last of the bottle. "If you're not afraid, your feet sweat and an insulating layer of steam forms between the bottom of your feet and the coals. There's nothing magic about it."

I laughed to save face. "I'm impressed with myself, anyway."

Next day, Jebi said Mr. Rai had suggested we go for another walk, but I declined, went back to my room and threw myself across the bed. Go like a pirate indeed. I wasn't going anywhere.

I changed out of my sweat pants into a blouse and skirt, walked to the main road, and waved down a taxi, giving Mr. Rai's office address.

He was answering letters on his manual typewriter, and looked up, worried, when he saw me. "*Allen?* What is wrong?"

"I feel stuck," I said. "Please tell me, honestly. If you think I don't have any talent for this, just say so. There's no point wasting more of your time — or mine."

SEVEN OCEANS FAR

Mr. Rai had long-distance service on his office phone. Eleven-thirty in the morning here was past Keri's bedtime in Portland, but Evans would know how she was. I picked up the phone and concentrated on placing my suddenly-shaking fingers in the right holes as I dialed the country code for the United States and the phone number that used to be mine.

"Y-allo," Evans answered as always. I pulled up a chair, needing suddenly to sit down.

The line hummed between us.

"Hello, who's there?"

"Hi, it's me, Ellen."

"Oh, you're back, are you?"

"No. I'm still in Kathmandu."

"How's the witch doctor business?"

"Oh, okay," I said, hoping my tone didn't betray my failure. "How are you?" I added, before the silence could stretch on too long, talking over the echo of my own voice as some relay in the phone line repeated my words.

"About the same."

"Is your back any better?"

"No."

"Well, how is everyone? Have you heard from Thorne and Keri?"

"Thorne's here. He's living in my camper."

"In the middle of winter?"

"All the rooms in the house are rented, and he needed a place to stay."

"He can stay with me when I get back. How's Keri?"

The delay on the line made it seem like ages until he answered. "Fine, I guess."

"Has she called?"

"I think about a week ago. I guess she's okay."

"Well, how did she sound?"

"You don't want to know," he said.

"Why, what's wrong?"

"...what's wrong?" My voice returned distorted, mocking.

"She just said she misses me. She misses her mommy and daddy."

I knew he wanted to hurt me. "But she's okay?"

"As okay as she can be."

"Mary's taking good care of her. You know that."

"I'm sure she is." I heard a soft pop as he sucked his cigarette, and then the sound of his breath, blowing smoke.

"I'll be back before much longer."

"...much longer." It sounded false, repeated back. That's what he was hearing. I felt myself shrink with shame.

"I'll see you when you get here."

"Tell Thorne and Keri I called," I said—as though I'd only phoned to leave a message for my children.

"Right. Well, goodbye."

"Goodbye."

"...*good bye*," the echo came.

He didn't hang up, and neither did I. The phone boomed faintly, a hollow cable snaking the long miles between us under the ocean.

Seven oceans far, a line from one of Maile's mantras for calling spirits a long way away. *Saat samundra tari.*

Mr. Rai looked at me sharply. "*Allen,* are you finished?"

I hung up the phone.

SHAKING

Maile brought two young women students, one tall with a smooth, narrow face and a single long black braid, the other a short, round-faced girl. They helped her set up her altar and dress up in her costume. As soon as she began her chant, the tall one started to tremble, averting her face as though ashamed, pressing both hands hard against her thigh to make the shaking stop. Within a few minutes the other student began to shake too, with a light vibration in both knees. I tried not to be jealous, and sat close to Maile as she blew mantras and threw rice grains at my head, stomach, and both knees— but still I failed to shake.

Drumming with hard, commanding beats, Maile jumped up and danced, whirling so that the hem of her costume flared and brushed my face. Over my head she circled a water pitcher, then a lighted oil lamp, as she stamped and shouted.

"What is she doing?" I asked.

"Something to unblock your way," Mr. Rai said. "I will explain you later."

The metal-clad point of her drum handle dug into the top of my head, bouncing painfully against my fontanel as she rotated around me, drumming, dancing, and loudly chanting. Both students shook violently. "*Hut!*" she cried out. "*Hut! Hashio!*" She sank down cross-legged on the floor, still shaking, and showered me with rice grains. When she had stopped her shaking, she dropped three grains into a glass of water, moved it close to her heart, blew a mantra on it, and told me to swallow everything, including the rice.

No one explained what it meant, and after the ceremony, I went to my room and prayed. Some previous tenant had left a rusty razor blade on the window ledge, and I picked it up and touched it to my wrist, lightly at first, then hard enough to open a tiny cut. I rubbed the beads of blood across the cast iron Shiva statue on my altar and vowed to fast until I shook.

Next day, though I'd hoped for Maile, Jebi was the one who came.
Santa Dev, who rented the room across the hall from me in Mr. Bharat's
house, showed up to be our translator.

Jebi talked about *baithung*, a healing method using a plate of rice
grains, an oil lamp and mala of rudraksha beads. The baithung healer
must send his spirit traveling in the three worlds, but doesn't set up an
altar, or drum—or shake.

Suddenly, Jebi raised his voice, and Santa jumped to his feet and
yelled a spate of angry words. Jebi yelled back. Santa dropped his head
and sulked.

"What's wrong?" I asked.

"Maybe I am not good translator. I am only trying to help by
coming here. Your shaman thinks I am ignorant." Santa shot a barrage
of angry Nepali in Jebi's direction.

Jebi backed down, explaining and appeasing.

"I am not a shaman," Santa said. "I know something because I am
Rai, but I know nothing about these baithung healers. I am Christian,
actually. How can I explain to you? I have never seen this done."

"You are a good translator," I assured him. "Much better than Mr.
Ganesh. Please don't go."

Mollified, he agreed to continue. Then Jebi sat me in front of his
altar and tried again, without success, to make me shake.

Thuli Kumari brought lunch. I thanked her and said I wasn't
hungry.

After Santa Dev had gone, Jebi acted out the fight they'd had and
laughed.

"Tell Mr. Rai I don't want dinner," I said. "I'll stay in my room and
study."

🙏

Later, Santa knocked on my door and said Mr. Rai wanted me to
be ready at five in the morning for a trip to Dakshin Kali, literally South
Kali, a shrine park dedicated to the worship of the goddess of blood. I
assumed it was just another of Mr. Rai's attempts to entertain me with
tourist attractions.

Bindu brought along a sack of rice and flowers, and Mr. Rai bought
more flowers and sweets for offerings from a roadside vendor at the
shrine. Early as it was, a long queue had already formed before the
gate of the fenced-off area where the goddess waited to receive her
offerings. The butchers' stalls had long lines too—people waiting with
living goats, sheep, and chickens to be sacrificed. The smell of outdoor

cooking filled the air as families who'd already been through the process scattered themselves over the grass of the large, park-like area, making small fires to roast and eat the meat of the animals they'd offered.

As the line moved forward, a scowling guard stepped out to block my way. "No foreigners allowed."

"Put your offering in Bindu's tray," Mr. Rai directed.

I laid two rupees among the flowers and rice.

"You pray outside here," Mr. Rai said. "Pray that, 'Mother Kali, you are my mother, please grace me with wisdom and power.'" I did so, bowing toward the statue, hands pressed together, face aflame with embarrassment, imagining the whole crowd watching with scorn. But no one really cared or noticed. Public prayer was the rule. Why else had any of them come?

I looked on the large stone face of the goddess behind her fence of iron palings and wept. She *did* look like a mother. My heart ached; tears ran down my cheeks. Of course I was crying because I felt rejected— but also because the prayer was real.

"Maile has been fighting Mother Kali for charge of your soul," Mr. Rai said. "Kali was trying to protect you, but Maile told her, 'Get out of the way. From now, I will take responsibility.'"

Back in the taxi, he reminded me of the dream he'd told me about, in which the two of us were shaking by a Shiva shrine. "We must go there to pray," he said. In fact, we were on our way. As we drove into the foothills, tears kept rolling from my eyes and dripping down my cheeks in a silent, steady stream I couldn't control.

The shrine was close to the paved road and crowded with worshipers. Heavy clouds pressed low. The damp cold crept beneath our coats as we climbed a short slope and stood before a square opening on a mossy rock wall. Across a pool of water, a bumpy, rounded rock face, with shapes said to resemble sacred cattle, rose up to a high cliff, and Mr. Rai said, "If your heart is pure, you can see spirit snakes down there in the water."

All I could see was the grey reflection of the sky.

"Light is from the wrong direction, and we are not standing in right place," he said, making excuses for me as usual. We made our offerings and bowed before another rock formation that was said to look like Shiva.

That night I dreamed of old sacred statues, crumbling and breaking to pieces.

The main room of Mr. Rai's house was full of people, that morning, though he, himself had left for work. I caught Thuli Kumari as she bustled toward the kitchen, and asked her not to make me breakfast.

Maile arrived in a faded yellow T-shirt and wraparound lungi rolled at the top and tucked into itself to form a great wad at the waist. She'd draped a navy blue cardigan on her shoulders against the early morning chill.

The screen by Bindu's bed was folded away, and the bed was neatly made with a white chenille bedspread. Bindu lounged against a pile of pillows, knitting; her teenage daughter, with a stylish Western hairstyle, flipped up at the ends, leaned on Bindu's shoulder, and a younger son perched at the bottom of the bed. Both children looked like her, with rounder eyes than their father.

I sat on the couch with Thuli Kumari and Mr. Rai's youngest sister, whose husband, Magchha, stood idly at the window, staring out on a scene of muted greens and greys beneath a cloudy sky. One of the neighbors leaned on the wall beside him. Gothic arcs of wire in a small electric heater near the couch glowed red and scorched the air by our legs, but the heat was quickly lost in the large, chill room. Still, it was warmer here than elsewhere, which was why everyone had gathered.

Maile bowed her namastes and lowered herself to the worn Tibetan rug beneath the window. From a blue plastic bag of the type local storekeepers gave out with purchases, she produced a small metal water pitcher of classic shape, holding it by its large, elephant-ear handle so that its bulging body gleamed. It held about two cups. Next, she brought out a metal dinner plate, which she filled with a layer of uncooked rice from a smaller plastic bag. She set a shiny new copper saucer into the rice, turning it to make it level.

Thuli Kumari took the pitcher to the kitchen, filled it with fresh water, and brought it back, along with an unlabeled bottle of yellow mustard oil. Maile poured oil into the saucer and twisted a wick from a puffy wad of raw cotton, laying one end into the oil and the other on the saucer's lip. She pinched up several grains of rice, held them close to her throat in the glow from her heart, closed her eyes in prayer, blew softly on them, and dropped them into the pitcher. Preparations finished, she turned and smiled, and motioned me beside her on the floor.

The sun was filtering through the clouds. In her pleasant musical voice, Maile made an unprecedented request, asking everyone to leave. "The deities are shy sometimes," she said, speaking slowly and simply so I could understand. With minimal fuss, the people left. Bindu put away her knitting and unplugged the heater and moved it out of the way, for by now the sun had warmed the room. Kumari shut the door behind her. I'd never before seen it closed.

I was comfortable in my sweater of loosely-knit wool, sweatpants, and long red socks, but the blue linoleum floor was cold. Maile handed me my drum and beater. "Bow three times to the altar," she directed, inclining her own head. "Beat the drum and begin reciting all the mantras and songs I've taught you." She flipped open my notebook and pointed to a mantra written in capital letters. It was one she'd given me. Though she could not read, even her own language, she had evidently been watching as I wrote the mantra down, and knew where it was. She demonstrated how I was to blow after each mantra, forcing air from deep in her belly in quick, emphatic bursts, at the same time seeming to gather power from above her head.

"All the mantras?" I asked.

"All."

"I have not yet learned them all."

"All the ones you know." She smiled.

With a match pulled from somewhere in the wad of cloth around her waist, she lit the oil lamp and announced, "Lord Shiva, the witness."

I gripped the drum handle, digging its point into the rug, and held it so the "OM" sign painted on its skin faced outward. I bent my body forward, and sent my intentions to the steady flame that was Lord Shiva, and the gleaming silver pitcher, the goddess Jari Wari Dolmo, feeling their holy presence glowing in the wintry light on Maile's clean, simple altar. "Please come into me, and make me shake." I prayed silently.

I settled my body into the floor, straightened my back, took a deep breath and tapped the drum on both sides, top and back, as Maile had instructed, whispering the formula to honor and bring it to life. Beginning a steady rhythm, no more than a light tapping, I softly recited the first mantra she'd taught me, the one for protection, and then the mantra for the malas of ritha and rudraksha beads, closing my eyes to concentrate.

Maile had never heard me say these mantras out loud, and, wondering how they sounded in my clumsy pronunciation, I faltered and forgot the next line. Forcing the thought of error from my mind, I continued, beginning the song she had said was "guaranteed to make me shake," picturing the page and a half of Tamang words as I'd written them out phonetically in red capital letters, and making up a melody in Maile's style, forceful at the beginning of each phrase, rising in pitch, and then falling to an authoritative ending. Maile sometimes actually growled with the power of this falling inflection, but I wasn't quite so bold.

The song told of riding on a little yak, sitting and shaking beneath a waterfall in a torrent of wisdom and energy. The long lines of the chant gathered power as they went on, sustaining, upholding, maintaining, enduring, accenting, affirming, ever stronger with the force of each new word. I tried to do the song justice, but faltered in places, and drained it of momentum.

Then, in Nepali, I sang Banjhankri's song—longer but easier to remember because I knew the meaning of each word, and next, the song for Bhairung, Shiva's angry aspect. I chanted mantras for cleansing, short healing mantras for joint pain and headache, diarrhea, and itching, and blew, and blew, and blew, forcing the air from deep in my lungs until I felt dizzy and light.

I came to the end of what I knew and stopped and opened my eyes. Maile sat patiently beside me, giving me her full attention. "Start again." She gestured with a sweeping motion toward the drum as though gathering the energy I'd carelessly allowed to spread outward as I relaxed, forcing me back to my task, giving me no chance to rest. My legs ached from folding.

I tapped the drum again, top, sides and back, recited the angbannu body-binding mantra and blew. I became aware of a yellow darkness, a small space inside the membranes of my closed eyelids, where the words of the mantras presented themselves in order, lining up to be spoken. I forgot the pain in my legs, no longer heard the clink of pans and dishes from the kitchen, nor even the sounds of the words as I spoke them, thinking only of the next word forming in that tiny inner space, and gradually becoming aware of a bright, yellow-white light entering the top of my head and extending down to the level of my eyebrows. I reached the Bhairung song once more: "Angry Bhairung, Hairy Bhairung, Black Bhairung," the chant flowed on hypnotically, gathering power as I recited the names and many aspects of this powerful god, locating each at a spot on my body—hands, forehead, shoulders, and finally, *whole body!*

A trembling started in my legs; they loosened. My knees lifted and fell, lifted and fell, resisted and gave in, resisted again, gave in again. My body shook, trembling in a discomfort of uncertainty, hot and sweating in its heavy clothes.

My voice gained strength as I repeated the song for Bhairung, feeling and seeing the fierce black face of Shiva. The shaking intensified as the angry god threw open the doors and windows of my body to receive the golden light. Yet still I resisted, for such sweetness, such intense beauty can never be endured. I welcomed the light and at once threw it off, with violent, involuntary spasms, then welcomed it again. So long as I welcomed the light, I could not help but close against it, and as soon as I closed, I longed to open. And so I shook.

Behind my eyelids, everything seemed small, precise and far away. I began to forget the words of the song, to hyperventilate and disconnect from the familiar feelings of selfhood. I could be anyone at all, She-Who-Shakes-Here-With-The-Gods—Ellen Winner from Colorado a forgotten construct.

Compared with that golden light, how low we humans are, down here in the middle world with all our dirty squirmings, beneath the notice of the gods. But they had noticed me now; had let me touch the border of their shining world.

"What did you feel?" Maile gently asked as I stopped and opened my eyes.

I set the drum carefully upright on its side. "A light, coming down on the top of my head. And here—." I held my stomach, meaning her to understand the shaky, scary feeling there.

"What color was the light?" She smiled.

"White and yellow."

"Mahadeo," she spoke the name of the Great God, and bowed toward the altar. I copied her, grateful, highly honored, not daring to think.

I straightened out my legs and groaned. I'd been chanting for two hours. Maile took up rice grains from the altar and pressed them into my third eye. I felt my forehead, big and smooth and white and clear and domed and noble from her touch, like her own high forehead, but without the scar. God looks at us in the forehead, I remembered from Swedenborg's writings, the dwelling place of divine love, while we look at God with our eyes, where divine wisdom has its seat, and by this, man and God are joined.

Thuli Kumari opened the door and came in smiling with our lunch. She knew I'd been shaking, I wasn't sure how. Bindu brought her knitting and settled on the bed once more. Mr. Rai's two sisters, Mr. Lok and the old, old man from the house in back, and several others drifted in, all seeming to know what had happened. They smiled and said "Swabash," well done.

Rice, lentils, and greens, the first food I'd eaten in two days, had never tasted so good.

After lunch, Maile again asked everyone to leave. This time, the shaking started sooner. "My leg is going to sleep," I complained, unfolding my left leg from under the right.

"When that happens, pinch the person near you," she said. "That will cure it."

"No!" I laughed.

"Ho," she insisted. But I certainly didn't intend to pinch Maile, my beloved guru. Now that I'd felt the energy she carried, my awe and respect for her doubled.

When the shaking started, I learned to consciously breathe to free up my stomach, and let the power move through me, but afterward, my head ached furiously. I went to my room to rest.

That evening, the living room was crowded with family and neighbors. Mr. Rai said, "Maile has told me you are shaking. This is good. You must work with her tonight to break your speech."

I considered begging off, wanting to bask in the day's achievements. I was so, so tired. But they were determined to keep up the momentum. The old man and woman from the house in back, Mr. Rai's two sisters and brother-in-law, his secretary, the secretary's wife and daughter, Sandeep from the trekking office, the old lama, Mr. Lok, and Bindu, Thuli Kumari and Sani Kumari, Santa Dev, the children who weren't away at school, the off-duty policeman, and others I knew only by face, had gathered to watch. Jebi was nowhere to be seen.

Again, Maile instructed me to recite the mantras and songs. I started in a whisper. The crowd was uncharacteristically silent, but gradually relaxed and began to chat as my low chant continued. This time, the light came down sooner, and as I concentrated, forgetting the audience, the shaking started in the first half hour.

"Who are you?" Maile asked in a quiet voice. "Who is on your body?"

No words came. It was enough to feel this power and shake.

"Who is it? You must tell. Tell us *who* you are!" Mr. Rai shouted in English. I could hear the audience behind me, loud and excited, but far removed. I concentrated on the songs and mantras, riding the sound of my own voice.

"*Ho ha!*" Mr. Rai cried at last, as a signal to stop drumming. Maile passed a handful of rice grains upward along the front of my body, and threw it on the altar to make the shaking stop.

"You are doing very well," Mr. Rai said. "I had no idea you have learned so many of mantras. Maile says your way has been cleared.

You are so straight, *Allen*, you are going to be a most good shaman."
He was clearly pleased. Everyone had thought he'd fail to make me a
shaman, but tonight they could see his success. By morning the whole
neighborhood would know.

I dreamed that night that Maile was teaching me a new mantra,
but when I woke, only one word remained: *trisul*—Shiva's trident. I
slept again and dreamed. Someone was calling my name from above. I
looked up. A host of crazy people leaned from upper and lower windows
of a brick asylum, cheering, smiling, calling good wishes, and shouting,
"Shakti, shakti, shakti"—power!

FATHER MILLER

Mr. Rai found a new translator, a tall young fellow named Gobinda Dakhal. Intelligent and westernized, he'd recently fled Bhutan as a political refugee, having taken part in a plot against the monarchist government. He looked like a revolutionary—healthy and idealistic—and told us he'd spent twelve days hiding out in a tea garden before finding a way to escape across the border to Nepal and send for his wife and two small children. He knew little of shamanism, but had a genuine curiosity not outweighed by ego. I liked him right away.

He interpreted for Maile. "She has had up to nine students at a time. She notes which spirits affect them, and which they are best at using. At first they may go crazy, especially during guru puja, running into fire or jumping into water. Hanuman may possess them so that they tear up the gardens. They may spend hours dancing on fire, or run to the river and come back. She travels with them on their soul journeys, sometimes seeing the same things they do. Her duty as their teacher is to give more power and blessing.

"When the students become independent, they get their own costumes, water pitchers, oil lamps, bells, and malas. They give their teacher gifts, and she blesses their shaman's tools. 'Now you are a full shaman,' she tells them. 'When you lose your way, or forget the words, come and ask me. I will give you power, knowledge, and energy in dreams. If you have trouble, call my name three times. I will know. I will come on your head and help you.'

"They have a graduation ceremony, and she pours out a little rakshi to the gods and passes the rest among the audience. 'Don't make mistakes,' she tells her students. 'Don't be greedy. Swear it that you won't. Don't be lazy. Swear! Follow all the rules. Before you wear this costume, remember what you swore.'"

"What about the gupha, the massan initiation in a cemetery?" I asked. "Does she do that with her students?"

"No, that is not necessary," she said.

I didn't need a translator to decipher the message in Maile's smile and the lilt of her voice: "This is all much simpler than you thought."

"Really? Not all shamans have to go to a cemetery to meet the massans?"

"I have never done this," she said.

I was relieved. Only a week and half was left on my visa.

"Maile," I said. "How long did it take from the time you started to shake until you spoke?"

"About two years," she said with a smile.

"Oh," I said.

But she went on as though nothing were wrong. "When you're shaking, take a bit of rice from the altar and put it on your head. Say, 'I am a shaman. Say, 'I am Mahadeo!'" She had me try it right then.

I recited mantras for twenty minutes, until I shook, and then held a bit of rice from the altar to my forehead and, frightened at my own audacity, whispered, "I am Mahadeo." The shaking intensified.

"Who are you?" Maile said, not shouting. "Who is there? Banjhankri? Devi? Who?"

As the shaking died away, I tried again, pressing another bit of rice to my forehead, saying silently, "I am Rakta Kali." The shaking increased, but only slightly. "I am Mahadeo," I tried again, and again shook harder. But still I could not speak.

"Now there is so little time, she must teach you as much as she can," Dakhal said. "She wants to explain how she calls the gods."

"The gods are above you as you sit," Maile said. "Your father and mother are on your shoulders, your family is in your stomach. Other shamans and foes you place beneath you." Cross-legged on the floor, she stomped her heel down hard on the rug and ground it in, as though crushing an enemy to dust. "The lower world is on both sides of you, on guard. While you are chanting, compare yourself to the whole universe. No one should touch you."

I scribbled furiously.

"The deities from the middle world come and speak to you, and the spirits of your ancestors. They say who they are, and how they died, and they tell you what is wrong with the patient."

She gave me the words of the song for traveling to the lower world, toward Yamalok, the land of the dead, describing what she saw on her travels—black birds, black wheat, black seeds, and tiny black humans, many thorns, beetles, plant sprouts—all tiny and black. Little yellow, green and black sheep and goats, none white. "The birds there are tiny," she said.

"There are seven stories to the lower world. The people and animals are small at the top, and get even smaller as she descends," Dakhal translated. "At the bottom are mongooses, centipedes, and scorpions. There are no barriers until the sixth level down, when she comes to Nargalok, home of Yama, the King of the Dead. He stops her and asks, 'Why have you come?'

"'I have just come to roam around, not to take anything away,' she says, so she won't have to give an offering.

"Sometimes she feels frightened and lonely in the lower world. She can get sick if her assistant beats the wrong rhythm. There is a special rhythm for the king and queen of the khadcos—the bad stars. Sometimes a big black ox stops her, but the more she goes forward, the more backward the ox goes.

"She is searching for Black Snake. He may be causing problems to her patient. She has already called Garuda, the fierce bird Vishnu rides, and put him on her body. Black Snake is stubborn and growls, but Garuda protects her. White Snake is also in the lower world but is not so dangerous as Black Snake. Black Snake looks at her fiercely and says, 'I am going to eat you.' He can kill, but Garuda protects her.

"Then she goes to the upper world to get power, to ask Mahadeo to be a witness and help heal the patient," Dakhal continued. "She feels her body is expanding, becoming light, as if floating, lit with miraculous fire. She sees souls. She must remember everything she sees—the Bhairungs and all the deities.

"Mahadeo has rudraksha beads on both arms and on his lock of hair. On his forehead is a trident marked in ash, in his right hand, a trident of metal, in his left a small drum. His face is dark brown. Snakes wind around his neck, and he wears a tiger skin and a yellow robe. Sometimes goddesses come and shed tears."

I searched her face. "They cry?"

"They cry." She nodded. "For the patient."

The next few nights, I worked with Jebi or Maile, and sometimes both, reciting mantras until I shook. Then they shouted questions, demanding that the possessing spirit speak and say who it was. Words pressed forward to be spoken, but were blocked. For as long as I could remember, I'd censored my speech to be sure it was true and not hurtful or, even worse, foolish, and now dared not turn my voice box over to an unknown entity.

I thought of nothing else. Each afternoon I memorized mantras, trying to feel my way into the sacredness embedded in their words and rhythms.

My visa would expire at the end of the week. Mr. Rai said it wouldn't be easy to renew, but Vhim had suggested that his old teacher, Father Miller at St. Xavier's, who had a long-standing interest in shamanism, might sponsor me through his Jesuit Research Foundation.

"Why not you say so before? We will call and see him. It happens I know Father Miller too," Mr. Rai said.

We put in a call, but Father Miller was out. Several more days passed, and finally Mr. Rai said we'd have to try to get the extension by ourselves.

Fortunately, it turned out the consular official knew Mr. Rai, and called for chia, which was served in delicate, flowered cups by a white-shirted office boy. As we sipped the tepid milk tea, Mr. Rai explained that I was learning shamanism and had begun to shake, but had not yet "broken my speech." We needed time for that to happen. The official laughed and said he thought all shamans were fake.

Mr. Rai laughed with him, and then got serious. "No, but this is very real. You know we are being straight with you. We could have lied and told you she is sick and cannot leave, but we have too much respect for you. You are very well able to tell when people are crooked." He nodded toward me—my cue to speak.

Jebi, Maile, and Ellen

"Yes," I said, clearing my throat. "I am very anxious to continue my studies. When I shake, I feel a yellow-white light coming in through the top of my head. I sit down in front of an altar with holy things, and say mantras until the critical part of my mind goes to sleep. Then I feel the light coming in, and my body starts to shake. I would like to be able to speak so I can be a full shaman and go home and heal people in America."

The official laughed again. "I will give you another month," he said. But that is all. You cannot come back when the month is gone and say you still have more to learn—or *even* that you are very sick." He filled out a form, signed it, stamped it twice, then stamped my passport and handed it to Mr. Rai. Mr. Rai made a joke in Nepali, and both men laughed.

"Swabash," Jebi said when Mr. Rai held up my passport to show him the fresh new stamp. "You will be speaking in ten or fifteen days," Jebi promised. "You will see pictures in your head as clear as television. I guarantee I will make you speak."

That night, Jebi had me recite his mantras until I shook, and Mr. Rai shouted, "Tell, tell who you are." Jebi showered me with rice. I saw a vivid vision of a cobra poised to strike.

"Basukinag," Jebi said, naming the great snake of the lower world. But I still didn't speak.

Father Miller finally returned Mr. Rai's call, and though we no longer needed his help with my visa, Mr. Rai arranged a visit to St. Xavier's. I was anxious to meet the teacher Vhim had spoken of so fondly.

St. Xavier's was in Godavari, at the edge of Kathmandu, housed in a large building at the end of a lane behind an iron fence. We drove in through the open gate. A black-robed student showed us into a large front room where Father Miller waited, thin and elderly, with light blue eyes and a kindly manner, and he greeted us warmly, coming out from behind his desk to sit with us on straight chairs in the middle of the room. A student brought tea.

Originally from America, Father Miller had been in Nepal so many years, he'd finally become a citizen. He and Mr. Rai discussed mutual acquaintances, and he told us about his school. Most of his class of novices had come from India and were studying drama, arts, and literature, in addition to religion.

"And why have you come to study our shamanism?" Father Miller's light eyes twinkled with tiny adjustments of light, as his rational American brain went about sorting, comparing, and mapping one thing onto another, finding common ground—eyes like my own, that made me feel at home.

"I guess I have the kind of mind that can't have faith unless I see it for myself," I said. "If there is a God, he has to be right here in the material world with us. Otherwise, what's the point?" I laughed a little, nervously, wondering if the priest would take offense.

"Doubts. Yes, I see."

"Teilhard de Chardin has always been one of my heroes," I offered.

Chardin had been a twentieth century paleoanthropologist and Jesuit monk. For most of his life, his major writings were suppressed by the Church, who feared heresy in his idea that consciousness evolves naturally from the complexification and involution of matter. Our kind of consciousness is no accident, he taught, but a natural inevitable flowering of the stuff of matter, whose ultimate destiny is union with God.

"The way he sees the material world as part of God, instead of separate and lost—it gave me hope," I said.

Father Miller bestowed a tolerant smile on my earnestness. "God's presence in the material world. The poet Gerard Manley Hopkins had the same idea."

"Glory be to God for dappled things," I quoted, as the line sprang to mind.

Father Miller turned to Jebi and asked in Nepali how long he'd been a shaman, and his caste, listening with full attention to his answers.

"I once saw a shaman do an exorcism," Father Miller said, switching back to English. "The shaman said a mouse had run over a dead man's body, so his ghost had to wander the world. The man's family was having a lot of trouble—ruined crops, children dying. The shaman said the ghost was causing all this harm because he was angry at his family for letting the mouse defile his body." Father Miller smiled at each of us in turn. "Hard to believe."

"That the ghost would do that, or that God would let it happen?" I asked, and without waiting for an answer, rushed on, "But just look at all the evil God lets happen."

Father Miller listened patiently. This probably wasn't the first time he'd been querulously taxed with explaining God's ways.

"God gives us free will," he said, but it sounded rote, like some standard Catholic answer.

"If He gives the living free will, why not the dead man too?" I challenged, looking forward to an intellectual discussion, and the fine, reckless feel of thoughts charging through my brain seeking an outlet.

"Ah, the problem of evil. I've come to the conclusion it's simply beyond our capacity to understand."

"It's beyond of *my* think," Mr. Rai said.

It wasn't beyond of mine, I thought, still making up arguments in the taxi home. I should have said, "Why call it evil? Evil for whom? Why do we think that God cares only for humans? Isn't He God of everything, ghosts too?" I tapped my fingers on the seat.

Jebi looked down at my hand, and then at me, his dark eyes deep and quiet. No dancing points of rationality there.

Who cared what I should have said? I stilled my hands and clasped them in my lap. Intellectualizing wouldn't help me channel the deity and speak.

HUNGER STRIKE

I dreamed I was driving a car, very carefully, because Santa Dev was quite ill in the passenger seat beside me. I woke to a pounding on my door. It was the real Santa Dev, holding a blood-streaked towel to his face. It was two in the morning.

"Can you help?" he asked in a low, scared voice. He was trembling.

I made him sit on the bed, and moved the towel aside. Twin streams of thick, dark blood ran from his nose.

"I have called Mr. Rai already," he said.

I tipped his head back and pinched the top of his nose as I used to do when my boys were little and came home with nosebleeds. Santa snuffled, and spat fastidiously into a bag, careful to keep the bed and the cuffs of his yellow sweatshirt clean.

Mr. Rai arrived with his third wife, Sani Kumari, and another young woman who sat on the bed with her back against Santa's and began to weep. The nosebleed stopped, and then started again. Santa sniffed.

"Don't keep sniffing. It only makes it worse," I said. But he couldn't seem to help it. The women exclaimed, both weeping now. Finally an ambulance came and they all left in a group.

It occurred to me only then that Santa might have waked me for shamanic healing.

The next day, Jebi and I bought oranges and apples from a small store near the hospital, and asked directions to Santa's room in the large, bare emergency room, where a row of unchanged beds with bloody sheets lined one long wall. A very sick old woman lay in one bed, next to a younger woman who coughed and spat into a bucket. The place was filthy and muggy, and smelled of blood and vomit, with no staff in sight to care for the patients. This was the Japanese Teaching Hospital, supposedly the best in town.

Santa was upset because, although the bleeding had stopped for the moment, the doctors had done nothing for him. "Have courage," Jebi said. "You'll soon be well."

Bindu came in then, cleaned up the mess of orange peel and bloody tissues around Santa's bed, and spoon-fed him a sort of gruel she'd brought in a metal camp pot wrapped in a towel. Evidently, no one with a choice ate hospital food. Jebi peeled him another orange. Santa was getting plenty of love and attention from his friends, even if the doctors ignored him.

It was clear that shamanic treatment made more sense under these conditions than Western medicine, at least the way it was practiced here, with insufficient drugs, supplies, and care. The doctors might give their patients a few moments of close attention, authoritative advice, and the feel of their cold, magical stethoscopes against their backs, but shamans had their own advice and magical tools, and provided compassion and a sense of holiness besides.

✤

It was Christmas day. Back at Mr. Rai's, I gave way to sadness, staring into space. "Your soul has gone traveling—home to see your children," Mr. Rai said.

Tears gathered in my eyes.

"They are fine," Jebi comforted. "They miss you, but they are fine."

"Elder brother," I said, taking advantage of Mr. Rai's rare calm mood, "I am a little upset. Time is running out, and I am determined to speak before I have to go home. I think I should fast."

"Hunger strike," said Jebi, showing off his English.

Mr. Rai agreed, and told Thuli Kumari not to give me dinner.

Later, Maile arrived with Mr. Lama and set up a small altar on a metal pie pan, in the center of which she placed a water pitcher with a bushy red flower. She instructed me to sip three times from the pitcher, then to begin reciting her mantras.

I concentrated. Someone was making weird noises behind me, but Maile had taught me to pay no attention to people in the room who mocked or didn't believe in shamans—to put them beneath me, under my seat. I could easily ignore the rude sounds.

I pictured splitting myself in two, put my critical, scientific self behind me on a tall stool, and asked it to be still and watch.

Maile spoke in Tamang while I shook. "Who are you, Singbon, Brabon, Dolmo, Lamo?" I knew these gods and goddesses from the words of her mantras, and understood what she said, but still I couldn't speak.

"*Allen* has decided to fast," Mr. Rai informed Maile and Mr. Lama when we finished. "She is determined to speak before she goes home."

Mr. Lama shook his head, frowned, and said something emphatic in Tamang. Maile nodded, waiting her turn to tell me I was wrong. "What are they saying?" I asked.

"They say there are many deities that live inside your body, and if you fast, you punish them. This is not good," Mr. Rai translated. "Why you want to do this?" they ask.

"For two reasons," I told them. "First, I know that fasting is how American Indian shamans get power. Second, I am trying to starve the more selfish parts of myself."

When Mr. Rai translated, everyone laughed.

"Why are they laughing?"

"Because they understand," he said.

"Maile was born to be a shaman. She was a shaman from early childhood," I said. "She didn't have to change herself. But I am not young, and I wasn't a shaman before. I have to change to be a shaman."

Maile laid her warm hand on my arm. "No," she said. "You must not starve and punish your deities. If you want to fast, do so only from sundown until after the evening ceremony. Don't eat any kind of meat except fish and chicken. Don't eat shishnu. Don't even try to pick it."

"Really?" I grinned, overjoyed at the idea of never touching shishnu again.

"We have to keep happy inside," Mr. Lama said. "Listen to your guru. If you are driving on a zigzag road, as long as you stay on the road you're okay, even if it's bumpy, but if you get off the road, you fall down. The road is your guru's teachings. Now your guru is telling you not to fast. You must follow that road. Don't worry. If you only eat clean food, you will stay clear." As Mr. Rai translated, I wished I had taken more time to seek out Mr. Lama for his wisdom.

"In the sacred pictures, Buddha is shown with water coming out of his belly button, and Shiva is shown with a river flowing from the top of his head," Mr. Lama went on. "This is clarity. In Buddhism we say a prayer and put water in our belly button to purify ourselves. It is important to stay clear. In shamanism, just as in Buddhism, we have to keep our inner gods happy. This is how we stay clear."

Everyone looked at me, smiling and nodding and wanting me to be happy. I bowed to Mr. Lama, and then to Maile, Jebi, Mr. Rai, and Bindu. "Namaskar," I said. "Tomorrow I will eat breakfast."

SPEAKING

A crowd had gathered in front of Mr. Rai's, watching as a shouting group of youths pushed a damaged car into the driveway. The rear fender had been dented in, the trunk lid bent and popped open, and the driver's door wouldn't shut. Mr. Rai's teenage son had backed a borrowed car too far too fast, across the grassy bank to the cliff edge. Witnesses described how the rear wheels had projected over the precipice, then slowly, the car had tipped backward, and half rolled, half fallen down the drop-off, coming to rest against a rock wall at the back of someone's property. After that, it refused to start, and Mr. Rai's son and his friends had pushed it through a gate, across a lawn, and around and up the steep road to the house.

"Thank God no one was hurt," Dakhal remarked.

The young men left and the crowd dispersed. We found Mr. Rai inside, scowling and taking short puffs on his cigarette, as Bindu and Thuli Kumari hovered, looking worried. "Where is he?" Mr. Rai demanded.

"Gone off with his friends," Dakhal said.

"He better come and face me." Mr. Rai clenched both fists.

The phone rang. Bindu answered and handed it to him.

"Yes, yes. I don't know." Then louder, "Why are you calling me? Is this my problem? I'm not the one for you to shout at." He put down the phone and called loudly for Magchha. "They say my brother-in-law is drunk and didn't show up for work." The phone rang again. I heard a man on the other end, talking fast and loud. Mr. Rai hung up. It rang again. "Don't call here any more," he shouted, holding the receiver away from his ear and adding in English, "Talking all nonsense about my family."

Bindu took the phone. "Papa, don't be angry. Why let them upset you?"

Instead of answering sharply, as I'd expected, Mr. Rai covered his face with his hands and began to weep. I was shocked. He, the strong one, always in charge, the one who knew exactly what to do—how could he give way like this?

"I try to do everything," he said in English. "I am here feeding these twenty-nine peoples, taking care of all these things. Now this happens. Of course no insurance. Will cost me ten thousands of rupees. Owner of car will be angry."

Bindu and Kumari sat stricken.

"I am paying for educating all these children, buying foods and clothing, everything. Now this. *Even*—I cannot do it."

Jebi was the one who went to comfort him, pouring whiskey, pressing Mr. Rai's fingers around the glass and raising it to his lips. "Don't worry, Elder Brother. Things will get better. Lord Shiva will help." I noticed Jebi didn't pour any for himself.

Bindu murmured then that it would be all right, and Kumari got up and headed to the kitchen to cook.

❧

Next day, Mr. Rai was unusually quiet, and Jebi was ill and frightened. "You're sick because you drink too much," Mr. Rai said to Jebi.

"I have already stopped drinking." Jebi pulled himself up straight.

It was true. I couldn't remember the last time he'd been drunk. But he was holding his stomach as though it hurt.

"Good man," Mr. Rai praised.

"It was a promise."

I wondered if it had to do with me—a bargain with the gods to let him be the first to make me speak.

We took Jebi to the Japanese teaching hospital, where a doctor felt his liver and ordered ultrasound, but the machine was broken. Instead, they led us into a small back room and inserted a long tube down his throat. It made him gag and groan. No one seemed to mind us watching. When it was finished, Jebi sat up shaking—but like a sick man, not a shaman.

"So far, I don't feel much damage to the liver," the doctor said, prescribing a medicine for tremors, and vitamin B6.

"He has promised not to drink," Mr. Rai said.

Jebi stood up staunch and square before the doctor, pulled his ears, and repeated, "I promise."

"Yes, good." The doctor folded his stethoscope into his pocket. "You should feel better soon."

❧

I practiced mantras in my room until the words began to blur, and then went outside. The light was low and wintry, but wildflowers still grew by the road. I picked a few and tossed them into the stream by Tunal Devi temple as an offering to Banjhankri, then turned and climbed uphill. The roads were never empty, but today they held little traffic.

My mind was on Banjhankri, riding on a bluish light I sensed and wanted to believe in, following me closely, just above my right shoulder. A third of the way up the hill, the feeling intensified, as though something had gripped me from behind. *"I think we can use her,"* the words sounded loud in my head. I knew I would soon speak.

That night I dreamed of a small woman shaman from the hills, wrinkled and very, very old. Her clothing was grubby, and her drum and sacred oil lamp were shiny with ancient dirt and smoke, for time had worked its magic on the grime, transforming it into a patina of respected age. She touched me, and I shook.

From the moment I opened my eyes, I felt calm and happy, like a child awakening on her birthday, knowing the day was mine.

Maile came alone that night, and set up a small altar. Jebi had gone out. It was cold in the room, but I knew I'd soon be warm. I peeled off my sweater, folded my shawl, and set them aside. Maile woke her mala with a mantra and hung it around my neck.

I took a deep breath, picked up my drum and held it upright, tapping the top and all four sides as I recited its mantra, and then began beating the Tamang rhythm—two taps and a slide, two taps and a slide—concentrating on fitting the new chant I'd memorized that day to the rhythm. Soon I began to shake, and the rhythm skittered out of control, becoming a fast, steady tapping, all I could manage as the shaking intensified.

"Who are you?" Maile shouted, pouring water from her sacred pitcher on my head.

I struggled against the force that blocked my throat, and when the words broke through, they came in a scream. *"Jhankri, jhankri!"* I am a shaman!

"Where do you play?" Mr. Rai shouted.

"In the tree," I answered in Nepali.

"What kind of tree?"

"The thorn."

"Where do you stay?"

"*Chandra!*" I used the Nepali word for moon, and wondered why, and then shouted, "*Nima!*" the Tamang for sun—for that was the image in my mind, a golden sun from Maile's song. "Sunset, sunset!"

"Which jhankri?" Mr. Rai shouted.

No answer came. They began to name different manifestations of Banjhankri, "Milk Jhankri? Black seed Jhankri? One-legged Jhankri, Golden Jhankri?"

"Yes, Golden Jhankri."*Suna* Jhankri!" I cried.

"What do you want?"

I knew I should demand an offering and call for incense, but nothing came to mind.

"*Gaiko dudh*, cow's milk?" Maile suggested.

"Gaiko dudh," I said. It sounded right. "And incense."

"What kind of incense? What kind of leaves?"

"Pine." The answer was there without thought.

"What do you want, and why are you here?"

No more answers came, neither pictures nor words. I fell silent and Maile stopped the shaking with a mantra. My body was slick with sweat. She took my hands in hers. "Cold hands," she said. "The Banjhankris always make our hands cold."

I felt a rush of gratitude. Though I'd spoken at last, I was still afraid I'd been lying, saying things simply because the words or pictures sprang to mind. I had no way to verify their truth. These were different rules for speaking than I knew. But my hands *were* cold. I couldn't have made them cold on purpose. It was a confirming sign.

Maile was very, very happy. She smiled, and her large teeth gleamed. "There are seven suns shining on your head," she said. "It is dark outside, but the sun is shining."

Dakhal translated as she went on, "Whenever I have a student, I suffer with her. Yesterday, I knew you would speak. I had a toothache because of it, but now the pain is gone."

"Now, put salt tika on your forehead and ask for help from God," Mr. Rai instructed, providing a little saucer of salt. "You will get more teaching in dreams, and now you will be able to do guru jokhanna."

GRADUATION

I had a chance to test my divinatory skills several days later when Bindu came down with cough and fever. Mr. Rai asked me to find out what was wrong. "Jebi, tell me what to do," I begged in sudden panic.

"It's easy," he encouraged. "Say from your heart, 'I may make mistakes; I may feel shame. Rude people may mock. Please give me the power to understand her sickness.' Worship Mahadeo. When you're shaking and people ask questions, the answers will come—from Banjhankri and Lord Shiva. You'll see the answers in the rice."

He began to arrange my oil lamp and water pitcher on the altar. "When you think you know, ask Bindu if it's true. If she says no, you have to go back to the altar and tell your deity he gave you the wrong answer. Dip the drum handle in the oil of your lamp and touch it to your forehead." He demonstrated, dabbing a shiny streak above his eyebrows. "Tell him, 'When you give the wrong answer it's just like killing God.'"

I sat before the altar, picked up my drum, and chanted until I shook. Mr. Rai shouted "Lo paramaswara!"

Bindu put a handful of uncooked rice on the drum, and I recited the jokhanna mantra, tapping the drum from underneath. The rice packed away from the center, moving to the lower left and upper right, and as I asked the deity for help, it began to become clear who Bindu was—the sweetness of her spirit, her deep religious devotion. I saw that she'd once been wounded when she lost a friend.

How long ago? I asked the rice. Five years? Ten? Fifteen?

Five years clearly wasn't right. Ten years felt more true—maybe fifteen. An area of blue moved away from where the rice was massed up on the lower left, replaced by red, floating down from the upper right.

I stopped drumming and asked out loud, "Did you lose a good woman friend about ten or fifteen years ago?"

"Ho," she said softly.

"This has left a hole in your heart, and makes you open to attack from wandering ghosts. That's why you get sick." I spoke with authority, though the thought had only then entered my head.

"What can we do?" Mr. Rai asked.

"Give a light blue cloth, maybe a sari, to someone who needs it. She is very much devoted to Mahadeo. She should ask Him to fill the hole in her heart." The idea was that when she gave away the blue cloth, she would be getting rid of excess blue energy, leaving room for someone with a surplus of red energy to give it to her to put her back in balance.

"Well done," Mr. Rai said, when the ceremony was over.

Later, his secretary told me that, indeed, fifteen years ago Bindu and a friend had become ceremonial sisters, but later they'd quarreled and never made up.

જ

Now that I was shaking and speaking, Jebi was willing to teach me everything. "How do you hypnotize the chicken?" I asked, guessing there must be some trick of squeezing its body.

"By the power of massan—with the mantra for Bir Massan," he said. "It is a very strong mantra, but you must have a massan bone. In fact, I will give you mine." He held it out.

"Oh, no." I drew back shocked. "After all you went through to get it?"

"I can get another at Pashupatinath," he said, "as easy as digging potatoes." The translator chuckled.

"No, that one is yours." Despite the scorch mark on the end of Jebi's bone, I didn't want to hear him say he hadn't really dug it from a grave, stark naked at midnight.

"There are sixty-four massans, but sixteen mantras are enough to control them," Jebi said, and dictated them all, including a mantra to wake the bone, a mantra to give it blood, and a mantra to put it back to sleep. "When you get your bone, cut your finger and feed it, and when you're finished, put it to sleep so it won't do harm," he said.

Dakhal brought clay from the garden, and Jebi mixed it with water and modeled rough little figures of massans, Banjhankri, Lemlemma, and other deities. "Give offering to massan to cure your patient's sickness," he said. "The other deities are there to witness. If you do this in America and don't want to sacrifice a real chicken, you can make one out of clay or use an egg. Say, 'I am sorry, I have no chicken. Please take this egg for a chicken.' Then break it and pour it out on Bir massan."

The sun came out, weak and watery, and we climbed to the roof to get warm. Thuli Kumari had spread fermented vegetables to dry on the flat, black surface for making *gundruk,* a favorite Nepali dish.

Jebi seemed quiet. So far, he'd kept his promise not to drink.

He taught me to cleanse a building of evil spirits by pounding four wooden stakes into the dirt at each outside corner, and spitting kerosene across a torch to blow fire into the inside corners. "When we finish and go out, we see small, black, baby-like things floating ahead of us — the bad spirits leaving." Later, in America, I used the ritual to purify Vhim's new restaurant, the Taj, a space in which four prior restaurants had failed; but his became a great success.

A large cloud moved across the sun, and the chill breeze drove us back inside. Jebi continued the lessons, explaining how he sucked out illness, letting Hanuman possess him as he sniffed for bad spots on the patient's body.

"How do you suck out blood?" I asked. "Do you hide chicken blood in your mouth?"

"No, no," he laughed. "If you suck the inside of your mouth hard enough, you will get blood." Dakhal, translating, burst out laughing too.

"Jebi, why are you wearing a glove in the house?" Mr. Rai asked. It was cold in the room. I huddled with Santa Dev and Mr. Rai's sisters over the heater near Bindu's bed. Jebi sat beyond the circle of warmth on the couch, but even earlier, on the roof in the sunshine, I realized, one of his hands had been covered with a single brown cloth work glove.

"Take it off," Mr. Rai ordered.

Jebi turned away, his body a curve of denial.

"Take it off. Come on, let me see."

Jebi peeled the glove down, revealing raw skin on the back of his left hand, wet with blood and serum.

"My God, what's happened?" At Mr. Rai's shocked tone, all three of his wives ran over to look. "How long has this been going on?"

Jebi kept his head down, shamed as though it were his fault.

"We are taking you to hospital," Mr. Rai said. "Right now."

But Jebi sank deeper into the couch and started to shake, and then fell over sideways and curled into a fetal position. Mr. Rai pulled at his legs and kept on scolding until he sat up and lifted his right pant leg to show another patch of weeping skin below his knee.

"I had an uncle that happened to," Santa said. "Right after he stopped drinking."

"Did it go away?" I asked.

"I don't know," Santa said. "He died soon after."

"Maybe it's because you stopped drinking." I knelt beside Jebi. "Your whole system has changed. All the germs that used to get killed by alcohol can live now. But after a while your body will adjust and start killing them." Thinking he'd probably never heard of phagocytes, I drew a circle with a wavy outline to represent a white blood cell, giving it big sharp teeth and mean eyes, with eyebrows drawn together at the center, but flaring upward at the sides to show it was really a good guy. "He's eating these little black germs in your blood," I said, and drew a few blobby spots close to its mouth. Jebi stared vaguely at the sketch, unable to take it in, and mumbled something to Mr. Rai.

"He wants you to do mantra."

I felt Jebi's forehead, hot with fever. His eyes were cloudy.

"Massan," he croaked.

I rushed to my room to fetch the rudraksha mala he'd given me, taking the opportunity to flip quickly through the sixteen massan mantras.

"I haven't memorized them yet," I admitted, bending over the couch where Jebi had curled into a tight little ball.

"Is okay," Mr. Rai said. "Do Bir massan mantra sixteen times."

At least I knew that mantra well. I swept Jebi's body with the mala, reciting the mantra under my breath, and counted to sixteen on my fingers, blowing on his hand and knee each time.

When it was finished, he sat up, able to focus. Some of the fear had left his eyes. He called for a porcupine quill, and Mr. Rai handed him one from the fence of crossed quills on his altar. Holding it to his forehead, pointed end out, Jebi recited a mantra, and, sighting down the length of the quill, hurled it across the room toward the door. He took a deep breath in and sighed, clasped his hands, stretched his arms between his legs, and looked up, clear-eyed and present with us once again.

Next morning, we took Jebi to the doctor and bought the medicines prescribed. Jebi was cheerful. The glove was off and the skin was drying out.

He held his usual teaching session, and gave me the mohini love spell mantras, and told me how to use them.

৵

Maile came later. The sun was bright and Dakhal suggested going to the roof.

"If the patient's eyelashes are tangled, you know the soul has gone away," she told me. She dictated a mantra and showed me how to call lost souls, placing a single flower in a small pitcher of water and setting it in the doorway. The mantra called for "this child's soul."

"What do we use to call back a grown-up's soul?" I asked.

"The same," she said. "Because we are all children."

As we basked, lifting our faces to the sun, Maile spoke of Banjhankri. "I give him offerings, incense, *sunpati* leaf from the mountains, rice, oil lamp, little flags. He tells me, 'If you are climbing a tree, I'll put a ladder there. If you are crossing a river, I'll put down a bridge. When you have to scale a cliff, I'll put my body there to climb on.'" She gazed off toward the horizon, and said, in a voice hypnotic and exalted, "The Banjhankris never die. They are living gods. Though they are small, they are kings of the mountains and forests of this world." Dakhal translated faithfully, preserving the rhythm and tone of her words. "As long as there are mountains, there will be Banjhankris—in every forest, every river, every lake, they will be there."

Overcome by a wave of feeling, I began to cry. Waterfalls of tears rolled down my cheeks. I groped in my pocket for a tissue. It had suddenly struck me how soon I'd have to leave. I studied Maile's face, trying to memorize her features—the scar on her forehead, the bright, clear eyes beneath, the tiny freckles on her nose—and wished with all my heart I could have known her as a child. We would have been best friends, joking and playing in the mountain sunlight, crouching under fallen trunks in games of hide and seek, sharing fresh milk and secrets in the cowshed, gossiping and pointing with our long upper lips as the Tamangs do, rolling, running, laughing—children together.

"The deity has come," she said gently. "Mahadeo."

Her words caught my heart and wrenched out yet another sob. I loved her so much, I felt as though we *had* been childhood friends, and grieved the loss of what had never been, more poignant than if the memories were real. I gulped and sobbed and hid my face between my knees to think of leaving the dearest friend I felt I'd ever known.

"When Mahadeo comes, sometimes it makes us cry."

How good of her to say I cried for holiness, when it was only selfish grief. I blew my nose.

"I used to cry all the time, when I was learning mantras from my human teacher," she said. "My students cry too, when they're learning."

A night was set for my formal graduation. A tailor had sewed up a red and white shaman's costume to Mr. Rai's order on his old treadle sewing machine, and I helped Jebi make a fresh altar. During the afternoon, we got a phone call from Wayne Parrott, a plant scientist I'd written patents for back home, from the University of Kentucky. He'd come to Kathmandu for an agricultural conference, and Mr. Rai invited him to witness the ceremony.

At dusk, the house filled with neighbors. Wayne arrived in a taxi with his camera, and Mr. Rai gave him a drink and seated him on the couch.

Jebi had begun calling Mr. Rai "Mahaguru," great guru, and deferred to his opinion as they discussed how the ritual should be performed. They summoned the old man from the house out back; as the oldest Rai man, his presence was essential. Magchha and Mr. Rai's sister arranged themselves nearby to help with drumming, and Maile arrived with Mr. Lama and got into costume.

Mr. Rai signaled Jebi to start, and he drummed and shook, and then led me to the center of the room, and Mr. Rai's wives and sisters and children, and Maile and Mr. Lama, people I'd come to know and love as family, gathered close.

Magchha beat the hypnotic middle world rhythm as they spiraled around me with sacred objects, water callas, kukhuri knife, oil lamp, gourd, and plates of offerings, holding them near the ground at first, and raising them higher and higher with every round, in the traditional Rai crest-raising ceremony. Bindu held a living chicken, passing it so close to my face each time she circled, that I could look right into its beady little eye. Everyone shouted, "Rogo, rogo, rogo," and sang a traditional, boisterous Rai song.

Mr. Rai handed me my new costume, folded on a plate beneath several malas. I pulled off my sweater and tied the costume over my T-shirt and sweat pants. Maile gave me a new string of bells and she and Jebi arranged them around my shoulders.

With my teachers beside me, I drummed and chanted mantras until I shook, and then handed off the drum to Magchha, and danced, and cut a piece of ginger with a single downward slice of the feather, though Jebi had to hold my wrist and add his force to the swing. As the bud of ginger bounced and came to rest cut side up, he fell against the wall shaking violently. Hands reached to support him, as flashes from Wayne's camera lit the scene like lightning.

"Now you are a real shaman," Mr. Rai said formally, so everyone could hear. "Be a good shaman. Always tell the truth. Go wherever you are called to heal." For the second time I saw him overcome with tears, and Jebi cried too.

BOOK FIVE

IN MY OWN COUNTRY

My plane touched down in Seattle after midnight, and I sped southward to Portland in a new rented car. I was nearly alone on the wide, empty freeway, and my soul expanded in the sense of space—America! Occasional northbound headlights passed silently, far away across the broad median. Lush pine forests massed in silhouette against the skyline, beyond a sweep of meadow. The tree branches came clear to the ground; no one had been cutting the lower limbs for firewood.

There'd been a goodbye party the night before I left, with Prem and Rita, Maile, Mr. Lama, Santa Dev, two fat government officials who had something to do with tourism, and another fat man in a suit whom Mr. Rai had invited, as well as the usual crowd of friends and neighbors. Mr. Rai asked Jebi and me to put on our shamans' costumes and show off to his important guests, and we did a short ritual, shaking and dancing like performing monkeys, and trading grins and enjoying ourselves a great deal more than the pompous fat men.

After the special guests left, someone put on a rock music tape and we danced, free-form like Americans, but with the graceful hand movements of Indian dancers. Old Mr. Lama had a few beers and stood up grinning, swanning his hands through the air and lifting his knees. Thuli Kumari slid into a writhing snake dance, and everyone stepped back and clapped. Mr. Rai's brother-in-law and younger sister played hand drums, and Jebi jumped around like a disco dancer. He still wasn't drinking, but his old fierce, happy look had come back.

I passed through the outskirts of Portland and turned onto the cliff road above the broad Willamette Valley. Ship and factory lights along the river twinkled with distance. I pulled up and parked in front of Mary's house.

She came to the door blinking, tying the belt of her bathrobe, and threw her arms around me and drew me in.

I leaned over Keri's bed and said her name.

"Mommy!"

I lifted her and hugged her sleepy little body close, breathing her faint sour smell of child's breath and freshly washed hair. "What big, long arms and legs."

"Stay here, Mommy." She dropped her head on my shoulder and drifted back to sleep.

Mary was eager to hear what I'd learned and, scoffing all the while at the very idea of spirits and deities, invited two friends to watch me perform. I told their fortunes with the drum and rice, using the patterns, like Tarot cards or tea leaves, to suggest issues for discussion.

As always, we spent long hours in the kitchen, cooking good American food, gossiping about old friends and ex-husbands, trading puns and literary references, and poking fun at each other. Nothing essential had changed. We walked the dog, played the piano and sang, and took the kids to the shore. It was great to be home.

Then Keri and I drove east to Colorado, where we collected Thorne and kept on going to visit my parents, leaving the freeway north of Lexington at Sadieville, Kentucky for the dark road that wound upward into the hills above Eagle Creek. The dogs set up a racket as we turned down the lane and passed the old black tobacco barn. Mom and Dad had been asleep, but got up to greet us. Dad's features, rounded with age to a classic Irish pattern, made him look like a giant leprechaun, red-faced and smiling, with wisps of white hair floating out around his bald spot, and thick, white eyebrows tufted over twinkling eyes. Mom was frailer than I remembered, and hugged us in a way that let us know she hadn't felt complete until we came. We helped ourselves to new-baked cookies in the kitchen. Mom coughed into a tissue. Her lungs had been weak since a long-ago bout with tuberculosis.

The sun came up white-gold above the hills and shone on a row of pill bottles lined along the kitchen window sill. Hawks wheeled over the wooded valley to the east. "I'm taking a course of antibiotics," Mom said, then dropped her voice, embarrassed, "A week ago, I coughed up blood."

"Don't these help?" I read the label on one of the bottles.

"It comes and goes. They rotate the prescriptions."

She fried bacon for the family. It smelled delicious. "My gurus said I couldn't eat pork," I said.

"All the more for the rest of us." She'd never been one to criticize, but I wondered what she really thought of my running off to Nepal to study shamanism. "What else did your gurus tell you?"

"They gave me lots of healing mantras—for joint pain, stomach aches, headaches."

"How about itching? I've got this skin rash on my back. It's giving me fits."

I thought she was joking, but she mentioned it again later, lifting her shirt to reveal an area of small, raised bumps on her upper back near the spine, spreading onto the shoulder blade.

"I can fix that," I boasted. "Take off your shirt." I did an extraction with a stick of incense, a little uncooked rice, and Maile's mantra.

"Thanks," she said, and scraped the shirt across her back to scratch it as she dressed.

But a few days later, as she crocheted red and white squares for an afghan and watched an old movie on TV, she muted the sound and gave a little cough. "I think your itching mantra worked," she said. "I don't suppose you have one for bad lungs?"

"Have you coughed up more blood?"

"No, but I'll need a new antibiotic." She let her hands fall idle in her lap.

"I did learn something—it's a whole big ceremony though."

"I'll tell you, Ellen, I'm willing to try just about anything."

❧

My oldest son, Tom, drove down from medical school in Champaign-Urbana, and Mom invited her friend, Liz Pattingill, and Liz's daughter Mary, to see the ritual. That's when I knew she wasn't just humoring me.

It was winter still. The leaves and flowers required for a traditional Rai altar were half a planet away, but the gods would accept substitutes. I spent the afternoon wandering the nearby woods and fields for evergreen branches to take the place of banana leaves, sticks from locust and elm for bamboo, and branches of thorn for porcupine quills. I crushed green leaves from Mom's house plants into a bowl of water to serve as plant gum, and ransacked the basement, finding a dried gourd from the garden and a prehistoric bone my father had found by Nebraska's Blue River. Down at the lake I scooped clay into a bucket, spread newspapers in the garage, and modeled little massan and Banjhankri figures as Jebi had prescribed.

What I lacked was a helper—someone to drum while I danced. The drumbeats were complex, but Thorne surprised me, picking up the tricky rhythms with easy confidence. He agreed to drum reluctantly, making it clear he didn't really hold with such nonsense.

I built an altar by the fireplace. The clay figures were dry on the outside now and held their shape. Mom's friends arrived, and the family gathered, Dad lingering until the last minute to watch the basketball game on TV. The Wildcats were ahead. Like Thorne, Dad didn't believe in spirits.

I got into my costume in the bathroom, trying not to feel silly as I came back jingling in the long white red-bordered skirt. The audience was quiet, politely expectant. I took my place at the altar and began to drum. None of them really believed in what I was doing, and I could imagine them snickering and exchanging glances behind my back, especially the kids.

But the mantras had their own momentum; I'd done this many times, and soon was shaking, making the bells around my shoulders ring. I handed off the drum and brass plate to Thorne, called for *"tharo sili,"* the lower world beat, and danced, whirling until the audience was a blur, focusing down on one single intent, the healing of my mother's illness.

"Dhukure sili," I ordered, and Thorne changed to the upper world beat as I "climbed" with little jumps. *"Paro sili"*— another change of rhythm, and I was there, dancing in the upper world, visualizing Lord Shiva and the sixty-four thousand deities. At last I called for *"kulchure sili,"* the middle world beat, and descended again to do my work.

I told fortunes for the audience like a real Rai shaman before the healing work, but Thorne and my father declined.

Outside, I scattered popcorn and grain as massan offerings, and whispered mantras. Inside, I passed the petrified bone over my mother's body to draw out her illness, shaking the bone toward the small clay figures on the floor. It took nearly twenty minutes, but everyone stayed quiet. Finally, with a silent apology to Bir Massan that it wasn't a chicken, I broke an egg and spilled its contents onto the largest clay figure.

"Take these things outside and throw them down the hill," I ordered Thorne—and he obeyed.

"How do you feel, Evaline," Liz asked in a too-bright voice.

"Oh, *quite* a bit better." Mom pushed up from her chair and headed for the kitchen to bring in pie and coffee.

"How *impressive,*" Liz gushed. "However could you remember all those mantras?" Thorne and Dad wandered back to the ball game. Tom, whose medical studies would include a Ph.D. in anthropology, said he thought it was interesting.

I didn't know what they really thought, but a year later Mom's lungs were still clear.

⚘

Back in Boulder, I moved into a new house and returned to work. Thorne left for college in Durango, and Vhim arrived from Nepal with his younger brother, Ek Raj, and plans to start a restaurant.

It was Vhim's idea for me to put on a demonstration of Nepali shamanism. He drew up a guest list that included my friends and co-workers as well as his own, and spent the day cooking special food—Indian curries, Thai chicken with peanut sauce, *momos*, vegetables breaded with chickpea flour and deep-fat fried. If nothing else, the event would advertise his restaurant.

I ironed my costume and fasted. Ek Raj knew the rhythms and agreed to drum and help set up the altar.

Our large front room filled to capacity. Shamans perform under normal house lighting in Kathmandu, but Vhim, knowing the American psyche, lit candles and switched off the overhead lights. He gave a short introduction. I panicked as I sat before the altar, but only for a moment until the familiar routine allowed me to focus down on what I had to do, scattering substitute liso of green leaves and water to circle the audience with protection, drumming, dancing, and performing jokhannas in Jebi's way, with rice on the drum, for those who asked.

"Tell them it's okay to talk," I whispered to Vhim during break. The silence seemed unnatural; I didn't want to be treated as an object of reverence.

"Okay," he said, but then somehow forgot. He probably thought Americans would lose respect for the process if we let them talk and move around as they pleased.

Donna, from my office, had a persistent bronchial infection, and volunteered to be the patient. I put her beside me and drummed, visualizing Hanuman, the monkey god, and asking him to possess me. When I began to feel in my body how he liked to jump and scamper, I got down on all fours and capered around Donna, sniffing at her upper chest, stomach and back, finding places where something needed to come out. My consciousness was split, gathering impressions through my nose, and at the same time maintaining awareness of the altar, the audience, and my patient, so as not to scare her or knock things over.

I sucked and spit blood, using a small white bowl so the red showed up nicely, and involuntarily gagged and choked every bit as dramatically as Jebi, as I visualized the disease coming out of Donna's body into my mouth.

When it was over, Vhim turned up the lights and handed me a glass of wine, which I sipped nonchalantly, secretly relieved no one had cried fraud.

The compliments began. "The dancing was incredible—so much energy."

"What you said about my issues with my husband was right on..."

"So exciting."

"Powerful."

They were actually impressed. My ego expanded dangerously.

"Will you quit work now and become a full-time shaman?" asked Lea from our office.

"Oh no," I laughed. "Most shamans have to keep their day jobs."

At this point, Jebi and Maile would have told people to come back for more work, but I kept quiet. The performance had taken a lot out of me.

Later Donna said the healing had helped her, and I let myself feel good—but tried not to forget that nature alone is the greatest healer.

A few months later, Jeannie McWilliams invited me to Colorado Springs to perform for her friends. Her husband, Glen, was an old climbing friend of Evans'. They had a beautiful old house, remodeled to preserve the original high ceilings and woodwork. We set up a simple altar with a brass plate, water callas, oil lamp, rice and flowers. I used Maile's ritual, which I preferred because of its quieter, more intimate feel, and felt her spirit with me.

As I divined for the guests, images and ideas arose, suggested by the patterns of rice on the drum, and I spoke of them easily, beginning to feel confidence, if not in their truth, at least in their usefulness.

The last of the guests placed his rice on the drum in a tight little pile, and said his name was George. He gave his date of birth when I asked. I was tired by now, and the images had slowed. All I got was a persistent idea that he was cheating on his wife. "Is there a problem at work?" I fished for something else to say.

"No."

"A problem with your health, your chest?"

"Not really."

"With your family?"

"No." But as Jebi would have said, he was hiding.

What does he need to know?' I asked my spirit guru, tapping the drum and watching the rice grains scatter. I dumped them off the drum and turned to face him, still waiting for inspiration. "I don't see much," I said finally. "Some problems with relationships. You're not at peace.

You must keep your promises—vows you may have made in the past—and tell the truth. Then your life will get to be more comfortable."

Then Jeannie asked Glen to have his fortune told. He'd been hanging back. "I don't believe in all this woo-woo stuff," he said. With his hard, muscular body and thick, nearsighted glasses, he was a strange hybrid of sensitive intellectual and high altitude Leadville tough. He came and sat beside me. "Will I be rich and famous?" I held the drum horizontal, and he dribbled his rice out slowly on its surface.

The rice grains jumped, bringing images of rocks, trees, water, blood and pain. Had someone fallen on the rocks? Was it Glen? Not Glen. "Be very careful in the wilderness," I said. "Someone may be badly injured, and you'll have to take care of them."

"Oh shit." He scooted back. "I think you just ruined my summer."

"It's really odd," Jeannie said when everyone had gone. "A few years ago when Glen was leading a raft trip in Alaska, someone got killed." She turned up the burner beneath the teakettle. "It wasn't his fault. This girl insisted on going off on her own and wouldn't follow directions. But he's really sensitive about it."

"That must be what I saw." I leapt at the idea. "The past, not the future." The teapot shrilled. A plume of steam came out.

Glen wandered in, opened the refrigerator, and grabbed a beer. "Ya wanna go on my Green River trip in June?" He mugged at me and pulled out a chair. "But seriously, do you really think something bad will happen?"

"I'm really sorry," I said. "It was just an image that came up—maybe something from the past, maybe a warning to be careful—maybe nothing at all. I don't exactly have a track record of accurate predictions, so don't take it seriously."

"Not me." He upended the bottle.

"I shouldn't tell fortunes," I went on as Jeannie poured a stream of bubbling water in my cup. "It may be all right in Nepal, in villages where the shaman knows everyone and uses it to get things out in the open and deal with them. But for strangers, it's more like just stroking their egos."

"Americans are narcissists anyway, especially in Bould*ah*," Glen agreed, his accent making fun of Boulder's influx of trendy people from back East.

Jeannie, an accomplished Tarot reader, changed the subject. "What really floored me, Ellen, was what you said to George. He's been having an affair for months with a woman from his office. His wife is really upset."

I shivered. But Glen got through the summer with no one hurt.

BANJHANKRI IN COLORADO

Vhim's mother came to Boulder from Florida, where she'd been staying with his sister. She was here to help set up the restaurant. A stocky woman of sixty, she climbed our inside steps with sturdy determination, her broad face beaming. "Wine *khanne?*" I offered, for she'd never learned English.

"*Na khanne,*" she said, still smiling. But Vhim had explained that when Nepalis refuse food or drink, the hostess is supposed to read their expressions. If they smile, it means they really want some. I poured us both a glass. We got on so well that Ama ended up renting a room in our house while Vhim and his brother and uncle and other assorted helpers stayed in a crash pad downtown.

I'd been wanting to invite Maile to America, but she spoke no English, and I hadn't known what she'd do all day while I was working. Now Ama could be her companion. Maile readily agreed to come, and she and Ama soon became fast friends.

Maile was an ideal housemate, calm, pleasant, quietly joyful, and never upset, her vibrations clear as a sweet, mellow note from a bell of precious metal. She could make you feel good just by being near.

When I got home from the office, Ama would leave to help Vhim at the restaurant, and Maile and I would have dinner and spend an hour or two as teacher and student. She gave me more mantras, and taught me the healing ritual that she used, without drumming or shaking, in her day-to-day practice, divining and extracting illnesses with incense and mantras.

We took long drives in the mountains, and hikes with the dogs; she liked to hold the leash and let Smoky, our rottweiler, pull her uphill. She didn't know how to read, but like most Nepalis, understood enough Hindi to watch rented Indian movies. Whatever I proposed to fill our time, she cheerfully agreed to, smiling, exposing her big white teeth, and saying, "hajur."

She was interested in our Harner-style drumming group, and agreed to join us, taking her turn as we smudged each other with sage.

Vann Hilty called in the spirits, shaking his rattle in the six directions. I explained that American shamans send their souls traveling to the upper and lower worlds, or another middle world where spirits live, while listening to a steady drumbeat.

That night, we worked on the pain in Mike Mitchell's foot. It came and went, he said, hurting so much at times that he had trouble walking, and no doctor had been able to diagnose or treat it.

"Now we travel to meet our teachers," I explained to Maile in my simple Nepali. "Some of us have animal teachers. We ask the teachers, 'What happened? This man's foot, why does it hurt? What can be done?'"

She smiled. "Hajur."

We lay on the floor to journey, covering our eyes, and Maile followed suit, easing herself down on one elbow and looking around to be sure she was doing it right.

After we had journeyed, we told what we'd learned. No one had a cure, though various remedies—salt baths, massage, and offerings to Mike's shaman ancestors from Samiland—were suggested.

"What did you see?" I asked Maile.

"Little tiny people in the lower world," she said.

"Did they say anything about Mike's foot?"

She smiled. "No, nothing." She wasn't embarrassed. She wouldn't have expected the spirits to give out information without the offerings or ceremonies they normally required.

Though she surely found it odd to be doing shamanism in a group, and with such simple methods, Maile seemed to respect it.

Everyone wanted to see Maile perform a real ceremony in the way of her people, so we rented space at the Unitarian Church, set a date, and recruited Ama and Vhim's uncle, and several Nepali waiters from the restaurant to help her set up the altar and shout "Lo paramaswara!" in the customary Nepali way when she began to shake.

It was a great success, and afterward, patients began coming to the house to see her every night. I did my best to translate. We suggested they put ten dollars in her altar for donations, and her bank account grew.

John Howard came faithfully, usually on Tuesdays and Saturdays, auspicious days for healing in the Nepali tradition. Though poor, he always brought some gift in return for his treatments, and would lay out laminated pictures of the deities he worshiped—Sai Baba, Jesus and Mary—next to Maile's altar. John was, energetic, athletic in build, with close-cropped red hair, and the competent manner of a military man—which he never could have been. For him, the spirit world was totally real. He had prayed to Sai Baba for a woman shaman to come, and believed it was Maile. "You can't always tell if the spirits around you are good," he explained. "Sometimes the bad ones trick you, pretending to be something else and saying things to confuse you. But Maile is good."

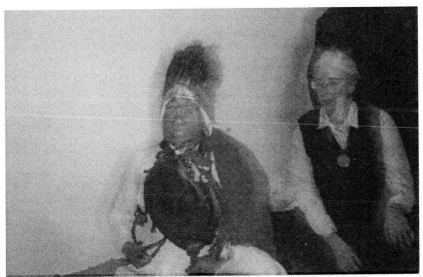

Maile and Ellen in America

Maile sang her long Tamang *gyasang* to the spirits, divined John's problem, offered rice and incense, and sang the special songs for each spirit that was bothering him, blowing mantras and passing an egg over his body. When she was finished, she blessed a few grains of rice and pressed them into the center of his forehead, which by now had completely smoothed out. Cracking the egg she'd used to remove the illness, she opened its small end, let the yolk slide into her hand, examined it under the light, and said, "Good."

Some patients came with long-standing pain, some with immune diseases like lupus, others with mysterious stomach ailments. Most had chronic problems their doctors couldn't cure. All said Maile's treatments helped.

Another class of patients was made up of those who believed they'd been contacted by flying saucer people, or were able themselves to channel beings from outer space. They wanted Maile to confirm their beliefs. No matter what they told her, she would simply smile as though she understood—she never contradicted anyone—and then do her healing rituals as usual.

Unlike Nepalis, American patients wanted explanations of her divinations. "She says you are afflicted by ghosts, and the Forest Shaman, and that your planets are out of alignment," I translated for a woman who complained of persistent headaches.

"Who are they? How does it work? What do you mean, my planets are out of alignment?" She searched my face. "I'm a Gemini. Venus is supposed to be retrograde right now, but what does it mean, 'my planets'?"

"Your inner planets. They're out of harmony with the cosmos." I struggled with my sketchy understanding. "She'll do a mantra to put them back into alignment." Anyway, I told myself, it was probably best left vague—more mysterious, not so easily categorized and dismissed. And it worked. When Maile finished, the headache was gone.

One night, an attractive large woman, no longer young, but with an air of smoldering, earthy sexuality, came for help to get a lover back. She told us that in her life so far she'd slept with more than two hundred men; that she had no trouble attracting them, but now there was only one she wanted, and he'd left her. "Can you do something?" she entreated.

Maile smiled, "Hajur," and began to speak to me in Nepali: "Tell her that next time she comes, she must bring a piece of candy or a cigarette—something she can give the man to put in his mouth. And tell her what I do should cost a lot of money. It's dangerous to do love spells—even for the shaman."

"I can't give him anything to eat or smoke," the woman said. "He's gone."

"Maybe you need a love spell taken away from you instead, of putting one on him," I suggested. "Maile can find out."

"Let me think about it," she said. "But since I'm here, I have this pain in my wrist..."

"Two hundred men!" Maile exclaimed when the door had closed behind her. In Nepal, woman were supposed to be virgins when they married, and if widowed, they were supposed to remain single the rest of their lives.

"Two hundred," Maile told Ama, as soon as she got home. *"Um um um."*

"Two hundred men," Ama echoed. *"Um um um um um."*

They discussed this amazing statistic at length, for among Nepalis a good story only improves in the telling, and each time, Ama narrowed her eyes into little half moon slits and laughed. "Two hundred men. *Um um um um um um um."*

"Here comes Two Hundred Men," Maile said when the patient came again.

Two Hundred Men came back many times, but we knew she was getting better when she stopped talking about getting her lover back, and asked for help to get over him.

&

Another patient, a doctoral student in anthropology, invited Maile to talk to her class, which was held in one of the old pink sandstone buildings on campus. Inside, down a long hallway paved with scuffed linoleum tile too old to take a shine, fifteen students waited in a circle of desks and chairs beneath a row of tall, west-facing windows.

Professor Deward Walker seated us near the door and took his place at the large front desk. Maile's patient introduced us. I felt a flutter of nervousness, hoping the students wouldn't ask anything too hard for me to translate.

"How do people tell the difference between a shaman and a sorcerer?" was the first question.

"Witches meet under *behar* and *pipul* trees, and learn the mantras of Parvati. You can see blue flames burning in the palms of their hands," Maile answered. So far so good. I knew the words.

"Shamans use the mantras of Lord Shiva," I added.

"Did Maile go through a psychotic period?"

"Yes, I go crazy when Hanuman comes on my body," Maile said.

She told how she'd been kidnapped by the Banjhankri, and I translated simply, as one tells a fairy tale to children.

"Does she literally believe she was kidnapped by a Wild Forest Shaman?" Someone had to ask.

I wasn't sure how to translate "literal belief," but whatever Maile thought I meant, she answered her usual "Hajur," of course.

"Is her healing effective? Do people actually get well?"

After all this time, I still had no miraculous cures to point to. "Most people say they feel better right away—but we haven't followed up."

❧

One weekend, Sharon Bonstadt from the drumming group invited us to a Lakota sweat lodge in the mountains. We set out in plenty of time, but ended up lost, driving back and forth near twilight, high on the side of Mt. Evans. A light rain fell, and a glorious rainbow spanned the rocky cliffs to either side. We were already late; it seemed the Lakota deities weren't anxious to meet Maile's gods.

Sharon had provided clear directions, but we kept on circling the area, unable to find the stone gate leading to the site, passing and repassing the same high grey granite canyon walls, horizontally grooved, as though a giant had slashed the point of his great knife along them.

It was nearly dark. The rainbow faded from the sky. Maile pointed to a spot on a cliff top high above the road to our left. "Banjhankri," she said.

"You see Banjhankri? Now?"

"Yes."

"Do you see him in your mind, or like a true person in front of you?" I struggled for the right Nepali words.

"Like a person," she said definitely. "Not in my mind."

I looked again where she'd pointed, searching for signs of rock climbers in the failing light, but the cliff face was bare.

"Sometimes I see him on high peaks and cliffs." She lifted her head and pointed with her long upper lip. "My guru," she added with affection.

❧

We never did find the sweat lodge, and on the way home, on impulse, I passed the turnoff to Boulder and took the exit to Evans' house. "My husband from before," I explained.

He was in his bedroom with the TV on. Maile namasted. It was quite warm inside and we took off our coats and piled them on a chair. One wall of his living room was lined with the old familiar books we'd had when we were married. I pointed out his paintings on the opposite wall, and he turned off the sound and joined us, seeming tired. When I suggested he show Maile his jewelry, he energized and brought out several pieces, including a jeweled tiara.

"For a queen," I said. "For playing." It was hard to explain to Maile how Evans spent his time.

Maile was suitably impressed, and expressed admiration in tones that needed no translation. Evans visibly brightened.

"We can't stay long," I said. "But I wanted you to meet my teacher. She's a healer, you know. If you're still having pain, maybe she could—."

"Cure me? Of a ruptured disc? I don't think so."

"Have you seen a doctor?"

"Have you forgotten? I don't have health insurance. Doctors like to be paid."

There was nothing to say. Maile namasted, and Evans responded with a wave. Outside, the cold air was a shock. It must have been eighty degrees inside.

"Tall man," Maile said in the car, pointing her long upper lip toward the house. "Good man."

She was quiet as we drove, and then, as we veered off onto Highway 36 toward Boulder, she said, "I could do a love spell to get you back together."

"I thought that was dangerous. For you."

"Not if it's for a husband and wife."

I flashed on a vision of Evans as he'd been when we met—gentle, playful, wise, full of puns and jokes and silly games. How full of consciousness and light he'd been—until he closed himself off. We drove on, cresting the final hill, and swooped down the long slope into Boulder Valley. I forced my thoughts ahead, to my new life here, and laughed, "Don't do it."

"You're happy alone." It wasn't quite a question.

"I'm happy."

"Me too," she said. We laughed together, friends.

❧

Maile had frequent toothaches, and I wanted to get her to a dentist before she went home. In Kathmandu, Mr. Rai had showed me a "dentist tree," shingled with overlapping layers of coins nailed to its thick slanting trunk by toothache sufferers seeking cures. Human dentists were rare and expensive in Nepal, but there were plenty in Boulder.

Dr. Armand had a thin, pinched face, a darkish complexion, and glasses that didn't sit quite true. He seated Maile in his big chair, pulled down a bright light, and poked into her mouth with hooks and picks, concluding that one of her molars would have to come out. "I'll numb the tissue with Novocain," he said.

As soon as she understood that a needle was involved, Maile protested. "Shamans should never get shots," Ama agreed. But Dr.

Armand insisted he couldn't pull the tooth without deadening Maile's pain. After a great deal of urging, she agreed to let him try.

He stuck the needle in her mouth at various angles, and pushed the plunger.

Maile's eyes squinched shut.

"Does it hurt?" he asked.

"It hurts."

He jabbed a few more times, and asked again. Again she said it hurt. The third time, he decided she must be imagining the pain, and got his pliers around the tooth and began to pull. Maile tensed and protested it still hurt, her words muffled by his hands, and the pliers, and the cotton he'd stuffed in her mouth. He kept on pulling. Suddenly her eyes rolled up and her body began to shake.

"Little sister, little sister!" Ama rushed to her side. "What's wrong?"

She groaned and cried out, *"Anhh, anhh, anhh."*

I froze.

"This is terrible," Ama said. "She shouldn't have had the needle. Shamans should never take the needle."

The dentist stepped back, alarmed, and Ama motioned me to help lift Maile upright. She kept on shaking, her eyes staring sightlessly.

"I'm calling 911," the dentist said.

"No," said Ama, very much in charge. Maile wasn't responding to our questions, but we stood her up, took her arms and led her outside, managing to get her into the car and home.

She stumbled into the living room, and still with that strange, unseeing stare, sat down on the floor, and called for *"Dhup, dhup!"* demanding incense.

Ama ran to the kitchen and made an altar on a dinner plate with a pile of uncooked rice and a piece of ginger. She lit Maile's oil lamp, and set it into the rice, and then held a stick of incense in the flame, and when it began to smoke, anchored it in a raw potato and placed it on the plate beside the rice. She set the whole thing on the floor in front of Maile.

Maile shook even harder, and prayed. She grabbed uncooked rice in handfuls, and held it to her chest, and then threw it out from her body to still the shaking. Then suddenly, she screamed, got down on all fours, and raced around and around the improvised altar on her hands and knees, crying out and panting, *"Anh, anh, anh, anh."*

"Hanuman," said Ama. "Hanuman has come on her body. Lo paramaswara!"

After five or ten minutes, the god finally left her. Maile stopped shaking and sat again before the altar. She prayed a bit more, and then allowed Ama to lift her and take her to her bed. We gave her aspirin and vodka to kill the pain, and she slept all through the afternoon and night.

The next day while I was at work, Ama tied a string around the tooth, fastened the other end to a doorknob, and pulled the tooth by slamming the door.

By evening, Maile was well enough to receive patients as usual.

Maile had been missing her little son, and when she began telling her patients that after she left, I would be their healer, I knew she had decided it was time to go.

"When you sit down to do a healing," she said, "think of me. I will come to help you."

I wept as she disappeared through the airport gate, her bag stuffed with presents for her family.

We found out later she had been cheated out of several hundred dollars in Bangkok, but had arrived safely home with the balance of her earnings. With this money, and a little more she was able to borrow, she was able to buy a house in Kathmandu.

WAIT FOR ME

Evans was drinking wine that Saturday when I dropped Keri off to spend the night with him in the little house in Denver he'd bought with his share of the proceeds from our family home. The TV was on in the bedroom, and two of his friends from the Society for Creative Anachronism perched at the foot of his bed watching—a slender man with lank, brown hair, and a soft, fleshy woman in a low-cut empire-style dress. They had a pasty look, as though they never went outside. The small room was grubby, and smelled of smoke and stale perfume. The fat girl's bosom displayed a fine Celtic cross I recognized as one Evans had made.

A young woman, slim and more attractive than the usual run of Evans' friends, edged around us from the kitchen and filled his glass. I thought she must be new, since none of his jewelry was hanging on her body. When he saw me in the doorway, he put an arm around her waist, wincing as his back changed position. Keri jumped onto the bed and snuggled into his other side.

"How's your back?" I asked.

"The same as always." He shot me a resentful look, as though it were my fault. "Annoying."

"Why don't you have Ellen say a mantra on it?" the fat girl suggested. "She really helped me."

I looked more closely, recognizing her now. One morning a few months ago she'd been on the couch complaining of a sick headache when I came to pick up Keri. On impulse, I'd offered to heal her with a Nepali mantra. I made passes over her body with a bit of uncooked rice cupped in the palm of my hand, and used a stick of burning incense to draw out the illness, whispering a mantra as I pinched her forehead toward the center and blew on it to transfer the holiness of the prayer.

Within minutes, the headache was gone. The mantra—and a cup of coffee—had fixed her up fine. I was surprised when it worked so well, but acted as though there'd never been the slightest doubt.

"Right," Evans drawled sarcastically, "a mantra."

It was all right. I didn't really want to test my powers on him. Shamanism worked for healing patients who had faith, whose problems could be psychosomatic; but his pain from the herniated disc was completely physical. It would take surgery to cure—or a miracle.

I left, feeling guilty at leaving Keri in the unhealthy atmosphere of Evans' house. Her father did love her, but love can't make up for everything, I reflected, driving up the narrow on-ramp. Not when it wants to enslave you to serve some other need. I'd loved him for making me sane, and he'd loved me back as his only link to the God he denied. Now he'd have to find his own connection. Or, more likely, die. If Jehovah himself came down out of the sky and offered to heal him, he'd probably refuse.

The view opened out on the high peaks to the west, crowned by strips of clean, smooth, high-tech clouds, golden pink in the sunset. By the time I topped the hill over Boulder, the few long clouds had gone dark, and the sky was otherwise clear and luminous against the mountain silhouettes. The city lights spread over the plain and partway up the foothills, just brighter than the sky, magically glowing as if a single, hidden source of light shone through the valley from beneath.

I unlocked my house. Only Keri and I lived here now; the boys were off at school, and the place had an empty feel. I made a cup of tea, carried it into the living room, and turned on an area light, leaving most of the room in darkness. I'd hung several drums on a beam over the stairwell and as the lamp warmed the air, the largest drum uttered a sudden sharp crack, protesting the heat and dryness. I started at the noise, then, realizing what it was, relaxed. This was the drum Evans had made for me, from cowhide stretched and laced over a strip of plywood he'd soaked in the bathtub and forced into a circle, as a peace offering to make up for being so angry when I took Michael Harner's course in core shamanism. The gift hadn't meant he'd changed his opinion, only that he wanted us to get along. And the drum had been a good one, with a deep, strong, singing voice that had powered my journeys for years—until Jebi gave me his own long-handled, two-sided drum of monkey-skin, which now lay on a shelf across the room.

I was thinking about how, when Keri and Thorne and I had first returned from Kentucky, we'd stayed several weeks with Evans in our old house. But I made it clear we were camping there only until I could find another place.

"Just like old times," Evans said, giving me one of those humorous, meaningful looks of his—the one that said "you're here."

We couldn't help resuming our old running dialog on faith, doubt, and reality, each trying to convince the other we were right. Our relationship still lived.

It was early spring, still cold in the great hall. An electric heater at the far end of the room sent occasional currents of warm, dry air against my legs. "Consciousness exists," I said. "We know it exists in us, if nowhere else, because we're conscious. Are you with me so far?"

"Go on." He poured wine into a matched set of jeweled goblets and handed me one.

"We're conscious. That's the first and *only* thing we know. The rest of what we think is happening—the material world, other people—that all comes later, as products of our consciousness." As I spoke, I closed my eyes and pictured the illusory forms of earthly experience blooming outward, as from the center of a flower.

"*Au contraire.* Consciousness is an epiphenomenon of our brains." He tapped his cigarette and knocked off an ash. "It's not *our* consciousness. That's meaningless. It's *my* consciousness, or *your* consciousness. There's no such thing as *our* consciousness. Where is it anyway?" He hit his empty wine glass on a thick plank of the table. "This is what's real."

"Your mind perceives a table and a knocking sound," I corrected. "That's all you know for sure."

"I know there's a table."

"You keep saying that, but you still haven't proved it." I spoke without heat.

"I have, but you won't listen." He answered by rote, but we both enjoyed this return to our familiar disagreement. It made a point of connection.

"I'll grant that what's inside your brain is real. It can affect me. But consciousness outside anybody's brain—it's fantasy," he said.

"I'll make you a bet," I challenged. "In a hundred years, when we're both dead, let's agree for our spirits to meet. Then we'll see who's right."

"Fine. And where do you propose to have this to happen?"

"At the top of Mt. Evans, of course."

"I'll be there if I can," he said.

❧

Oh, Evans, Evans, wait for me.

A DREAM OF BUGS

At the grocery store, I ran into Joe O'Laughlin, Evans' old climbing friend—the one who'd used Mr. Rai's trekking services in Nepal. "I hear you're a shaman now," he said. "Sacrificing chickens down at the law office, are you?"

After Maile had gone home, her patients kept calling. I performed the rituals she had taught me, summoning her presence to mind, but with increasing discomfort at diagnosing things like hunter spirits, witches, and planets out of alignment—things with no meaning for Americans. Usually, I suggested that people come to our drumming group so everyone could work on them.

"Nepali shamanism doesn't seem to translate well," I said to Joe. "Americans don't want to sit around and watch the shaman perform like they do in Nepal. They want to take an active part."

"It must have been quite an experience, though." He seemed to hesitate, and then said, "Have you seen Evans lately?"

"Of course—the kids see their dad."

"Is he sick?"

"You mean his back?"

"He seems really weak. I saw him at Tori's last weekend, helping her put up screens. I know he doesn't have much stamina because of all that smoking, but he could only work about ten minutes before he had to sit down and rest. Is that normal?"

"He seems okay," I said. "We're all getting older."

But it didn't surprise me after that, when Keri had her nightmare. She cried out sharply a little past midnight. I woke at once and ran to her room. She was sitting up, clutching her covers to her neck, her white face stark against her long dark hair, her eyes gleaming with horror. A bar of moonlight lit the wall above her bed.

"I dreamed I saw Daddy," she gasped. "He was lying down, and great big black and red bugs were crawling all in and out of his body."

She began to sob. "I'm scared." I sat on the bed and pulled her close. "Mommy, I'm frightened. Something's wrong with Daddy."

I started to tell her not to worry the way my father had done for me—to say it was only a dream and not real—but remembered in time how little comfort that had been. A dream like that should be respected, not brushed aside. "Daddy doesn't really have bugs inside him, honey. But he may be sick." I kept on hugging her. "You may be sensing it. Sometimes sickness looks like bugs in dreams."

"What's wrong with him?"

"I don't know," I said, but I had a bad feeling. "Let's tell him to get a checkup."

"I don't want anything to happen to Daddy." She sobbed and clung tight to my neck, gasping until she hyperventilated, putting herself into a panic.

"Sh-h, it's all right. Take a deep breath. Tomorrow we'll call him, and you can ask if he's okay." I got her to lie down and squeezed into bed beside her.

"Sickness looks like bugs?" She burrowed her forehead into my shoulder. "They were horrible...I don't want Daddy to be sick." Her voice began to drag with sleep as she talked herself away from the awfulness of the dream, pulling out of it with words. She knew what "sick" was—when you threw up or had a fever, and got better the next day. It couldn't be that bad.

"It's all right, honey, everything's all right." I held her until she settled into the deep stomach breathing of sleep.

But it wasn't all right. She was close to her father. Her vision might well be real. In the morning, we'd call him. If I got up the courage, I'd offer to pull out the bugs with a shamanic extraction.

❧

The next day was Saturday, and Keri and I slept in. She stumbled upstairs as I was pouring coffee. "Shall we call your Dad?" I asked.

"Oh—my dream." Her eyes darkened as she remembered.

"Go ahead, call him," I urged.

She leaned into me. "I don't want to."

"I'll do it." He might still be asleep, but I didn't want to wait.

"Y-alloh." He sounded normal.

"Hi. Uh, how are you feeling?"

"Fine, I guess."

"Joe said you seemed tired."

"I am. My back hurts too, but I'm okay. Just getting old."

"How long since you had a physical?"

"I don't like doctors."

"I know, but do me a favor and see one."

"I'll think about it."

Keri took the phone. "Daddy, are you okay?"

His answer came scratching through the earpiece like an insect's buzz.

"Daddy, I want you to go to the doctor like Mommy said."

The buzzing rose to a higher pitch. He was annoyed, and Keri looked upset, but in a moment she brightened. "Sure, I guess. Mom, can I go to Dad's? There's an SCA party tonight."

I didn't see why not.

Paul, Thorne's friend from high school, was at Evans' polishing the silver decoration on a long leather scabbard with precise efficiency. He was always there lately, like an old-time apprentice, learning the art of metalworking from Evans.

"Look what I made." Paul leaned across the work table to hand me a sheath encased in silver lacework, studded with great chunks of turquoise set in bezels of some yellowish metal.

"Very nice."

"He's talented," Evans said, from the stack of pillows on which he lay propped, as he smoked and sipped lukewarm coffee. "This is his best piece yet." Evans extended an arm for Keri, and she snuggled onto the bed beside him.

"Can I see my costume?" She tapped his thin, bare wrist where it emerged from the unbuttoned sleeve of his flannel shirt. Parallel slants of straight dark hairs curved in at the dent between his bones.

"It's by the sewing machine."

Paul went off to fetch it, and came back with a cloud of blue gauze. "You'll be an Arab princess," Evans said.

I asked him, "Are you losing weight?"

"You can't fatten a greyhound," he said, repeating what his mother, Anna Kennedy, used to say when was little, and people would remark how thin he was.

I left Keri there, and headed out to the Flatirons trailhead. I shrugged into my daypack and hiked across a small dry gully and over a brown grass meadow, leaving the trail to wander through a stand of Ponderosa pine. It was cold, and I put up my hood and thrust my hands in my jacket pockets, finding a bag of loose tobacco left over from an outing last summer with the drumming group. Holding up a pinch of the moist brown tendrils, I let them go in the wind as an offering to the spirits of this place, real or not.

Maybe they were only in my mind, but why should that matter? The whole place—with its trees, its large-crystalled rocks encrusted with tiny inverted fingernails of grey-green lichen, the dried-out tongues of prickly pear among the sparse brown grass, a croaking raven overhead, the sun itself—might all be nothing more than an elaborate projection of my mind. How could I know?

I sank down by a boulder and shivered, huddling out of the wind behind the big rock. Microscopic droplets pricked in and out of existence in the cooling air, dotting my cheeks and upper lip with tiny points of cold. Dense grey clouds were massing to the west above the mountains. I wished I could go back to Evans' and hear him tell me I was wrong.

Instead, I drove home and fixed myself a can of soup. I picked up a novel and tried to read, but couldn't get rid of the image from Keri's dream of the red and black bugs in her father's body. Mr. Rai had said that telling dreams could make them lose their power, and I'd heard that the Iroquois held a similar idea—that a bad dream should be told or acted out to use up its force so it couldn't come to pass. Keri had told her dream, had talked it out until she was no longer frightened and it was only words and fading images with no more power to harm.

It was easy to believe, here in my own house with the familiar shapes of couch and chair standing guard, the refrigerator humming its soft song, and the dog snoring at my feet, that nothing bad could happen. The snow kept falling, loading trees that overhung power lines all over the city. Thick, wet flakes drifted by the window. By morning the yard would be full of broken branches. The lights flickered. I lifted the phone to check for a dial tone. It was dead.

Next morning, I woke to a deep blue sky above a landscape buried in sparkling snow, shapes rounded and melting at the edges. The digital clock was blinking, showing 3:00 a.m. The power had been out quite a while, but the phone was back on, ringing. "Mom, Mom, why didn't you answer the phone last night?" It was Keri.

"It wasn't working. Because of the storm."

"I wanted you, Mom. Daddy didn't feel good."

"How is he now?"

"He's sleeping."

"Is Paul there?"

"No, he left last night. Mom, come and get me."

The roads were clear and steaming in the sun. Keri met me at the door, her eyes dark with smeared mascara. Evans was asleep, and no one else was in the house. She'd slept in her costume, a shiny blue polyester shift covered with blue netting, tied loosely at the waist with a soft golden rope.

"What happened, honey? Was somebody mean to you?"

"No, they were nice, but Daddy got sick and went to bed, and nobody cared. They said he was drunk."

I'd never seen him drunk. High, but never out of control or sick.

He woke then, and groaned.

I got him coffee. "I hear you were sick last night."

"It doesn't matter." He propped his pillows up and shut me out.

"Yes, it does."

"Who to?" He lit a smoke and sucked.

"To you, if no one else."

He narrowed his eyes and gave me a look Mr. Rai would have called the evil eye. I felt his resentment like a physical blow. Because I'd left him, this was all my fault.

I felt guilty—then angry, and scrubbed at Keri's face with a wet paper towel. "Get dressed, honey," I told her, "Let's go."

DOUBT

Our drumming circle met on alternate Saturdays to practice core shamanism, using a minimum of ritual, and working on anyone who came to ask for healing. I'd shown the group what I'd learned in Nepal, of course, and they'd watched how Maile played the spirits, but everyone preferred the methods Harner had taught us, journeying to helping spirits to ask what to do for each case on the spot, rather than learning a complex set of foreign rituals. I felt it was hogging the show to perform like a Nepali shaman, and had become so sensitive to the feeling, I rarely volunteered to act as healer, even in the Harner way.

But one night I felt strong, and the patient stirred my compassion. She was thin, and neatly dressed in a black sweater and trousers, with short brown hair that curled around a face too young to be permanently marked by the tension that immobilized her expression.

As the others drummed and chanted, *"Ah-way, Ah-way, away, away, away,"* I called my helping spirit from the Lower World, merging with him until I could visualize the illness like a knot of tangled white snakes in the patient's stomach. I made clawing motions in the air above her, willing the image of my helper's spirit hands to reach inside her body and remove the snakes. A feeling of life and power surged through me.

The patient shook and spasmed. As my spirit helper pulled out the writhing mass of snakes, I lifted my arms and threw them toward the lake to the west, emitting involuntary grunts and keeping my attention focused until the snakes were completely drowned. The patient heaved; her back arched, and she started to sob. When all the snakes were gone, I passed my hands down over her aura to smooth it. Someone brought a glass of water; she drank it and we hugged. "My stomach always hurts, *always*, and now it doesn't," she told the group.

"It *did* hurt, but it's all better," I said to seal in the healing. "Sometimes it takes more than one treatment. You can always come back if you need to."

꧁

Larry and Sharon stayed behind after drumming for a glass of wine. Sharon was my neighbor, an intense, part-Cherokee social worker, whose daughter, Cheyenne, was Keri's best friend. Larry, a long-haired free spirit with a full beard and a PhD from Yale, eked out a tiny living as a substitute flutist for the Denver Symphony and spent his days on the prairie with binoculars, keeping track of breeding pairs of eagles.

"I can't help feeling like a fraud sometimes," I said, halfway through a second glass of wine. "We don't know if we really helped that woman."

"But we do know it works. Look at my father," Larry said. We'd done a long-distance healing to slow the proliferation of retinal blood vessels that threatened his diabetic father with blindness. "I told you how amazed the doctor was at the improvement in his eyes."

"And what about Vann's mother? Every time we drum, her white count goes down," Sharon said.

"And that guy with the soul loss," Larry added.

"And the woman with the headaches." Sharon put her hand over her glass as I offered more wine.

"We hardly ever hear back," I pointed out. "So how do we really know?"

Larry stared into his glass and Sharon fiddled with a cuff button. I knew I should shut up. I'd wanted them to reassure me, not lose their faith. "I know people feel better right after we work on them—and maybe that's enough. At least we don't charge money." I managed a laugh.

"The doubting shaman," Larry said.

"I guess so," I muttered.

"You won't believe it until you see a miracle," he said, trying to make it seem all right.

"But you won't see a miracle till you believe it," Sharon pointed out.

A few weeks later, a friend of a friend, a Buddhist named Peg, called to ask for healing, trying to sound matter-of-fact, but unable to disguise the worry in her voice. "It's a lump in my right breast. It showed up on X-ray, and they scheduled surgery right away—next week."

"Why don't you come to our drumming circle," I suggested.

She turned out to be an attractive woman in her early forties, nervous, but with an overlay of studied calm. I introduced her to Mike, Sharon, Don, Merle and Larry, offered them chai, and left them to chat while I spread a white, lacy cloth of Bindu's making on the floor for an altar and laid out objects representing the four elements: a candle to the east for fire, a feather to the south for air, a small cup of water to the west, and a chunk of sandstone to the north for earth.

We took our places in a circle around the simple altar, and smudged each other with burning sage. Mike, selected by a twirl of the drumstick as tonight's leader, rattled to the four directions, and skyward and earthward, to call in the spirits. We drummed together, raising energy.

Peg told the group of the lump her mammogram had showed.

Sharon drummed and we journeyed, asking our power animals and teachers for help, and then took turns telling what we'd learned. Larry, opposite Peg in the circle, said he'd seen the lump in his journey and had asked his spirit helper to remove it, as had I. Don, a shy man with a deep voice, sitting to the right of Peg, reported, "I asked my Bear to help. He came and knocked her down. He sniffed all around her, poked his nose into her belly, and her breast, and then opened his jaws and ate the lump." Merle and Mike, to Peg's left, said they hadn't even seen the lump, or anything at all to indicate disease.

Later that week Peg phoned.

"Did you have the surgery?" I asked. "Are you okay?"

"I did," she said. "They cut me open and—you're not going to believe this—they couldn't find a thing."

That night I couldn't sleep. The streetlight by the bike path cast a barred shadow of the blinds on the opposite wall. No traffic moved. Had it been a miracle? I didn't know what to think. You could say it was telepathy; that no tumor had ever been there, that Peg had known it, and we read her mind. You could say that time was circular, and we were only remembering what happened last time around. You could say the spirits really came and helped. But the simplest, most parsimonious explanation was this—the one who thought it all happened, the one thinking right now, was the one who had made it up. Only me. As always, always, only me. Why postulate an other, when I was quite capable of making up the whole drama, starring myself as a great and powerful shaman, and moving the others like puppets on a set.

I swung my feet to the floor and switched on the light to banish the thought. I couldn't afford to think like this. If I started in again believing everything was illusion—children, work, friends, and the objects of my everyday life—it would soon turn ugly. I wouldn't relive those bad old days for anything.

Work was my solace. It kept me sane, but writing patents takes logical thought, and old habits of doubt came flooding back. I decided Peg had probably had a cyst that disappeared on its own.

⁕

John came often for Maile's kind of treatment, bringing little gifts. I invited him to drumming group but he insisted I tell him what the rice grains had to say, sighing and settling into himself as I lit the incense and began Maile's gentle, rhythmic Tamang chant. When I was finished, I searched the egg yolk for breaks in the gel, blood spots, white streaks, and other signs Maile had taught me, letting the slippery yellow globe slide off my fingers into the bowl. "A lot of bad stuff came out," I told him, feeling like a fraud.

But John obviously felt better. What more did I want? I scraped the side of my hand across the carpet to gather scattered grains of rice, and threw them out in the yard for the birds.

"I can feel Maile when you're working," John said, putting on his jacket. "You miss her, don't you? You don't seem as confident as you were right after she left. But the energy's still right."

"Well, actually, I haven't been doing much shamanism."

He shrugged into his pack. "You ought to," he said.

⁕

Mr. Rai telephoned that Christmas Eve. He said his shaman school was doing well and wished me Merry Christmas.

"And *Allen*," he said, "you are practicing healing as you learned from Jebi and Maile?"

"Well not so much."

"You should do, you know."

"I know. But it isn't easy. You don't know how hard we have to work here at our jobs. No one has spare time to sit around for long ceremonies like they do in Nepal."

"I know you are busy, but you have learned all these things. You have to be our shaman in America."

DEATH

Evans fell one day and couldn't get up. His sister, Elaine, came out from Maryland to take charge. At sixty, two years younger than he, she looked no more than forty-five, except for the haunted expression in her eyes. She wore a blue T-shirt neatly tucked into a trim waistband; her short, wavy hair was finely striped with even strands of black and white, her clear skin stretched taut over a high, round forehead with shapely eyebrows she never had to pluck. Her cheekbones were well-defined, and her brown eyes lucid, fringed with naturally dark lashes. She met Keri and me at the door.

Keri grabbed my arm and peered into her father's bedroom. It smelled of cigarettes, but not enough to mask the smooth, heavy, undertone of illness. "Mom! Is he dying?" Her voice held outrage, as though some grownup ought to make it right.

Paul jumped up from his seat beside the door, blocking Keri's way, and without moving his jaw, hissed out, "He isn't dying."

"It was so good of you to come out to take care of him," I told Elaine, feeling fatuous. "I don't know what he would have done."

Her short silence said it all—if you hadn't left him, this wouldn't have happened. Why aren't *you* the one watching, waking up at night to give him pills and turn him. But what she actually said was, "He's my big brother," the slight sentimental drag to her voice reassuring me that she'd taken on his care as a rightful duty. I could watch.

I handed her my offering—a bag of adult diapers.

She set it on the chair and moved aside to let us see. Evans was sleeping. "We've given him pain pills, but he ought to wake up soon."

Keri squeezed past me to stand beside the bed. Evans had curled into a fetal position and lay quiet, taking shallow, regular breaths. His skull shone pink through thin wisps of hair. "Daddy's getting bald," she said.

"It's the chemotherapy," Elaine explained. "The doctors are giving him chemicals to make him better."

He must have heard us, for he moved and groaned. Gleaming slits appeared between his eyelids, but he didn't lift his head. Paul brought in a dish of ice cream, arranged pillows to prop him, and lifted the spoon to his mouth. He advanced his chin slightly to meet it, his mouth and tongue making all the right movements, enjoying the dessert in an unconscious sort of way.

He let his head fall back, opened his eyes, looked vaguely around, and raised one arm. "Oh, you're here." He closed his eyes again.

Keri threw me an imploring look.

"You're lucky he recognized you," Elaine said.

Paul took the dish away.

Evans' body slipped sideways, and I reached beneath his back to pull him straight. "Ooh don't. Don't touch," he groaned. His eyelids flickered.

Paul appeared at once and arranged the pillows to support Evans in the crooked position. "It hurts him to breathe," he said, settling the blankets with a proprietary gesture and checking the time on the dusty clock radio. "He gets another pain pill in an hour."

Keri backed slowly toward the wall. I took the chair by the bed. Evans lay quiet, focused inward, breathing gently in and out.

"Om." The word welled up unbidden, from a place of help. I wanted so to heal him. I said a silent mantra for protection and moved my attention into his body, the inflamed lungs, something dark, heavy, and implacable encroaching into space that should be free—a malevolent, unguided force. Could it be attacked and broken? I began to probe it for weakness.

But his eyes were open, on me now in full awareness. My concentration broke. "Oh, it's you," he said again, awake. It was really him—that old knowing look, conscious, alert, as dear as life. Recognition sparked between us. I wouldn't be blowing mantras on him now, fooling with his innards while he watched me with those eyes. I shouldn't have intruded in the first place, since he hadn't asked.

"Coffee?" he croaked.

I took his cup to the kitchen, threading past a jumble of sleeping bags and foam pads on the floor, where Paul and Elaine were camped for the duration. A low table opposite the workroom door held a saki set and two candles. Above it, a jeweled drinking horn hung on the wall. On a long table inside the workroom, I made out pieces of a sword and a jeweled hilt that Paul had been making. Evans' tools were lined up neatly—grinders, polishers, saws and welding torches; his latest projects—pieces of chain link armor, brooches, and hammered cups set with great cabochons of semi-precious stones—lay undisturbed, as though he might get up any time and finish them. Some of these things might be valuable.

When Evans had been diagnosed, three weeks ago, he could still walk, though only when he had to, leaning on furniture to make his way back and forth to the bathroom. Elaine had arrived within days.

"I made a list of my things," he had told me. I ran my eyes down the inventory of artwork, jewelry he'd made, old climbing gear, books and long-playing records. Friends' names were penciled in beside each item. He owned no real estate except the house held in joint tenancy with his sister—nothing valuable enough to trigger probate. "Can you make it legal—write a Will to say who should get what?"

"Of course." I folded the list and put it in my purse. "What about a Living Will, if you don't want life support?"

He thought a moment, and then nodded.

"He can decide later," Elaine said, briskly setting a tray across his stomach.

She had refused to accept the death sentence, and immediately found a new doctor who started him on steroids and chemotherapy. He'd improved miraculously—at first. His breathing eased, and he walked without falling. He cheered up and began to ask for his friends, joking that he wanted his wake while he was still alive to enjoy it.

"A party," Elaine had said brightly. "That *would* be fun."

So on a Saturday night in early February, Keri and I had driven down to Denver against determined lines of snow that slanted against the windshield. Evans' house was full of people I didn't know, many in costume—capes of satin trimmed in fake fur, lacy empire dresses for the women, and for the men, blousy-sleeved, collarless shirts under weskits, and tight pants. Evans presided from his bed, almost like his old self, lifting his glass and holding forth on the politics of whatever historical period the costumes represented.

The phone rang and Elaine passed it to him.

"Francine." His face lit up. "Oh, I'm sorry. There's no way at all? I wish I had the money, I'd send a taxi for you." He hung up. "I really wanted her here—for my wake," He said, and added, "I may never see her again."

"Where does she live?" I was hooked, as always, on that pitiful upcurve of his eyebrows, signaling need.

"Oh, far—way out in Lakewood."

"I suppose I could pick her up."

He brightened at once. "I'll call her back."

Paul offered to come along and show me the way. We took

everyone's orders for fast food, as long as we were going out anyway, and set off into the storm.

"Who is Francine?" I asked.

"Francine and Jackie. They're dancers." He meant the kind who show their bodies to men in clubs.

Several inches of snow had accumulated on the main roads. Traffic crawled. Paul pointed me off to a side street where the snow was even deeper, but we made steady progress. "It's really wonderful the way you're helping with Evans," I said to break the silence, "giving up your job and everything."

"He's my teacher. I don't mind."

"What will you do after he dies?"

"He isn't going to die," he said quickly. "I don't believe in death."

I glanced in amazement at his rigid profile, the short straight nose, nearly bridgeless, the pointed scrag of dark hair jutting from the sloped line of his forehead, the eyes locked straight ahead. "You don't believe people die?"

"Have you actually ever seen it happen?"

"Well, no, not being there right at the moment," I admitted. "But I saw my grandfather's body. I saw them put it in the ground."

"That's what you *thought* you saw." He clamped his jaw tight shut, and I drove on through endless snowy streets. An hour later, we arrived at Francine's apartment building. I waited in the car while Paul got out. Snowflakes blanketed the windows.

After a while the car doors opened and let in a blast of cold air. Paul and two young women got in. Under their coats, thrown over their shoulders like capes, the women wore tights and leotards decorated with beads and feathers, topped by short bolero jackets. Francine was a tall, leggy blonde with shoulder-length hair flipped up at the ends and stiff with spray. Her face in profile was long-nosed and rabbity, with a receding chin. Her companion, Jackie, pushing strings of lank, dark hair out of eyes, was smaller, and wore too much makeup. She had a sullen, bad-girl face that made Francine look wholesome. They set their long legs into the back seat like sticks they were obliged to carry with them, rather than parts of their own bodies, and treated their arms the same way, pressing outward with their elbows first, as though making space for their wrists and hands. Their long, thin fingers pushed deliberately against the air. The effect was sophisticated—cool.

I had no idea how to talk to girls like these. "It's good of you to come," I said. "It means a lot to Evans."

"We care about him," Francine said.

I started to ask how long they'd known him, and then realized I didn't want to know. We drove in silence through the snow. I felt suspended, grief and time held back for a brief merciful space we'd been granted in which to make Evans happy. It didn't surprise me that these young women loved him. They probably saw him as gentle and Daddy-like—in control but non-threatening. And because he used them in a different way than most men, they probably believed he was simply there for them, not using them at all.

Keri was asleep when we got back to the party, but woke to the general applause that greeted our bags of hamburgers and french fries.

Francine and Jackie hurried at once to Evans' bed, and smoothed his hair and held his hands and stroked them. I didn't begrudge them. Love has its own power, beyond ideas of good and bad. I had to respect it. But I didn't offer to take them home.

After his "wake," Evans started chemotherapy and quickly weakened. Elaine and Paul talked hopefully about recovery, but he himself said little. We watched old movies; he spoke about the history of the Celts, geology, or whatever subject came to mind from his wide reading. But he'd lost the ability to control his thoughts, and through them, his emotions. The mention of a friend's name, a familiar piece of music, a remembered rock climb or trip, a mountain range in the background of a cowboy movie, these things of earth he would never see again, would trigger intense nostalgia, an emotion that seemed to give rise to some internal swelling, and he would moan, "It hurts, it hurts," as the tumors pressed his lungs. "Say something neutral. Quick."

We kept a ready supply of intellectual topics to engage his mind. "There was a story on the news earlier, about a dinosaur bone they found in Wyoming. Do you remember how old they said it was?" Elaine might say, and his pain would ease as he answered.

Once, as he looked down at our joined hands on the blanket, a congestion of blood gathered in his face. I spoke quickly. "You don't really have to give up everything, you know. Your body may die, but your spirit will live on." His face cleared, showing interest. "I truly believe there are spirits," I went on. "I saw one once."

Elaine waved and beckoned from the doorway. "Don't talk about things like that," she whispered when she had me out of his hearing. "He doesn't believe in them, and it'll just upset him."

"There's no point stirring him up," Paul added.

I had to defer to their judgment. They were the ones, after all, who had to cope with his upsets. The initial steroid effect had worn off. They took turns getting up at night to change his diapers and give him pain pills, and their faces and tempers showed the strain.

"Shouldn't we call hospice?" I suggested. "You two are exhausted."

But Elaine put me off. "It would seem like giving up."

Paul glared at me like a hated enemy. "No!"

On our next visit, Evans was propped on his pillows, feeling better because the course of chemotherapy had ended and the poisons were washing from his system. "Sit here on the bed. Careful. As long as I don't move, it's all right."

"I wish you didn't have to suffer." I covered his hand with mine, feeling thin bird bones beneath the skin.

"I wish I could have made you happy," he said.

"I always loved you." I could hardly speak. "I still do."

"I love you, Daddy," Keri said.

"I wish I could give you something. I never did know what you needed," he said sadly.

"You *are* giving me that painting," I reminded him. "Did you ever sign the Will? Or the Living Will?"

"Elaine has it." He made a slight head movement toward the other room. "I don't think I signed it yet. I don't remember very well."

Keri slipped around the bed and held his other hand.

"I know we'll see each other again," I said, totally believing it. "You'll see. Remember, we have a date on top of Mt. Evans in a hundred years. We haven't finished our karma with each other yet—we just did as much as we could stand for one lifetime." I gave a nervous laugh and stopped.

"You may be right." He had no energy to argue, but he wasn't upset.

"Did I ever tell you my vision about dying?" I picked up a bit of the sheet and twisted it around in a tent-like point. "We're like this twist. The sheet is everything there is—all consciousness, God, the universe and everything. And our consciousness, our selves—what we think of as ourselves—is just this little piece, twisted around and around until one twist can look back on the twist just below it and say, 'That's me.' We're twisted so tight, we forget we're part of the whole big sheet. Then, when we die—," I released the twist and the sheet smoothed out. "A-a-ah. What a relief! All at once we understand what we were all along—the whole sheet—consciousness itself. We only imagined we were separate."

Evans' head, stiff on its neck, turned carefully to watch my demonstration, so as not to disturb his body's delicate balance.

ॐ

Now, as I stirred the coffee Evans had asked for, Elaine came into the kitchen and began moving dishes from the drainer to the cupboard. "He probably won't drink that," she said. "He's been mostly out of it for days—confused, not recognizing anyone. We think it's the pain pills." I'd left the lid off the coffee jar, and she screwed it back on. "One of Paul's friends, Jenny, was here a couple of days ago, telling us how confused she got when she had to take morphine for a broken leg. She said you get into a sort of hellish twilight state where you're suffering and feeling pain, but you can't tell anyone, or do anything about it."

My spoon stopped moving in the cup.

"She said she'd rather not have had the drugs," Elaine finished in a dry, reasonable voice.

"But she knew she was going to get better, didn't she?" I protested. "She was young and knew she'd heal."

"Evans knows he'll get well too." Paul stood in the doorway, his hands on his hips.

"I've known Evans my whole life," Elaine said. "You've known him a long time too. You know the last thing he'd want is to be drugged unconscious. He always wanted to keep thinking, no matter what."

"He was awake just now," I said. "He knew us."

"It's working, then," Paul said.

"We asked the doctor if we could cut down on the pain pills," Elaine finished. "He said go ahead and see what happens."

ॐ

Next day when I phoned, I could hear Evans groaning in the background.

"It takes time for the morphine to wear off," Elaine said. "He may not really be in pain. It may just be memory of pain. He's too dopey to know."

I left Keri with Sharon and rushed over. Evans was still groaning, and thrashing, though always before he'd tried to hold himself completely still. "Evans, I'm here." I leaned above his bed. "It's Ellen."

"Can't somebody help?" he cried. "Oh, help." Elaine stood in the doorway, her eyes wide and tragic.

"*Elaine,*" I said.

"We were giving him morphine at night," she said, "but we

stopped so he could get completely clear of drugs. He'd want it that way." I followed her to the kitchen. She filled the tea kettle with slow, controlled motions and set it on the stove.

"*Aah-aah-ah*," Evans cried from the bedroom. "Have pity. Help."

"How can you stand it?"

A pained look flickered across her face. "I can't." She wiped her hands on a dish towel. "I don't know what to do. We just try different things."

"I'm sorry," I said. "I know you're doing the best you can." After all, it obviously took more courage to listen to him cry and groan than to shut him up with pills.

She rubbed her eyes.

"I'll just sit with him a while." I steeled myself, entered the bedroom and took the bedside chair, letting my eyes adjust to the dimness.

He lay on his back. "Oh, stop, oh stop!" he cried.

I calmed my breathing. "Om," I said inside myself. I thought of Maile, imagined her comforting presence.

"*Oh, oh-oh-oh*," he groaned, dispelling any thought of calm.

I tried again. "Om," I prayed silently, concentrating on the words of Maile's protection mantra, blowing it toward him. He groaned. I thought of Jebi's deep compassion, the insistent pounding of his drum.

Evans lifted an arm, brought it down hard on the mattress, and shouted, "*Ah!*"

I pictured Maile's face, its image giving me the power to focus — her high smooth forehead with the scar, the reverence of her gestures. Reciting the words inside my mind, I said the Banjhankri mantra for healing every ill, and breathed it toward his body, softly so Elaine wouldn't hear.

A sense of Maile's spirit and Tamang deities filled the room with an atmosphere as white and thick and sweet as cream. As long as I kept on reciting her mantras, it stayed. I kept my breathing deep and even, asking for healing to fill in every space in the room and in Evans' body. His face smoothed out. His ragged breathing calmed as I visualized the whiteness moving into his lungs.

I remembered how I'd prayed for Keri when she'd been hit by the car, how fiercely I'd concentrated, with no other thought — the whole world shrunk to that one time and place — her small dark head on the pillow all that existed as I willed her to be whole, no matter if universe had to turn on its axis to make it happen. I wasn't praying like that now. I didn't believe Evans could get well. I was only praying for his comfort, without that same time-stopping concentration I'd used for Keri. And the world moved on in its blind, cruel progress, dragging us all along with it.

❧

Keri asked to see her father, but I put her off. I couldn't let her see him like this. I'd never felt so stretched and tense. I prayed to every deity I knew, asking for Evans' comfort and release. In my distracted state, Sai Baba was easiest to visualize, with his bright orange robe and sphere of black hair bushing out around his broad, brown face that radiated warmth.

One afternoon, I took Keri and her friend Cheyenne swimming at the East Boulder Recreation Center, a beautiful new building with a panoramic view of the mountains through floor-to-ceiling windows in the pool. It was April, and still light at five o'clock. I swam laps, watching the shadows deepen on the rocky hillsides and snowcapped peaks, and wishing Evans could share this beauty one more time.

The light was gone when I went out to the car to wait for the girls. I closed my eyes and prayed. "Please help him." In my vision, the orange-robed figure of Sai Baba descended from a dark sky, picked up Evans' wasted body like a baby, and floated upward. They rose to a height of twenty feet, and Evans, suddenly realizing he had survived his death, straightened his arms and legs in a movement of joy.

Triggered by the darkness, the bright new streetlights in the parking lot came on, broken to shards by my tears. I sobbed with relief. The girls ran toward me laughing, swinging their bags.

I started dinner, turning down the burner to catch the phone. "You'd better meet us at the hospital," Paul said, sounding official, like a rescue worker. "We just put Evans in an ambulance."

By the time we got there, he was in intensive care, hooked to a machine that breathed his body.

"We took him for chemotherapy," Paul said. "Everything was fine. He was sitting up in his wheelchair, but suddenly, he slipped down to the sidewalk and stopped breathing."

"Paul did CPR," Elaine chimed in. "He was pounding on Evans' chest, crying and shouting over and over, 'You can't die, I won't let you.' Tears were literally flying from his eyes. I've never seen anyone work so hard. Paul got his heart going, and we called the ambulance, and here we are."

"What time did all this happen?" I asked.

Paul checked his watch. "About seven."

Exactly the time of my vision in the parking lot.

Paul took Evans' hand and chafed it, but he didn't respond.

"I saw his soul," I said. "I had a vision of his soul leaving his body just when you said he collapsed. He was happy."

Elaine, staring at her brother's face, didn't bother to look up. She didn't have time for my sweet little daydreams. A doctor beckoned from the doorway, and she left.

We watched in silence, the only sound, the whoosh of the machine. Evans lay unmoving, his eyes closed.

"You're not unplugging him," Paul flatly announced when Elaine returned.

"Of course not."

I found a phone and arranged for Thorne to take the next flight home from Durango, then stopped a doctor to ask what would happen. He showed me a set of X-rays. "These dark masses are tumors," he said, pointing out fist-sized shadows. "They're pushing up against his heart. That's what gave him the heart attack." The doctor wanted me to know there was no hope of recovery.

"I'm not in charge," I said. "His sister is. She'll never let you turn off the life support."

The sickroom filled with Evans' friends — Francine, Jackie, an older woman with iron-gray hair, and numerous others, only some of whom I recognized. Paul sat closest to the bed, saying over and over, "We know you hear us, Evans. We love you. Please come back."

"Please come back," the others echoed. "We love you."

I could well understand how much they longed to see that flash of recognition one more time, that conscious look that made them real. But Evans gave no sign or word. The ventilator rasped on. A plastic bag below the bed slowly filled with dark gold fluid from his bladder.

Near midnight the crowd thinned out. Thorne arrived from the airport and everyone left to give him time with his father, to say what had to be said between them.

By morning Evans still hadn't moved. The machine kept his chest rising and falling; a digital readout displayed blood pressure and heart rate. When the numbers fell too far, an alarm would go off, and a nurse would come in to change the bag of fluids dripping into his bloodstream.

Paul sat beside him, forehead pressed against the bed rails, holding Evans' hand. "I know you're there," he said from time to time. "Just give us a sign."

"Give us a sign, Daddy," Keri echoed, her eyes fixed on her father's wasted face.

Finally I could stand it no longer. "You need to tell him it's all right to go on." I said. "Let him go."

"Not while I can help it." Paul shot me an angry look.

The day wore on. Friends came and went. My son Aaron arrived and stood beside me for a while, comforting me with his presence.

"We love you, Daddy," Keri said.

In the early evening, a single tear rolled from Evans' left eye and down his cheek.

"Daddy!" Keri cried.

"We know you love us." Paul's energy revived. "We know you hear us. Just open your eyes." He put the bed rail down and rubbed Evans' hand, lying blue and unresponsive on the sheet.

Evans made no sign. His face was still, his suffering flesh like stone. A nurse came in and changed the drip bag. "This is the last of the stimulants," she said. "They won't work after this."

Paul laid his forehead on the mattress. His shoulders shook. "It's all right," he said at last, lifting a face wet with tears. "If you want to, you can go."

"Daddy, it's all right, you can go," Keri said, with the generosity of someone much older.

The monitor went on blinking numbers for an hour, telling us the heart still beat, the blood still flowed, as the last of the fluid dripped out; and then the numbers rapidly fell: 90, 85, 70, 65, 58, 55, 40, 45, 40, 30, 20, 17, 12, 5, 0. The line went flat, but the rasping sound went on and on, still breathing for Evans' body. An alarm shrilled and an attendant ran in to shut it down.

"He was a good man," the grey-haired lady said. One by one, the people left. Keri reached out and touched the top of that strange, bald, mottled head, turning purple as the blood pooled up beneath the skin.

We put on our coats and left, riding the elevator in silence, surprised that the world could still exist.

Outside, it was dark, a whole day gone by unnoticed. Keri sat in the passenger seat, head down, her shoulders heaving. "I never even got to say goodbye," she sobbed.

"I think he did say goodbye," I comforted. "You saw that tear." The vision I'd had of his soul being borne off by Sai Baba had obviously been wrong—a fantasy contrived from wishful thinking. He'd been in his body all the time. The tear had proved it. "He won't be suffering now."

She stared straight ahead. In back, Thorne laid his head against the seat. I started the car.

ALL ROADS LEAD HOME

I gave up drumming group. It was a chore, and I'd rather stay home and read.

Sharon said, "I know you're grieving, but maybe we can help."

"It isn't only that," I said. "It just seems like, what's the point? Besides, I'm basically an introvert. I thought shamanism might change that, but let's face it, it didn't."

"Listen, I'm shy too. I know what it's like. But you can't just give in. You went to Nepal, you learned so much, got so much power."

Power? My throat closed down on what I might have said. "I don't have power. I don't have a clue. I wasn't any help to Evans—couldn't even give him faith when he was dying."

"Do you think he would have accepted help from anyone? You need to let it go."

"You're psychobabbling, Sharon." I wasn't usually that rude, but I'd start to scream if she kept on. How could someone like me—who couldn't think a single thought without triggering another thought that said, "that's wrong"—help anyone? I'd never once let him rest in his own unquestioned reality. No wonder he died.

"Well, call when you feel like talking," Sharon's voice had gone tense.

"Okay," I said, but she'd hung up.

❧

I should have tried to heal him, shouldn't have backed down because I feared to hear him say, "You're wrong." Why hadn't I prayed as hard for him as for Keri? So much for *power.*

We grieved all through that summer. I lost myself in work, and after work read novels for escape. Thorne was mostly with his friends, and Keri took to hanging out with bad kids on the mall—as though if we stayed away from each other, we wouldn't be reminded.

I had no patience for anyone.

Ama came for jokhanna and phukne, complaining of pain in her legs. I couldn't turn her down, but had to force myself through Maile's routine. Afterward, Ama bathed me in her warm, contagious smile and said she felt better. I smiled back, thinking *psychosomatic*.

Then it was fall, and Thorne went back to school. On Halloween, the night our European forebears honored their own ancestral spirits, Keri set the carved wooden head that looked like her father on the porch, and balanced one cigarette after another on its lips, lighting each one and watching it burn down until the whole pack was finished. The smell of his tobacco comforted her.

I wished I could believe his spirit had come to enjoy the smoke, but felt no sign of his presence. Nothing was left now but grief. I tried to dream of him but never could. I prayed for a message, a dispatch from the universe to let us know he still existed. I felt death pulling, as though in dying he'd showed the way, teaching me how to follow. Sometimes my heart would start to pound, speed up, and feel pierced with sudden pain. But none of the spiritual techniques I'd learned, not journeying, nor chanting, nor calling, could help. He was gone. The one person who'd ever convinced me I wasn't alone.

I couldn't do more than make it through each day, but I'd signed up for Michael Harner's three-year course in shamanism, and we were due to meet again in upstate New York. It was easier to learn these advanced techniques in the context of my own culture than it had been in Nepal—but it hadn't stilled my doubts. I called my usual roommate, Prue Kestner, and said I didn't think I could make it.

"Oh, Ellen, please come," she said. "The circle isn't complete without all of us. We need you—and you need to be there." Prue was something of a hero to me, international teacher of yoga, shamanic practitioner, and artist. In her sixties she still kept her day job in the D.C. office of the American Bar Association, heading up their mediation project.

The fall colors were fading as I carried my bags to the upstairs barracks room we'd been assigned. Prue was somewhere around. Her bed was made up and her bag set neatly in the closet. She'd picked up my sheets and towels from the laundry and left them on my bed. I found her in the lunchroom with Evvie, Allie, Tom, and Big Al. There were hugs all around, and when she said "I'm glad you came," I felt glad too.

"I know you feel bad about your husband's death," she said as we walked back to our room.

"Ex-husband."

"I know, but it doesn't really matter after so many years together." We got into bed. "Would you like me to journey to see if I can find out where his soul has gone, and if he needs help?"

"No," I said. "I don't even want to think about it." I had my own memories and didn't want them distorted by someone who'd never even known him. Whatever she might report from her journey, I wouldn't know if it was genuine or only some fantasy she'd concocted. Anything she said would seem a desecration. Something of this must have come through in my tone, because she didn't answer.

"I guess I'm not a very good roommate this time," I offered. "I'm feeling negative about everything, and I don't like myself very much."

"It's all right dear, I understand." She was so kind, but she never said a thing she didn't mean, and that was a comfort. We got quiet then, and I knew she was praying, probably for me. The room was rich with inaudible, sustained organ chords, like being in church.

The days of the class dragged by. I went through the motions at our sessions, walked the valley by myself, climbed the trail to Lookout Point and kept on going, finding fresh bear scat at the very top. I spent time by the stream just sitting, watching water run downhill and trying not to think. Deer were protected here and the whitetails were tame. I could have fed them from my hands if I'd cared.

On one of these solitary walks, I came across Carol, a member of our class, meditating on a rocky strand. She heard me and looked up. "I know something's been bothering you," she said. She had dark hair and a pretty, long face with narrow eyes, like someone whose ancestors had evolved in cold climates. The sunlight glinting from the water turned them green.

Something in her quiet sympathy, and the peace of the place, allowed me to tell her about Evans' death. "I should have been able to heal him," I said, "but I couldn't."

"It's not your fault." She fished a tissue from her pocket and handed it over. "Remember when Sandy Ingerman taught us soul retrieval— how she explained that you can be holding on to a part of someone's soul without realizing it, because you don't want to lose them?"

"I guess I do." I wiped my eyes.

"It isn't good. It steals your energy, and holds the other person back from where he needs to go." I felt myself responding to her kindness, her shaman's will to help. "Let him go," she said.

Many of our activities centered around re-creating techniques other cultures used to contact spirits, and halfway through the week, Michael Harner announced we would try the Ozark practice of table-walking. We arranged ourselves around three tables set up in the large classroom, our hands resting lightly on their surfaces. Michael rattled to the four directions and called the spirits.

I knew the members of our circle were honest, down-to-earth, good people. Nevertheless, as the table began to shake beneath my fingers, and then to violently rock back and forth, I studied their hands for stretched tendons or other evidence of deliberate pushing, but the hands were all relaxed and smooth, resting on the table tops, like mine, without tension. Some of the group, more sensitive than I, had already felt the spirits' presence. Beside me, Roslyn was channeling in a voice unlike her own.

I wasn't aware of the presence of any particular spirit, but my upper legs began to shake. I felt a sudden shock of energy, like a bright bolt of lightening flashing within my very core—not painful but intense, like nothing I'd ever felt before. This was totally different from the pleasant glowing sensation of light coming into my forehead from above that had happened in Nepal. Stronger than joy, stronger than sex, it occupied the very quick of me, illuminating a place I hadn't even known existed—not static, but moving like life itself, distilled, essential, not to be denied. I began to groan, knowing I groaned for the spirit because it so needed to groan, without words in overwhelming sadness and despair. I surrendered to the need to give it voice. It felt so good to let those feelings out.

"Don't let them possess you," Michael said, coming around the table.

"We know you are suffering, but there's a better place, a loving place. You must go, now. This is not your body." Someone was helping, encouraging the spirit to depart. With an effort of will, and no little reluctance, I pushed it out and felt it leave.

The table rocked; the others spoke to spirits, reminding them of loved ones waiting in the upper world, moving them on. I stood bereft, wanting to groan and groan and keep on groaning, but knowing I'd done right to send the spirit on.

"It was the strangest feeling," I said later. We'd gathered in the lunch room, raiding the dark kitchen for cookies and bananas, everyone talking at once about what had happened. "It was totally real, like white, liquid fire. Pure life."

Back in our room, Prue got into her nightgown and sat on my bed. "It made me want to groan," I said. I couldn't stop thinking about it. I twisted the front of my T-shirt, wadding it in my fists, "Like someone dying, like...like Evans when he was—." I quit squeezing the shirt and stared out the window.

"Do you think it was him?"

I wanted to say something light and ambiguous, but there was no way to pass this off like some experience that might, or might not, have happened to another person. It had been so real, that grief...

"Don't think about it," she said quickly. "You don't want to call it back. Don't say his name."

"I don't know...who it was." I pulled the T-shirt off and shrugged into my pajama top.

"He's gone," Prue said. "You pushed him out. He's gone."

I turned back the covers and inserted myself inside, like a letter into an envelope, sealed off and safe. Prue stood and kissed me on the forehead.

My thoughts had simplified. I guarded the clear, clean space within, a fresh, empty darkness free of complexity, and refused to think of him or what he would have had to say about spirit possession; refused to let myself wonder if what had happened made sense.

On our last day of class, we recreated another spiritual practice that had been described by ethnographers studying Inuit and Central Asian cultures. The shaman would have himself tied up in a blanket, and then when the lights went off, he would escape—supposedly with spirit help. The written accounts speculated about accomplices. We would try it ourselves to see if it could be done without trickery. "If anyone is claustrophobic, or if you have a heart condition," Michael cautioned, "don't do it."

The class divided into two groups, the ones who were to be tied up, including me, kneeling to let our partners throw a blanket over our heads and tie us in with clothesline, crossing our wrists behind our backs and binding our ankles with the same long rope. If I had a fleeting thought that my recent chest pain and irregular heart beats might be considered a heart condition, I dismissed it.

Michael explained what we must do to invoke the spirits to help us get free. The lights went out, and the drumming began. I'd been bound with real knots, but my partner was inexperienced, and as I struggled, the rope came loose at once. By the time the drumming stopped, all but two of us had worked ourselves free. I felt sorry for Frank who didn't make it, but he'd been tied by Big Al who obviously knew knots, probably from sailing.

"I was amazed when the ropes came free," Prue marveled.

"I wasn't," I said. "I don't think I was tied that well."

I got permission to try again with the second group, and approached Big Al. At least six foot two, and almost completely bald, he could have doubled as a movie bad guy, but was actually a medical doctor with a heart as large as the rest of him—and more to the point, he was quite strong. "You seem awfully good with knots," I said. "Would you be willing to tie me up? I want to find out if it *really* works."

"How's your heart? Can you stand it?"

I laughed. "Thanks doctor, but I did it before all right. And no, I've never been diagnosed with heart trouble." It wasn't literally a lie. "Tie me as tight as you can."

I knelt on the floor, and he settled the blanket over my head, closing me in with my resolve. He bound my wrists behind my back, with knots tight and sure. "Tighter," I said. "I can still move my arms." He pulled until the ropes cut my wrists, grunting as he yanked them tight, and then bound my ankles and wound the rope around and around my body, tying it securely. I couldn't move at all. It was hard to breathe through the blanket. I began to feel claustrophobic.

Michael turned off the lights and drummed. My heart lurched in my chest. I called on spirits, prayed for help. I struggled, and felt the knots tighten. I called on Lord Shiva. I couldn't catch my breath. I started to panic. With every movement, the thin cord pulled tighter, cutting off the circulation in my wrists, making my hands weak and numb.

I remembered Mr. Rai in Nepal, shouting, "Concentrate yourself!" My world collapsed into one mighty effort—this moment here and now. All thought of gods and spirits disappeared, for thought had no place here. Nothing existed but the pain in my wrists, the pain in my chest, the brightness behind my eyes, driving me inward, a raw desire for freedom arrowing into the very core of being. Then suddenly, miraculously, the